C-962   CAREER EXAMINATION SERIES

This is your
PASSBOOK for...

Court Assistant II

Test Preparation Study Guide
Questions & Answers

NATIONAL LEARNING CORPORATION®

COPYRIGHT NOTICE

This book is SOLELY intended for, is sold ONLY to, and its use is RESTRICTED to individual, bona fide applicants or candidates who qualify by virtue of having seriously filed applications for appropriate license, certificate, professional and/or promotional advancement, higher school matriculation, scholarship, or other legitimate requirements of education and/or governmental authorities.

This book is NOT intended for use, class instruction, tutoring, training, duplication, copying, reprinting, excerption, or adaptation, etc., by:

1) Other publishers
2) Proprietors and/or Instructors of "Coaching" and/or Preparatory Courses
3) Personnel and/or Training Divisions of commercial, industrial, and governmental organizations
4) Schools, colleges, or universities and/or their departments and staffs, including teachers and other personnel
5) Testing Agencies or Bureaus
6) Study groups which seek by the purchase of a single volume to copy and/or duplicate and/or adapt this material for use by the group as a whole without having purchased individual volumes for each of the members of the group
7) Et al.

Such persons would be in violation of appropriate Federal and State statutes.

PROVISION OF LICENSING AGREEMENTS – Recognized educational, commercial, industrial, and governmental institutions and organizations, and others legitimately engaged in educational pursuits, including training, testing, and measurement activities, may address request for a licensing agreement to the copyright owners, who will determine whether, and under what conditions, including fees and charges, the materials in this book may be used them. In other words, a licensing facility exists for the legitimate use of the material in this book on other than an individual basis. However, it is asseverated and affirmed here that the material in this book CANNOT be used without the receipt of the express permission of such a licensing agreement from the Publishers. Inquiries re licensing should be addressed to the company, attention rights and permissions department.

All rights reserved, including the right of reproduction in whole or in part, in any form or by any means, electronic or mechanical, including photocopying, recording, or by any information storage and retrieval system, without permission in writing from the Publisher.

Copyright © 2025 by
National Learning Corporation

212 Michael Drive, Syosset, NY 11791
(516) 921-8888 • www.passbooks.com
E-mail: info@passbooks.com

PASSBOOK® SERIES

THE *PASSBOOK® SERIES* has been created to prepare applicants and candidates for the ultimate academic battlefield – the examination room.

At some time in our lives, each and every one of us may be required to take an examination – for validation, matriculation, admission, qualification, registration, certification, or licensure.

Based on the assumption that every applicant or candidate has met the basic formal educational standards, has taken the required number of courses, and read the necessary texts, the *PASSBOOK® SERIES* furnishes the one special preparation which may assure passing with confidence, instead of failing with insecurity. Examination questions – together with answers – are furnished as the basic vehicle for study so that the mysteries of the examination and its compounding difficulties may be eliminated or diminished by a sure method.

This book is meant to help you pass your examination provided that you qualify and are serious in your objective.

The entire field is reviewed through the huge store of content information which is succinctly presented through a provocative and challenging approach – the question-and-answer method.

A climate of success is established by furnishing the correct answers at the end of each test.

You soon learn to recognize types of questions, forms of questions, and patterns of questioning. You may even begin to anticipate expected outcomes.

You perceive that many questions are repeated or adapted so that you can gain acute insights, which may enable you to score many sure points.

You learn how to confront new questions, or types of questions, and to attack them confidently and work out the correct answers.

You note objectives and emphases, and recognize pitfalls and dangers, so that you may make positive educational adjustments.

Moreover, you are kept fully informed in relation to new concepts, methods, practices, and directions in the field.

You discover that you are actually taking the examination all the time: you are preparing for the examination by "taking" an examination, not by reading extraneous and/or supererogatory textbooks.

In short, this PASSBOOK®, used directedly, should be an important factor in helping you to pass your test.

COURT ASSISTANT II

DUTIES

Under direct supervision, performs court clerical work at a level above routine office clerical duties in accordance with well-defined methods: answers over-the-counter and telephone inquiries from attorneys and litigants; interviews complainants and litigants for purpose of preparing summonses; accepts papers filed with the court; may receive payment and issue receipts for court fees or fines; prepares simple court forms; prepares routine court activity reports; may supervise a small clerical unit performing routine entry-level duties; may be authorized by rule or order as provided by law to administer oaths, take acknowledgments and sign processes of the court; may maintain docket books; performs related duties in courtroom or at outlying court location and court office.

SCOPE OF THE EXAMINATION

The written test will cover knowledge, skills and/or abilities in such areas as:

1. Office practices and procedures;
2. Legal terminology, documents and forms;
3. Preparing written material;
4. Understanding and interpreting written material;
5. Arithmetic; and
6. Supervision.

HOW TO TAKE A TEST

I. YOU MUST PASS AN EXAMINATION

A. *WHAT EVERY CANDIDATE SHOULD KNOW*

Examination applicants often ask us for help in preparing for the written test. What can I study in advance? What kinds of questions will be asked? How will the test be given? How will the papers be graded?

As an applicant for a civil service examination, you may be wondering about some of these things. Our purpose here is to suggest effective methods of advance study and to describe civil service examinations.

Your chances for success on this examination can be increased if you know how to prepare. Those "pre-examination jitters" can be reduced if you know what to expect. You can even experience an adventure in good citizenship if you know why civil service exams are given.

B. *WHY ARE CIVIL SERVICE EXAMINATIONS GIVEN?*

Civil service examinations are important to you in two ways. As a citizen, you want public jobs filled by employees who know how to do their work. As a job seeker, you want a fair chance to compete for that job on an equal footing with other candidates. The best-known means of accomplishing this two-fold goal is the competitive examination.

Exams are widely publicized throughout the nation. They may be administered for jobs in federal, state, city, municipal, town or village governments or agencies.

Any citizen may apply, with some limitations, such as the age or residence of applicants. Your experience and education may be reviewed to see whether you meet the requirements for the particular examination. When these requirements exist, they are reasonable and applied consistently to all applicants. Thus, a competitive examination may cause you some uneasiness now, but it is your privilege and safeguard.

C. *HOW ARE CIVIL SERVICE EXAMS DEVELOPED?*

Examinations are carefully written by trained technicians who are specialists in the field known as "psychological measurement," in consultation with recognized authorities in the field of work that the test will cover. These experts recommend the subject matter areas or skills to be tested; only those knowledges or skills important to your success on the job are included. The most reliable books and source materials available are used as references. Together, the experts and technicians judge the difficulty level of the questions.

Test technicians know how to phrase questions so that the problem is clearly stated. Their ethics do not permit "trick" or "catch" questions. Questions may have been tried out on sample groups, or subjected to statistical analysis, to determine their usefulness.

Written tests are often used in combination with performance tests, ratings of training and experience, and oral interviews. All of these measures combine to form the best-known means of finding the right person for the right job.

II. HOW TO PASS THE WRITTEN TEST

A. NATURE OF THE EXAMINATION

To prepare intelligently for civil service examinations, you should know how they differ from school examinations you have taken. In school you were assigned certain definite pages to read or subjects to cover. The examination questions were quite detailed and usually emphasized memory. Civil service exams, on the other hand, try to discover your present ability to perform the duties of a position, plus your potentiality to learn these duties. In other words, a civil service exam attempts to predict how successful you will be. Questions cover such a broad area that they cannot be as minute and detailed as school exam questions.

In the public service similar kinds of work, or positions, are grouped together in one "class." This process is known as *position-classification*. All the positions in a class are paid according to the salary range for that class. One class title covers all of these positions, and they are all tested by the same examination.

B. FOUR BASIC STEPS

1) Study the announcement

How, then, can you know what subjects to study? Our best answer is: "Learn as much as possible about the class of positions for which you've applied." The exam will test the knowledge, skills and abilities needed to do the work.

Your most valuable source of information about the position you want is the official exam announcement. This announcement lists the training and experience qualifications. Check these standards and apply only if you come reasonably close to meeting them.

The brief description of the position in the examination announcement offers some clues to the subjects which will be tested. Think about the job itself. Review the duties in your mind. Can you perform them, or are there some in which you are rusty? Fill in the blank spots in your preparation.

Many jurisdictions preview the written test in the exam announcement by including a section called "Knowledge and Abilities Required," "Scope of the Examination," or some similar heading. Here you will find out specifically what fields will be tested.

2) Review your own background

Once you learn in general what the position is all about, and what you need to know to do the work, ask yourself which subjects you already know fairly well and which need improvement. You may wonder whether to concentrate on improving your strong areas or on building some background in your fields of weakness. When the announcement has specified "some knowledge" or "considerable knowledge," or has used adjectives like "beginning principles of…" or "advanced … methods," you can get a clue as to the number and difficulty of questions to be asked in any given field. More questions, and hence broader coverage, would be included for those subjects which are more important in the work. Now weigh your strengths and weaknesses against the job requirements and prepare accordingly.

3) Determine the level of the position

Another way to tell how intensively you should prepare is to understand the level of the job for which you are applying. Is it the entering level? In other words, is this the position in which beginners in a field of work are hired? Or is it an intermediate or advanced level? Sometimes this is indicated by such words as "Junior" or "Senior" in the class title. Other jurisdictions use Roman numerals to designate the level – Clerk I, Clerk II, for example. The word "Supervisor" sometimes appears in the title. If the level is not indicated by the title, check the description of duties. Will you be working under very close supervision, or will you have responsibility for independent decisions in this work?

4) Choose appropriate study materials

Now that you know the subjects to be examined and the relative amount of each subject to be covered, you can choose suitable study materials. For beginning level jobs, or even advanced ones, if you have a pronounced weakness in some aspect of your training, read a modern, standard textbook in that field. Be sure it is up to date and has general coverage. Such books are normally available at your library, and the librarian will be glad to help you locate one. For entry-level positions, questions of appropriate difficulty are chosen – neither highly advanced questions, nor those too simple. Such questions require careful thought but not advanced training.

If the position for which you are applying is technical or advanced, you will read more advanced, specialized material. If you are already familiar with the basic principles of your field, elementary textbooks would waste your time. Concentrate on advanced textbooks and technical periodicals. Think through the concepts and review difficult problems in your field.

These are all general sources. You can get more ideas on your own initiative, following these leads. For example, training manuals and publications of the government agency which employs workers in your field can be useful, particularly for technical and professional positions. A letter or visit to the government department involved may result in more specific study suggestions, and certainly will provide you with a more definite idea of the exact nature of the position you are seeking.

III. KINDS OF TESTS

Tests are used for purposes other than measuring knowledge and ability to perform specified duties. For some positions, it is equally important to test ability to make adjustments to new situations or to profit from training. In others, basic mental abilities not dependent on information are essential. Questions which test these things may not appear as pertinent to the duties of the position as those which test for knowledge and information. Yet they are often highly important parts of a fair examination. For very general questions, it is almost impossible to help you direct your study efforts. What we can do is to point out some of the more common of these general abilities needed in public service positions and describe some typical questions.

1) General information

Broad, general information has been found useful for predicting job success in some kinds of work. This is tested in a variety of ways, from vocabulary lists to questions about current events. Basic background in some field of work, such as sociology or economics, may be sampled in a group of questions. Often these are principles which have become familiar to most persons through exposure rather than through formal training. It is difficult to advise you how to study for these questions; being alert to the world around you is our best suggestion.

2) Verbal ability

An example of an ability needed in many positions is verbal or language ability. Verbal ability is, in brief, the ability to use and understand words. Vocabulary and grammar tests are typical measures of this ability. Reading comprehension or paragraph interpretation questions are common in many kinds of civil service tests. You are given a paragraph of written material and asked to find its central meaning.

3) Numerical ability

Number skills can be tested by the familiar arithmetic problem, by checking paired lists of numbers to see which are alike and which are different, or by interpreting charts and graphs. In the latter test, a graph may be printed in the test booklet which you are asked to use as the basis for answering questions.

4) Observation

A popular test for law-enforcement positions is the observation test. A picture is shown to you for several minutes, then taken away. Questions about the picture test your ability to observe both details and larger elements.

5) Following directions

In many positions in the public service, the employee must be able to carry out written instructions dependably and accurately. You may be given a chart with several columns, each column listing a variety of information. The questions require you to carry out directions involving the information given in the chart.

6) Skills and aptitudes

Performance tests effectively measure some manual skills and aptitudes. When the skill is one in which you are trained, such as typing or shorthand, you can practice. These tests are often very much like those given in business school or high school courses. For many of the other skills and aptitudes, however, no short-time preparation can be made. Skills and abilities natural to you or that you have developed throughout your lifetime are being tested.

Many of the general questions just described provide all the data needed to answer the questions and ask you to use your reasoning ability to find the answers. Your best preparation for these tests, as well as for tests of facts and ideas, is to be at your physical and mental best. You, no doubt, have your own methods of getting into an exam-taking mood and keeping "in shape." The next section lists some ideas on this subject.

IV. KINDS OF QUESTIONS

Only rarely is the "essay" question, which you answer in narrative form, used in civil service tests. Civil service tests are usually of the short-answer type. Full instructions for answering these questions will be given to you at the examination. But in case this is your first experience with short-answer questions and separate answer sheets, here is what you need to know:

1) Multiple-choice Questions

Most popular of the short-answer questions is the "multiple choice" or "best answer" question. It can be used, for example, to test for factual knowledge, ability to solve problems or judgment in meeting situations found at work.

A multiple-choice question is normally one of three types—
- It can begin with an incomplete statement followed by several possible endings. You are to find the one ending which *best* completes the statement, although some of the others may not be entirely wrong.
- It can also be a complete statement in the form of a question which is answered by choosing one of the statements listed.

- It can be in the form of a problem – again you select the best answer.

Here is an example of a multiple-choice question with a discussion which should give you some clues as to the method for choosing the right answer:

When an employee has a complaint about his assignment, the action which will *best* help him overcome his difficulty is to
  A. discuss his difficulty with his coworkers
  B. take the problem to the head of the organization
  C. take the problem to the person who gave him the assignment
  D. say nothing to anyone about his complaint

In answering this question, you should study each of the choices to find which is best. Consider choice "A" – Certainly an employee may discuss his complaint with fellow employees, but no change or improvement can result, and the complaint remains unresolved. Choice "B" is a poor choice since the head of the organization probably does not know what assignment you have been given, and taking your problem to him is known as "going over the head" of the supervisor. The supervisor, or person who made the assignment, is the person who can clarify it or correct any injustice. Choice "C" is, therefore, correct. To say nothing, as in choice "D," is unwise. Supervisors have and interest in knowing the problems employees are facing, and the employee is seeking a solution to his problem.

2) True/False Questions

The "true/false" or "right/wrong" form of question is sometimes used. Here a complete statement is given. Your job is to decide whether the statement is right or wrong.

SAMPLE: A roaming cell-phone call to a nearby city costs less than a non-roaming call to a distant city.

This statement is wrong, or false, since roaming calls are more expensive.

This is not a complete list of all possible question forms, although most of the others are variations of these common types. You will always get complete directions for answering questions. Be sure you understand *how* to mark your answers – ask questions until you do.

V. RECORDING YOUR ANSWERS

Computer terminals are used more and more today for many different kinds of exams.

For an examination with very few applicants, you may be told to record your answers in the test booklet itself. Separate answer sheets are much more common. If this separate answer sheet is to be scored by machine – and this is often the case – it is highly important that you mark your answers correctly in order to get credit.

An electronic scoring machine is often used in civil service offices because of the speed with which papers can be scored. Machine-scored answer sheets must be marked with a pencil, which will be given to you. This pencil has a high graphite content which responds to the electronic scoring machine. As a matter of fact, stray dots may register as answers, so do not let your pencil rest on the answer sheet while you are pondering the correct answer. Also, if your pencil lead breaks or is otherwise defective, ask for another.

Since the answer sheet will be dropped in a slot in the scoring machine, be careful not to bend the corners or get the paper crumpled.

The answer sheet normally has five vertical columns of numbers, with 30 numbers to a column. These numbers correspond to the question numbers in your test booklet. After each number, going across the page are four or five pairs of dotted lines. These short dotted lines have small letters or numbers above them. The first two pairs may also have a "T" or "F" above the letters. This indicates that the first two pairs only are to be used if the questions are of the true-false type. If the questions are multiple choice, disregard the "T" and "F" and pay attention only to the small letters or numbers.

Answer your questions in the manner of the sample that follows:

32. The largest city in the United States is
    A. Washington, D.C.
    B. New York City
    C. Chicago
    D. Detroit
    E. San Francisco

1) Choose the answer you think is best. (New York City is the largest, so "B" is correct.)
2) Find the row of dotted lines numbered the same as the question you are answering. (Find row number 32)
3) Find the pair of dotted lines corresponding to the answer. (Find the pair of lines under the mark "B.")
4) Make a solid black mark between the dotted lines.

VI. BEFORE THE TEST

Common sense will help you find procedures to follow to get ready for an examination. Too many of us, however, overlook these sensible measures. Indeed, nervousness and fatigue have been found to be the most serious reasons why applicants fail to do their best on civil service tests. Here is a list of reminders:

- Begin your preparation early – Don't wait until the last minute to go scurrying around for books and materials or to find out what the position is all about.
- Prepare continuously – An hour a night for a week is better than an all-night cram session. This has been definitely established. What is more, a night a week for a month will return better dividends than crowding your study into a shorter period of time.
- Locate the place of the exam – You have been sent a notice telling you when and where to report for the examination. If the location is in a different town or otherwise unfamiliar to you, it would be well to inquire the best route and learn something about the building.
- Relax the night before the test – Allow your mind to rest. Do not study at all that night. Plan some mild recreation or diversion; then go to bed early and get a good night's sleep.
- Get up early enough to make a leisurely trip to the place for the test – This way unforeseen events, traffic snarls, unfamiliar buildings, etc. will not upset you.
- Dress comfortably – A written test is not a fashion show. You will be known by number and not by name, so wear something comfortable.

- Leave excess paraphernalia at home – Shopping bags and odd bundles will get in your way. You need bring only the items mentioned in the official notice you received; usually everything you need is provided. Do not bring reference books to the exam. They will only confuse those last minutes and be taken away from you when in the test room.
- Arrive somewhat ahead of time – If because of transportation schedules you must get there very early, bring a newspaper or magazine to take your mind off yourself while waiting.
- Locate the examination room – When you have found the proper room, you will be directed to the seat or part of the room where you will sit. Sometimes you are given a sheet of instructions to read while you are waiting. Do not fill out any forms until you are told to do so; just read them and be prepared.
- Relax and prepare to listen to the instructions
- If you have any physical problem that may keep you from doing your best, be sure to tell the test administrator. If you are sick or in poor health, you really cannot do your best on the exam. You can come back and take the test some other time.

VII. AT THE TEST

The day of the test is here and you have the test booklet in your hand. The temptation to get going is very strong. Caution! There is more to success than knowing the right answers. You must know how to identify your papers and understand variations in the type of short-answer question used in this particular examination. Follow these suggestions for maximum results from your efforts:

1) Cooperate with the monitor

The test administrator has a duty to create a situation in which you can be as much at ease as possible. He will give instructions, tell you when to begin, check to see that you are marking your answer sheet correctly, and so on. He is not there to guard you, although he will see that your competitors do not take unfair advantage. He wants to help you do your best.

2) Listen to all instructions

Don't jump the gun! Wait until you understand all directions. In most civil service tests you get more time than you need to answer the questions. So don't be in a hurry. Read each word of instructions until you clearly understand the meaning. Study the examples, listen to all announcements and follow directions. Ask questions if you do not understand what to do.

3) Identify your papers

Civil service exams are usually identified by number only. You will be assigned a number; you must not put your name on your test papers. Be sure to copy your number correctly. Since more than one exam may be given, copy your exact examination title.

4) Plan your time

Unless you are told that a test is a "speed" or "rate of work" test, speed itself is usually not important. Time enough to answer all the questions will be provided, but this does not mean that you have all day. An overall time limit has been set. Divide the total time (in minutes) by the number of questions to determine the approximate time you have for each question.

5) Do not linger over difficult questions

If you come across a difficult question, mark it with a paper clip (useful to have along) and come back to it when you have been through the booklet. One caution if you do this – be sure to skip a number on your answer sheet as well. Check often to be sure that you have not lost your place and that you are marking in the row numbered the same as the question you are answering.

6) Read the questions

Be sure you know what the question asks! Many capable people are unsuccessful because they failed to *read* the questions correctly.

7) Answer all questions

Unless you have been instructed that a penalty will be deducted for incorrect answers, it is better to guess than to omit a question.

8) Speed tests

It is often better NOT to guess on speed tests. It has been found that on timed tests people are tempted to spend the last few seconds before time is called in marking answers at random – without even reading them – in the hope of picking up a few extra points. To discourage this practice, the instructions may warn you that your score will be "corrected" for guessing. That is, a penalty will be applied. The incorrect answers will be deducted from the correct ones, or some other penalty formula will be used.

9) Review your answers

If you finish before time is called, go back to the questions you guessed or omitted to give them further thought. Review other answers if you have time.

10) Return your test materials

If you are ready to leave before others have finished or time is called, take ALL your materials to the monitor and leave quietly. Never take any test material with you. The monitor can discover whose papers are not complete, and taking a test booklet may be grounds for disqualification.

VIII. EXAMINATION TECHNIQUES

1) Read the general instructions carefully. These are usually printed on the first page of the exam booklet. As a rule, these instructions refer to the timing of the examination; the fact that you should not start work until the signal and must stop work at a signal, etc. If there are any *special* instructions, such as a choice of questions to be answered, make sure that you note this instruction carefully.

2) When you are ready to start work on the examination, that is as soon as the signal has been given, read the instructions to each question booklet, underline any key words or phrases, such as *least, best, outline, describe* and the like. In this way you will tend to answer as requested rather than discover on reviewing your paper that you *listed without describing*, that you selected the *worst* choice rather than the *best* choice, etc.

3) If the examination is of the objective or multiple-choice type – that is, each question will also give a series of possible answers: A, B, C or D, and you are called upon to select the best answer and write the letter next to that answer on your answer paper – it is advisable to start answering each question in turn. There may be anywhere from 50 to 100 such questions in the three or four hours allotted and you can see how much time would be taken if you read through all the questions before beginning to answer any. Furthermore, if you come across a question or group of questions which you know would be difficult to answer, it would undoubtedly affect your handling of all the other questions.

4) If the examination is of the essay type and contains but a few questions, it is a moot point as to whether you should read all the questions before starting to answer any one. Of course, if you are given a choice – say five out of seven and the like – then it is essential to read all the questions so you can eliminate the two that are most difficult. If, however, you are asked to answer all the questions, there may be danger in trying to answer the easiest one first because you may find that you will spend too much time on it. The best technique is to answer the first question, then proceed to the second, etc.

5) Time your answers. Before the exam begins, write down the time it started, then add the time allowed for the examination and write down the time it must be completed, then divide the time available somewhat as follows:
    - If 3-1/2 hours are allowed, that would be 210 minutes. If you have 80 objective-type questions, that would be an average of 2-1/2 minutes per question. Allow yourself no more than 2 minutes per question, or a total of 160 minutes, which will permit about 50 minutes to review.
    - If for the time allotment of 210 minutes there are 7 essay questions to answer, that would average about 30 minutes a question. Give yourself only 25 minutes per question so that you have about 35 minutes to review.

6) The most important instruction is to *read each question* and make sure you know what is wanted. The second most important instruction is to *time yourself properly* so that you answer every question. The third most important instruction is to *answer every question*. Guess if you have to but include something for each question. Remember that you will receive no credit for a blank and will probably receive some credit if you write something in answer to an essay question. If you guess a letter – say "B" for a multiple-choice question – you may have guessed right. If you leave a blank as an answer to a multiple-choice question, the examiners may respect your feelings but it will not add a point to your score. Some exams may penalize you for wrong answers, so in such cases *only*, you may not want to guess unless you have some basis for your answer.

7) Suggestions
    a. Objective-type questions
        1. Examine the question booklet for proper sequence of pages and questions
        2. Read all instructions carefully
        3. Skip any question which seems too difficult; return to it after all other questions have been answered
        4. Apportion your time properly; do not spend too much time on any single question or group of questions

5. Note and underline key words – *all, most, fewest, least, best, worst, same, opposite,* etc.
6. Pay particular attention to negatives
7. Note unusual option, e.g., unduly long, short, complex, different or similar in content to the body of the question
8. Observe the use of "hedging" words – *probably, may, most likely,* etc.
9. Make sure that your answer is put next to the same number as the question
10. Do not second-guess unless you have good reason to believe the second answer is definitely more correct
11. Cross out original answer if you decide another answer is more accurate; do not erase until you are ready to hand your paper in
12. Answer all questions; guess unless instructed otherwise
13. Leave time for review

b. Essay questions
1. Read each question carefully
2. Determine exactly what is wanted. Underline key words or phrases.
3. Decide on outline or paragraph answer
4. Include many different points and elements unless asked to develop any one or two points or elements
5. Show impartiality by giving pros and cons unless directed to select one side only
6. Make and write down any assumptions you find necessary to answer the questions
7. Watch your English, grammar, punctuation and choice of words
8. Time your answers; don't crowd material

8) Answering the essay question

Most essay questions can be answered by framing the specific response around several key words or ideas. Here are a few such key words or ideas:

M's: manpower, materials, methods, money, management
P's: purpose, program, policy, plan, procedure, practice, problems, pitfalls, personnel, public relations

a. Six basic steps in handling problems:
1. Preliminary plan and background development
2. Collect information, data and facts
3. Analyze and interpret information, data and facts
4. Analyze and develop solutions as well as make recommendations
5. Prepare report and sell recommendations
6. Install recommendations and follow up effectiveness

b. Pitfalls to avoid
1. *Taking things for granted* – A statement of the situation does not necessarily imply that each of the elements is necessarily true; for example, a complaint may be invalid and biased so that all that can be taken for granted is that a complaint has been registered

2. *Considering only one side of a situation* – Wherever possible, indicate several alternatives and then point out the reasons you selected the best one
3. *Failing to indicate follow up* – Whenever your answer indicates action on your part, make certain that you will take proper follow-up action to see how successful your recommendations, procedures or actions turn out to be
4. *Taking too long in answering any single question* – Remember to time your answers properly

IX. AFTER THE TEST

Scoring procedures differ in detail among civil service jurisdictions although the general principles are the same. Whether the papers are hand-scored or graded by machine we have described, they are nearly always graded by number. That is, the person who marks the paper knows only the number – never the name – of the applicant. Not until all the papers have been graded will they be matched with names. If other tests, such as training and experience or oral interview ratings have been given, scores will be combined. Different parts of the examination usually have different weights. For example, the written test might count 60 percent of the final grade, and a rating of training and experience 40 percent. In many jurisdictions, veterans will have a certain number of points added to their grades.

After the final grade has been determined, the names are placed in grade order and an eligible list is established. There are various methods for resolving ties between those who get the same final grade – probably the most common is to place first the name of the person whose application was received first. Job offers are made from the eligible list in the order the names appear on it. You will be notified of your grade and your rank as soon as all these computations have been made. This will be done as rapidly as possible.

People who are found to meet the requirements in the announcement are called "eligibles." Their names are put on a list of eligible candidates. An eligible's chances of getting a job depend on how high he stands on this list and how fast agencies are filling jobs from the list.

When a job is to be filled from a list of eligibles, the agency asks for the names of people on the list of eligibles for that job. When the civil service commission receives this request, it sends to the agency the names of the three people highest on this list. Or, if the job to be filled has specialized requirements, the office sends the agency the names of the top three persons who meet these requirements from the general list.

The appointing officer makes a choice from among the three people whose names were sent to him. If the selected person accepts the appointment, the names of the others are put back on the list to be considered for future openings.

That is the rule in hiring from all kinds of eligible lists, whether they are for typist, carpenter, chemist, or something else. For every vacancy, the appointing officer has his choice of any one of the top three eligibles on the list. This explains why the person whose name is on top of the list sometimes does not get an appointment when some of the persons lower on the list do. If the appointing officer chooses the second or third eligible, the No. 1 eligible does not get a job at once, but stays on the list until he is appointed or the list is terminated.

X. HOW TO PASS THE INTERVIEW TEST

The examination for which you applied requires an oral interview test. You have already taken the written test and you are now being called for the interview test – the final part of the formal examination.

You may think that it is not possible to prepare for an interview test and that there are no procedures to follow during an interview. Our purpose is to point out some things you can do in advance that will help you and some good rules to follow and pitfalls to avoid while you are being interviewed.

What is an interview supposed to test?

The written examination is designed to test the technical knowledge and competence of the candidate; the oral is designed to evaluate intangible qualities, not readily measured otherwise, and to establish a list showing the relative fitness of each candidate – as measured against his competitors – for the position sought. Scoring is not on the basis of "right" and "wrong," but on a sliding scale of values ranging from "not passable" to "outstanding." As a matter of fact, it is possible to achieve a relatively low score without a single "incorrect" answer because of evident weakness in the qualities being measured.

Occasionally, an examination may consist entirely of an oral test – either an individual or a group oral. In such cases, information is sought concerning the technical knowledges and abilities of the candidate, since there has been no written examination for this purpose. More commonly, however, an oral test is used to supplement a written examination.

Who conducts interviews?

The composition of oral boards varies among different jurisdictions. In nearly all, a representative of the personnel department serves as chairman. One of the members of the board may be a representative of the department in which the candidate would work. In some cases, "outside experts" are used, and, frequently, a businessman or some other representative of the general public is asked to serve. Labor and management or other special groups may be represented. The aim is to secure the services of experts in the appropriate field.

However the board is composed, it is a good idea (and not at all improper or unethical) to ascertain in advance of the interview who the members are and what groups they represent. When you are introduced to them, you will have some idea of their backgrounds and interests, and at least you will not stutter and stammer over their names.

What should be done before the interview?

While knowledge about the board members is useful and takes some of the surprise element out of the interview, there is other preparation which is more substantive. It *is* possible to prepare for an oral interview – in several ways:

1) Keep a copy of your application and review it carefully before the interview

This may be the only document before the oral board, and the starting point of the interview. Know what education and experience you have listed there, and the sequence and dates of all of it. Sometimes the board will ask you to review the highlights of your experience for them; you should not have to hem and haw doing it.

2) Study the class specification and the examination announcement

Usually, the oral board has one or both of these to guide them. The qualities, characteristics or knowledges required by the position sought are stated in these documents. They offer valuable clues as to the nature of the oral interview. For example, if the job involves supervisory responsibilities, the announcement will usually indicate that knowledge of modern supervisory methods and the qualifications of the candidate as a supervisor will be tested. If so, you can expect such questions, frequently in the form of a hypothetical situation which you are expected to solve. NEVER go into an oral without knowledge of the duties and responsibilities of the job you seek.

3) Think through each qualification required

Try to visualize the kind of questions you would ask if you were a board member. How well could you answer them? Try especially to appraise your own knowledge and background in each area, *measured against the job sought*, and identify any areas in which you are weak. Be critical and realistic – do not flatter yourself.

4) Do some general reading in areas in which you feel you may be weak

For example, if the job involves supervision and your past experience has NOT, some general reading in supervisory methods and practices, particularly in the field of human relations, might be useful. Do NOT study agency procedures or detailed manuals. The oral board will be testing your understanding and capacity, not your memory.

5) Get a good night's sleep and watch your general health and mental attitude

You will want a clear head at the interview. Take care of a cold or any other minor ailment, and of course, no hangovers.

What should be done on the day of the interview?

Now comes the day of the interview itself. Give yourself plenty of time to get there. Plan to arrive somewhat ahead of the scheduled time, particularly if your appointment is in the fore part of the day. If a previous candidate fails to appear, the board might be ready for you a bit early. By early afternoon an oral board is almost invariably behind schedule if there are many candidates, and you may have to wait. Take along a book or magazine to read, or your application to review, but leave any extraneous material in the waiting room when you go in for your interview. In any event, relax and compose yourself.

The matter of dress is important. The board is forming impressions about you – from your experience, your manners, your attitude, and your appearance. Give your personal appearance careful attention. Dress your best, but not your flashiest. Choose conservative, appropriate clothing, and be sure it is immaculate. This is a business interview, and your appearance should indicate that you regard it as such. Besides, being well groomed and properly dressed will help boost your confidence.

Sooner or later, someone will call your name and escort you into the interview room. *This is it.* From here on you are on your own. It is too late for any more preparation. But remember, you asked for this opportunity to prove your fitness, and you are here because your request was granted.

What happens when you go in?

The usual sequence of events will be as follows: The clerk (who is often the board stenographer) will introduce you to the chairman of the oral board, who will introduce you to the other members of the board. Acknowledge the introductions before you sit down. Do not be surprised if you find a microphone facing you or a stenotypist sitting by. Oral interviews are usually recorded in the event of an appeal or other review.

Usually the chairman of the board will open the interview by reviewing the highlights of your education and work experience from your application – primarily for the benefit of the other members of the board, as well as to get the material into the record. Do not interrupt or comment unless there is an error or significant misinterpretation; if that is the case, do not hesitate. But do not quibble about insignificant matters. Also, he will usually ask you some question about your education, experience or your present job – partly to get you to start talking and to establish the interviewing "rapport." He may start the actual questioning, or turn it over to one of the other members. Frequently, each member undertakes the questioning on a particular area, one in which he is perhaps most competent, so you can expect each member to participate in the examination. Because time is limited, you may also expect some rather abrupt switches in the direction the questioning takes, so do not be upset by it. Normally, a board member will not pursue a single line of questioning unless he discovers a particular strength or weakness.

After each member has participated, the chairman will usually ask whether any member has any further questions, then will ask you if you have anything you wish to add. Unless you are expecting this question, it may floor you. Worse, it may start you off on an extended, extemporaneous speech. The board is not usually seeking more information. The question is principally to offer you a last opportunity to present further qualifications or to indicate that you have nothing to add. So, if you feel that a significant qualification or characteristic has been overlooked, it is proper to point it out in a sentence or so. Do not compliment the board on the thoroughness of their examination – they have been sketchy, and you know it. If you wish, merely say, "No thank you, I have nothing further to add." This is a point where you can "talk yourself out" of a good impression or fail to present an important bit of information. Remember, *you close the interview yourself.*

The chairman will then say, "That is all, Mr. _____, thank you." Do not be startled; the interview is over, and quicker than you think. Thank him, gather your belongings and take your leave. Save your sigh of relief for the other side of the door.

How to put your best foot forward

Throughout this entire process, you may feel that the board individually and collectively is trying to pierce your defenses, seek out your hidden weaknesses and embarrass and confuse you. Actually, this is not true. They are obliged to make an appraisal of your qualifications for the job you are seeking, and they want to see you in your best light. Remember, they must interview all candidates and a non-cooperative candidate may become a failure in spite of their best efforts to bring out his qualifications. Here are 15 suggestions that will help you:

1) Be natural – Keep your attitude confident, not cocky

If you are not confident that you can do the job, do not expect the board to be. Do not apologize for your weaknesses, try to bring out your strong points. The board is interested in a positive, not negative, presentation. Cockiness will antagonize any board member and make him wonder if you are covering up a weakness by a false show of strength.

2) Get comfortable, but don't lounge or sprawl

Sit erectly but not stiffly. A careless posture may lead the board to conclude that you are careless in other things, or at least that you are not impressed by the importance of the occasion. Either conclusion is natural, even if incorrect. Do not fuss with your clothing, a pencil or an ashtray. Your hands may occasionally be useful to emphasize a point; do not let them become a point of distraction.

3) Do not wisecrack or make small talk

This is a serious situation, and your attitude should show that you consider it as such. Further, the time of the board is limited – they do not want to waste it, and neither should you.

4) Do not exaggerate your experience or abilities
In the first place, from information in the application or other interviews and sources, the board may know more about you than you think. Secondly, you probably will not get away with it. An experienced board is rather adept at spotting such a situation, so do not take the chance.

5) If you know a board member, do not make a point of it, yet do not hide it
Certainly you are not fooling him, and probably not the other members of the board. Do not try to take advantage of your acquaintanceship – it will probably do you little good.

6) Do not dominate the interview
Let the board do that. They will give you the clues – do not assume that you have to do all the talking. Realize that the board has a number of questions to ask you, and do not try to take up all the interview time by showing off your extensive knowledge of the answer to the first one.

7) Be attentive
You only have 20 minutes or so, and you should keep your attention at its sharpest throughout. When a member is addressing a problem or question to you, give him your undivided attention. Address your reply principally to him, but do not exclude the other board members.

8) Do not interrupt
A board member may be stating a problem for you to analyze. He will ask you a question when the time comes. Let him state the problem, and wait for the question.

9) Make sure you understand the question
Do not try to answer until you are sure what the question is. If it is not clear, restate it in your own words or ask the board member to clarify it for you. However, do not haggle about minor elements.

10) Reply promptly but not hastily
A common entry on oral board rating sheets is "candidate responded readily," or "candidate hesitated in replies." Respond as promptly and quickly as you can, but do not jump to a hasty, ill-considered answer.

11) Do not be peremptory in your answers
A brief answer is proper – but do not fire your answer back. That is a losing game from your point of view. The board member can probably ask questions much faster than you can answer them.

12) Do not try to create the answer you think the board member wants
He is interested in what kind of mind you have and how it works – not in playing games. Furthermore, he can usually spot this practice and will actually grade you down on it.

13) Do not switch sides in your reply merely to agree with a board member
Frequently, a member will take a contrary position merely to draw you out and to see if you are willing and able to defend your point of view. Do not start a debate, yet do not surrender a good position. If a position is worth taking, it is worth defending.

14) Do not be afraid to admit an error in judgment if you are shown to be wrong

The board knows that you are forced to reply without any opportunity for careful consideration. Your answer may be demonstrably wrong. If so, admit it and get on with the interview.

15) Do not dwell at length on your present job

The opening question may relate to your present assignment. Answer the question but do not go into an extended discussion. You are being examined for a *new* job, not your present one. As a matter of fact, try to phrase ALL your answers in terms of the job for which you are being examined.

Basis of Rating

Probably you will forget most of these "do's" and "don'ts" when you walk into the oral interview room. Even remembering them all will not ensure you a passing grade. Perhaps you did not have the qualifications in the first place. But remembering them will help you to put your best foot forward, without treading on the toes of the board members.

Rumor and popular opinion to the contrary notwithstanding, an oral board wants you to make the best appearance possible. They know you are under pressure – but they also want to see how you respond to it as a guide to what your reaction would be under the pressures of the job you seek. They will be influenced by the degree of poise you display, the personal traits you show and the manner in which you respond.

ABOUT THIS BOOK

This book contains tests divided into Examination Sections. Go through each test, answering every question in the margin. We have also attached a sample answer sheet at the back of the book that can be removed and used. At the end of each test look at the answer key and check your answers. On the ones you got wrong, look at the right answer choice and learn. Do not fill in the answers first. Do not memorize the questions and answers, but understand the answer and principles involved. On your test, the questions will likely be different from the samples. Questions are changed and new ones added. If you understand these past questions you should have success with any changes that arise. Tests may consist of several types of questions. We have additional books on each subject should more study be advisable or necessary for you. Finally, the more you study, the better prepared you will be. This book is intended to be the last thing you study before you walk into the examination room. Prior study of relevant texts is also recommended. NLC publishes some of these in our Fundamental Series. Knowledge and good sense are important factors in passing your exam. Good luck also helps. So now study this Passbook, absorb the material contained within and take that knowledge into the examination. Then do your best to pass that exam.

EXAMINATION SECTION

EXAMINATION SECTION

TEST 1

DIRECTIONS: Each question or incomplete statement is followed by several suggested answers or completions. Select the one that BEST answers the question or completes the statement. *PRINT THE LETTER OF THE CORRECT ANSWER IN THE SPACE AT THE RIGHT.*

Questions 1-5.

DIRECTIONS: Questions 1 through 5 are to be answered on the basis of the following fact pattern.

When Family Court opens on Monday morning, Desiree rushes to the clerk's desk in a panic. Her ex-boyfriend, Alex, has made threats against her and her children and she would like to file a restraining order as soon as possible. She has never been in court before and does not have any idea of what to expect or what she may need, but she is in fear of her and her children's lives.

1. While Desiree fears for her safety, she cannot obtain a final order of protection against Alex. Why? 1.____
   A. A judge has not yet been assigned to the case.
   B. A judge has not been assigned, so there has been no finding of a family offense being committed and Alex has not agreed to the order.
   C. Desiree's children should be present for the request to the court unless they are under age 18.
   D. Alex has not agreed to the order.

2. A temporary restraining order only lasts until 2.____
   A. the close of the case
   B. the beginning of an appeal
   C. the next time the petitioner is in court
   D. it is extended indefinitely

3. Desiree asks how long a final order of protection lasts. The MOST appropriate response is 3.____
   A. two or ten years
   B. two or five years
   C. one year
   D. six months

4. Which party is responsible for drafting the petition to the judge for a temporary restraining order? 4.____
   A. The judge
   B. The party seeking the order
   C. The clerk
   D. A spectator

5. After Desiree starts her case, Alex is served with a summons. Three weeks later, Desiree returns to the courthouse to say that she has changed her mind and no longer fears for her safety.
Desiree must
   A. withdraw her petition for a restraining order
   B. start an anger management program
   C. withdraw her petition with prejudice as she will not be able to file again
   D. recuse herself

6. Jamie has hired legal counsel to represent him in the purchase of commercial buildings across New York State. With his attorney's help, he has secured the purchase of nine different office buildings totaling $2 million. Last week, Jamie discovered that his attorney forged his signature on the sale of four of those properties and collected the proceeds. Assume the threshold for filing a suit in Albany County is $50,000, Nassau County is $200,000, and New York County is $500,000.
Where can Jamie sue his attorney for malpractice?
   A. New York County   B. Albany County
   C. Nassau County   D. All of the above

7. Which of the following matters is LEAST likely to be heard in the Albany County – Commercial Division?
   A. Commercial class actions
   B. Transactions governed by the Uniform Commercial Code
   C. Divorce
   D. Shareholder derivate action

8. Which of the following matters is LEAST likely to be heard in Suffolk County District Court?
   A. Small claims matter of $1,000,000   B. Arraignment in a felony case
   C. Petty larceny (theft of $200)   D. Shoplifting

9. Which of the following is LEAST likely to be heard in the Landlord and Tenant Court?
   A. Non-payment proceedings   B. Hold-over proceedings
   C. Evictions   D. Adoptions

10. Dave approaches the clerk's desk and insists that he has a tenant in his building who refuses to pay rent and will not vacate the premises.
Dave seeks assistance on initiating _____ proceedings.
   A. Annulment   B. Hold-over   C. Numeration   D. Abandonment

11. John and Jill need to file for bankruptcy and would like to do so together. John and Jill would file which type of petition?
   A. Separate   B. Tenants   C. Survivor   D. Joint

12. Rich would like to know what advice he can give his brother who was arrested last night for driving under the influence of alcohol. Rich's brother is scheduled to be arraigned this morning. While you may not be authorized to give legal advice, it is prudent to know that a plea of nolo contendere has the same effect as a plea of _____, but is not an admission of guilt.
    A. acquittal B. remorse C. not guilty D. guilty

13. Emily arrives in court for her bankruptcy hearing. Emily is not working, does not have any savings. She does not own any property, jewelry, collectibles, or other precious items of value.
    Emily's bankruptcy petition will MOST likely be classified as a _____ case.
    A. nolo contendere B. no asset
    C. no prohibition D. Chapter 13

14. Assume the same facts as above. Emily is a full-time student and took out a student loan before filing bankruptcy.
    The trustee has informed Emily her student loan is a _____ debt.
    A. dischargeable B. non-dischargeable
    C. immediate D. short term

15. A party in interest in bankruptcy is defined as a party who
    A. has standing to be heard in a matter to be decided in the bankruptcy case
    B. standing to disrupt the court
    C. intends to file a brief
    D. intends to petition for early release

16. A petty offense is one that is punishable by _____ or less in prison.
    A. six months B. one year C. three years D. four years

17. Town and village courts have jurisdiction over
    A. vehicle and traffic matters B. small claims
    C. civil matters D. all of the above

18. The highest civil court in New York is the
    A. Supreme Court B. City Court
    C. Civil Court D. Court of Appeals

19. The highest criminal court in New York is the
    A. New York City Criminal Court B. Court of Appeals
    C. County Courts D. Village Courts

Questions 20-23.

DIRECTIONS: Questions 20 through 23 are to be answered on the basis of the following fact pattern.

Amy is a Guardians ad Litem ("GAL") for the New York Housing Court. She volunteered for the Court because she wanted to help people resolve their housing disputes. The judge has appointed Amy as Gerald's GAL in his case. Gerald is involved in a minor dispute with his landlord.

20. Amy believes that Gerald's housing issues stem from his poor money management. Can Amy manage Gerald's checkbook and other personal finances as they relate to his housing case?
    A. Yes, because his finances relate to his housing case
    B. Yes, because he clearly cannot manage his money on his own
    C. Yes, but only if Gerald asks her to
    D. No

21. Amy is NOT allowed to do which of the following things?
    A. Meet with Gerald
    B. Meet with Gerald's landlord
    C. Allow Gerald's landlord into Gerald's apartment
    D. Ensure the landlord completes repairs as promised

22. A GAL works in which party's best interest?
    A. Gerald's landlord
    B. Gerald
    C. The appointed party
    D. The judge

23. Amy has fallen ill and cannot meet her obligations as a GAL. Which party can remove Amy as Gerald's GAL?
    A. Gerald
    B. Gerald's landlord
    C. The judge
    D. The clerk

24. Pro per is another term for _____ or a self-represented person.
    A. pro tem   B. pro se   C. qui tam   D. quid pro

25. Sanctions are defined as a
    A. penalty or other type of enforcement used to bring about compliance with the law
    B. penalty specific to international trade law
    C. federal penalty reserved for those who lie under oath
    D. misdemeanor crime punishable by more than four years in prison

KEY (CORRECT ANSWERS)

1.	A	11.	D
2.	C	12.	D
3.	B	13.	B
4.	C	14.	B
5.	A	15.	A
6.	D	16.	A
7.	C	17.	D
8.	A	18.	D
9.	D	19.	B
10.	B	20.	D

21. C
22. C
23. C
24. B
25. A

TEST 2

DIRECTIONS: Each question or incomplete statement is followed by several suggested answers or completions. Select the one that BEST answers the question or completes the statement. *PRINT THE LETTER OF THE CORRECT ANSWER IN THE SPACE AT THE RIGHT.*

Questions 1-5.

DIRECTIONS: Questions 1 through 5 are to be answered on the basis of the following fact pattern.

Edwin has been served with a lawsuit from his former accountant, Bob. Bob claims Edwin never paid him for his accounting services after he filed Edwin's personal income tax and business income tax returns. Edwin has come to the clerk's desk confused and angry.

1. Edwin wants to know what the basis of Bob's legal claim is against him. Where can Edwin find more information about the case?
    A. The internet
    B. The complaint
    C. The subpoena
    D. The arraignment

    1.____

2. Edwin claims that he was audited by the IRS shortly after Bob filed his personal income taxes. Edwin wants to sue Bob in connection with his being audited. In order to do so, Edwin would need to
    A. re-sue   B. re-file   C. countersue   D. cross-claim

    2.____

3. Bob filed taxes for Edwin and Edwin's wife. While Edwin's wife is not listed on the Complaint in Edwin's suit against Bob, Edwin's wife would also like to appear as a party to the case. Is this possible?
    A. No, because Edwin's wife may be unavailable for trial
    B. No, because Edwin's wife is not initiating the suit
    C. No, because Edwin can only sue Bob himself
    D. Yes

    3.____

4. Which of the following courts is MOST appropriate for Edwin's suit against Bob?
    A. Housing Court
    B. Surrogates Court
    C. Civil Court
    D. Criminal Court

    4.____

5. Which of the following is MOST likely to be the legal basis of Bob's suit against Edwin?
    A. Breach of contract
    B. Negligence
    C. Assault
    D. Defamation

    5.____

6. The Housing Court is made of parts. The resolution part presides over all pre-trial matters in a case and attempts to settle the case. Jeremy appears at Housing Court for his trial that begins this morning.
Is Jeremy's case appropriate for the pre-trial part of the Housing Court?
    A. Yes, as pre-trial matters preclude this
    B. Yes, as a check in before the trial can start
    C. No, the trial part is separate and distinct from the pre-trial part of Housing Court
    D. No, the trial part only hears cases on Mondays

Questions 7-8.

DIRECTIONS: Questions 7 and 8 are to be answered on the basis of the following text.

Jenny received a notice from the marshal that she is being evicted from her apartment. She wants to ignore the notice, but comes to the courthouse at the urging of her boyfriend.

7. Her boyfriend warns her that if she does not take care of the notice, she and her _____ may be _____ from the apartment.
    A. property; removed
    B. removed; property
    C. property; removal
    D. assets; removed

8. At the courthouse, the clerk instructs Jenny to complete an affidavit in support of a(n)
    A. order for removal
    B. petition
    C. order to show cause
    D. justification

9. Because Jenny never answered the original petition for eviction from her landlord, her landlord obtained a _____ judgment against her. Jenny now needs to complete an affidavit in support of an order to show cause to _____ a judgment based on failure to answer.
    A. vacate; default
    B. vacate; demand
    C. default; vacate
    D. default; validate

10. A clerk in the Resolution Part of Housing Court can do all of the following EXCEPT
    A. answer questions about the court calendar
    B. answer questions about the judge's rules
    C. assist the judge as necessary
    D. provide detailed legal analysis and/or advice

11. A judge may direct parties in a dispute to mediation, which is a form of
    A. neutrality
    B. alternative dispute resolution
    C. alternative judgment
    D. non-binding analysis of the legal dispute

12. Joel and Rachel would like to place their daughter into foster care.
    Do Joel and Rachel need an attorney to represent them in court?
    A. Yes, as foster care placements are complicated
    B. Yes, unless they do not have money to hire a lawyer
    C. No, legal representation is not required but they do have a right to have the court appoint an attorney if they cannot afford one
    D. No, unless they change their minds after the placement has taken place

13. The New York Court of Claims is the only court where one can seek damages against
    A. the State of New York or other state-related agencies
    B. New York City
    C. municipalities in Richmond County
    D. New York State colleges

14. While City Courts such as Binghamton City Court handle criminal and civil matters, the amount in dispute can only be up to
    A. $20,000,000   B. $15,000   C. $1,000,000   D. $5,000,000

15. Beatrice is having issues understanding her mother's will. Her mother is living, but Beatrice wants to ensure she understands all of the terms of the will while her mother is still alive.
    Beatrice is not the named executor, which is defined as
    A. someone named in the will appointed to wind up the affairs of the deceased person
    B. the person who inherits all of the deceased person's property
    C. the attorney of the estate
    D. the judge who presides over the estate

16. A person who is named in the will to inherit money or other property is the
    A. executrix   B. devisee   C. custodian   D. beneficiary

17. Matters of will and probate are heard in which court?
    A. Civil Court   B. Family Court
    C. Surrogates Court   D. Criminal Court

18. A revocable trust is a trust that can be
    A. rescinded by the grantor after creation
    B. overruled by a judge
    C. nullified by the beneficiaries
    D. canceled outright without warning to the trust remainders

19. James approaches the clerk's desk seeking assistance regarding a child support matter. James lost his job a few months ago and can no longer pay his child support.
    What is the LEAST appropriate advice you can give James?
    A. He is prudent for coming to the court to seek assistance as there are serious penalties for non-payment of child support.
    B. A support order can be modified.

C. Without income, he cannot possibly pay child support, so he should wait until he is found in contempt of court.
D. Penalties for non-payment include interception of tax refunds, suspension of personal and business licenses, and seizure of bank accounts.

20. As a clerk for the New York Court of Appeals, you are asked to determine whether a case from one of the trial courts has been upheld or reversed. If the case has been upheld, it is recorded in the docket as
    A. remanded   b. retained   C. affirmed   D. affiant

21. If a case has been reversed or sent back to the trial court from the New York Court of Appeals, the word _____ will be recorded in the docket.
    A. retained   B. reversed   C. remanded   D. replevin

22. Sue does not agree with the finding of the Family Court. She asks if an order can be appealed.
    The MOST appropriate response is:
    A. No, as all orders are final
    B. No, as Family Court does not pose any legal issues requiring appeal
    C. No, given that Sue is not represented by an attorney
    D. Yes, she may appeal from an order

23. Joe, John, and Beth are involved in a paternity suit. Joe believes he is the father of Beth's baby, Sarah, but John maintains that he is the father.
    What document would be MOST helpful for the court in resolving this matter?
    A. John and Beth's marriage license
    B. Joe and Beth's marriage license
    C. Sarah's birth certificate
    D. Beth's medical records

24. Abel is concerned that his cousin, Ted, is not able to afford legal representation in his trial for armed robbery. Ted must be considered _____ or otherwise unable to afford to hire a lawyer before defense counsel is appointed by the court.
    A. responsible   B. indigent   C. not guilty   D. petty

25. Which of the following is heard and determined outside of the courtroom?
    A. Hearing   B. Plea bargain
    C. Testimony   D. Evidence

KEY (CORRECT ANSWERS)

1.	B		11.	B
2.	C		12.	C
3.	D		13.	A
4.	C		14.	B
5.	A		15.	A
6.	C		16.	D
7.	A		17.	C
8.	C		18.	A
9.	C		19.	C
10.	D		20.	C

21. C
22. D
23. C
24. B
25. B

EXAMINATION SECTION
TEST 1

DIRECTIONS: Each question or incomplete statement is followed by several suggested answers or completions. Select the one that BEST answers the question or completes the statement. *PRINT THE LETTER OF THE CORRECT ANSWER IN THE SPACE AT THE RIGHT.*

Questions 1-5.

DIRECTIONS: Questions 1 through 5 are to be answered on the basis of the following fact pattern.

Bill initiated a lawsuit against his landlord, Amy, last year. Bill claims Amy did not upkeep common areas in the four-apartment building where Bill resides. These common areas include the hallway, entryway, and parking lot of the building. Bill is not represented by an attorney, but Amy is represented by Maureen. The parties have failed to settle the matter outside of court. Bill, Amy, and Maureen are ready to move forward with court proceedings.

1. The magistrate judge sets the pre-trial conference between the parties for March 30 at 9:30 A.M. The parties required to attend the pretrial conference are
    A. Maureen, Bill, and the judge
    B. the judge only
    C. Bill and Amy
    D. Bill, Amy, and Maureen

1.____

2. During the pre-trial conference, the judge wants the parties to stipulate to as many issues as possible before trial. The judge instructs the parties to focus on undisputed facts. An example of a stipulation would be:
    A. Both parties agree the parking lot is not a common area
    B. Maureen files a motion to vacate
    C. Bill wants to expedite the case and start trial the following Monday]
    D. Amy files a counterclaim against Bill for failure to pay rent on time

2.____

3. A pre-trial conference is attended by the required parties if the case does not settle before trial. However, a pre-trial conference cannot be set until
    A. the jury is selected
    B. the attorneys have entered appearances
    C. initial pleadings, including the complaint and answer, have been filed
    D. the court clerk is selected

3.____

4. Which deadline is MOST likely to be set by the judge during the pre-trial conference?
The deadline
    A. to decide which juror will serve as foreperson
    B. to decide which courthouse the trial will take place
    C. for all discovery to be completed
    D. for the judge to select a law clerk to transcribe court proceedings

4.____

5. Bill will be appearing as a
   A. defendant
   B. pro se litigant
   C. respondent
   D. en banc party

Questions 6-9.

DIRECTIONS: Questions 6 through 9 are to be answered on the basis of the following fact pattern.

Adam, Barbara, Cameron, and David appear for jury duty on June 15. Adam and Barbara have each served on a trial before; Adam served on a criminal trial while Barbara served on a civil trial. The trial Adam served on lasted three months, and he would prefer not to serve on a trial ever again. Cameron and David have never served on a trial before and are unsure of what to expect.

6. While prospective jurors wait to be called by the clerk, Adam and Cameron spark up a conversation. Adam tells Cameron that if he were selected to be a juror Cameron may be isolated from his family and friends for weeks.
   What is Adam referring to?
   A. Ex-parte communications, which prohibit jurors from speaking with anyone else during the trial
   B. Voir dire, which may require one to be questioned in judge's chambers about past dealings
   C. Jury sequestration or juror isolation from the public to prevent contact with outside influences
   D. Individual depositions of jurors prior to the start of a trial

7. Barbara overhears the conversation between Adam and Cameron and interjects. She explains that not all juries operate the same way. She explains that in the middle of the trial in which she served, the defendant filed a motion requesting a bench trial.
   A bench trial is a trial without a
   A. plaintiff's attorney
   B. jury
   C. defendant's attorney
   D. bailiff

8. The court's clerk finally begins jury selection. He or she calls how many jurors from the jury selection list?
   A. 9
   B. 6
   C. 10
   D. 12

9. Cameron and David are selected and take a seat in the jury box. The judge provides an overview of the case and tells the prospective jurors that the case involves armed robbery. As a teenager, David was mugged at gunpoint while walking home from school. He raises his hand and tells the judge he may be biased in the trial because of his personal experience.
   The defendant's attorney will ask that David be excused
   A. with good reason
   B. for cause
   C. without prejudice
   D. with prejudice

10. Which of the following does NOT occur during the judge's charge to the jury? 10.____
    A. A discussion of the standard of proof jurors should apply to the case
    B. A reminder that opening and closing arguments are considered evidence
    C. A note that jurors should base their conclusions on the evidence presented at trial
    D. A reminder that jurors are required to adhere to the relevant laws in rendering a verdict

11. Which of the following does the court reporter NOT record 11.____
    A. testimony of the witnesses
    B. objections made by the attorneys
    C. the judge's respective rulings of objections
    D. ex-parte communications

Questions 12-16.

DIRECTIONS: Questions 12 through 16 are to be answered on the basis of the following fact pattern.

Michael is accused of felony theft of an automobile. The vehicle was taken from an 18-unit apartment building parking lot sometime during the night of August 15. The vehicle was driven for approximately five miles before the driver crashed it into a parked car. The driver fled the scene. The owner of the vehicle, Jeffrey, was asleep in his apartment during the time the vehicle was stolen. Michael and Jeffrey are represented by counsel.

12. Given the charge of felony theft of an automobile, Michael now faces how long a term of incarceration? 12.____
    A. One year or more
    B. One year or less
    C. Six months
    D. Five years or more

13. During Jeffrey's testimony, one of the jurors, Samantha, realizes she was in the building where the car was stolen on the night of the theft. She was sleeping over her sister's apartment for the night and remembers seeing a bright blue Porsche – Jeffrey's car – in the parking lot before bed. She immediately informs the bailiff who tells the judge. 13.____
    How will the judge MOST likely move forward in the case?
    A. Declare a mistrial
    B. Acquit Michael of all charges
    C. Excuse the juror and replace here with an alternate juror and continue the trial
    D. Demand the attorneys in the case submit post-hearing briefs on the issue

14. In open court, the judge asks Samantha details about why she was in the apartment at the time Michael allegedly stole Jeffrey's car and what, if anything, she remembers about that night. Samantha says she did not see or hear anything suspicious, but does remember Michael being in the apartment building in one of the common areas. Michael's attorney files a motion for a mistrial after Samantha's testimony to the court. Why? 14.____

A. Samantha's testimony has substantially prejudiced the other jurors who heard Michael was in the building on the night of the theft.
B. There is not enough substantive evidence to continue the trial against Michael.
C. Samantha should have been removed as a juror at the beginning of the trial.
D. The case must be filed in the court closest to where the car was found, not where it was allegedly taken.

15. If the judge declares a mistrial, what effect would that determination have on the jury verdict?
    A. No effect; the jury must still render a decision on the merits
    B. The jury need only to determine damages.
    C. The jury does not need to render a verdict.
    D. Only six jurors need to serve after the judge declares a mistrial.

16. After all evidence has been presented, it is clear Michael did not commit the crime. Michael was in another state at the time of the theft and could not have committed felony theft of Jeffrey's automobile. Before the case is submitted to a jury, Michael's attorney submits a motion that argues no reasonable jury could find for Jeffrey. Michael's attorney asks the judge to instruct the jury to find Michael not guilty.
    Michael's attorney is requesting a(n) _____, because Michael clearly did not commit the crime.
    A. reduced charge
    B. substitute charge
    C. acquittal
    D. directed verdict

17. During the direct examination of one of the plaintiff's witnesses, the defendant's attorney objects. Defendant's attorney believes opposing counsel asked a leading question. The judge sustains defendant's objection.
    How must plaintiff's counsel proceed?
    A. The witness may answer the question as asked.
    B. Plaintiff's counsel must re-phrase the question in a proper form or ask another question.
    C. Plaintiff's counsel must stop his or her line of questioning completely.
    D. The witness may step down.

18. An expert is permitted to
    A. review the plaintiff's evidence, draw a reasonable conclusion, and give testimony to that effect
    B. review the defendant's evidence, draw a reasonable conclusion, and submit his or her opinion in writing to the judge
    C. give his or her opinion based on the facts in evidence and provide the reasoning for that opinion
    D. provide an opinion in open court

19. Which party, as a matter of right, is entitled to a rebuttal in closing arguments?
    A. The plaintiff
    B. The defense
    C. The defense, but only after the plaintiff has given their closing argument
    D. The defense, but only if the plaintiff waives their right to make a closing argument

20. When a jury cannot agree on a verdict, a(n) _____ occurs and the result is a(n) _____.
    A. mistrial; acquittal
    B. mistrial; hung jury
    C. hung jury; mistrial
    D. acquittal; mistrial

21. Generally speaking, the role of the foreperson, also known as the presiding juror, is to
    A. announce the verdict
    B. preside over discussion of the jurors
    C. preside over the votes of the jurors
    D. all of the above

22. A request to poll the jury serves what purpose?
    Jury polling
    A. ensures the verdict to be recorded is accurate
    B. allows jurors to resolve any conflicts of interests prior to the start of trial
    C. helps the jury selection process move faster
    D. allows the judge to ensure each juror will be impartial and unbiased while hearing evidence

23. In which of the following scenarios would a bailiff MOST likely intervene?
    A. The plaintiff and defense attorneys are chatting with one another outside the courtroom.
    B. The judge and his or her law clerk are overheard talking about the case in judge's chambers.
    C. One of the jurors is talking with the defense attorney inside the courtroom before others have entered the room.
    D. The plaintiff and the defendant's attorney are heard talking in the hallway.

24. Which of the following would be submitted only after a verdict is rendered?
    A. Motion to dismiss
    B. Motion in limine
    C. Motion to exclude
    D. Motion in arrest of judgment

25. In many jurisdictions, a motion for a new trial must be filed before a party can file a(n)
    A. exculpatory plea
    B. motion for mistrial
    C. acquittal by default
    D. appeal

KEY (CORRECT ANSWERS)

1.	A	11.	D
2.	A	12.	A
3.	C	13.	C
4.	C	14.	A
5.	B	15.	C
6.	C	16.	D
7.	B	17.	B
8.	D	18.	C
9.	B	19.	A
10.	B	20.	C

21. D
22. A
23. C
24. D
25. D

TEST 2

DIRECTIONS: Each question or incomplete statement is followed by several suggested answers or completions. Select the one that BEST answers the question or completes the statement. *PRINT THE LETTER OF THE CORRECT ANSWER IN THE SPACE AT THE RIGHT.*

Questions 1-5.

DIRECTIONS: Questions 1 through 5 are to be answered on the basis of the following fact pattern.

James and Sean started an accounting practice five years ago. Business quickly soured and James and Sean decided to each start their own competing business practices. While James' business flourished, Sean's practice has floundered. Sean believes James spoke poorly about him to their mutual friends, ruining his professional reputation, and went behind his back to steal clients. Sean now wants to sue James civilly.

1. How would Sean begin a civil suit against James?   1.____
   A. Sean needs to file an interpleader to compel James to court.
   B. Sean must file a motion to compel proceedings.
   C. Sean must file a complaint against Sean in the proper court.
   D. Sean can outline the facts of his case to the clerk who will transcribe the issues.

2. Sean must also file a summons with the clerk.   2.____
   What is the role of the summons in initiating a lawsuit?
   A. It puts the other party on notice that a lawsuit has been filed against them.
   B. It compels discovery in a court of proper jurisdiction.
   C. It requires the other party to answer by initiating a cross-motion.
   D. It gives the other party extended time to file a counterclaim.

3. Sean's attorney and James' attorney begin the process of exchanging   3.____
   information about the witnesses each side plans to call and the evidence that
   will be presented at trial.
   This process is called
   A. interrogation   B. discovery   C. compulsion   D. demurrer

4. One of James' and Sean's former clients is moving to London. James' and   4.____
   Sean's attorneys agree to take her deposition now and use it at trial in the
   event she will not be able to appear.
   At trial, her testimony will be _____ and part of the record.
   A. read into evidence   B. ex parte
   C. sequestered   D. assumed credible

5. After being notified that a lawsuit has been filed against him, James has an   5.____
   opportunity to answer the _____ that has been filed against him.
   A. pleadings   B. motion to compel
   C. interpleader   D. complaint

6. Venue refers to the district or county within a state where the
   A. lawsuit began
   B. lawsuit must be heard
   C. plaintiff resides
   D. plaintiff is domiciled

7. After both parties have agreed on a jury, the jurors are _____ by the court clerk before they are impaneled.
   A. instructed to take notes
   B. sworn in
   C. fingerprinted
   D. arranged

8. Can the prosecution compel a defendant in a criminal trial to take the stand and testify?
   A. Yes; he or she must explain what happened in open court
   B. Yes; he or she must take the stand and testify they are using their Fifth Amendment right against self-incrimination.
   C. Yes; he or she must take the stand but they can refuse to answer any question they choose.
   D. No.

9. Criminal charges are brought against a person in all of the following ways, EXCEPT
   A. citation
   B. information
   C. indictment
   D. subpoena

Questions 10-15.

DIRECTIONS: Questions 10 through 15 are to be answered on the basis of the following fact pattern.

Jason's brother, Andrew, has been arrested. Jason appears at the courthouse as soon as he hears this news. He does not know why Andrew has been arrested, but suspects it may be related to his tumultuous relationship with his ex-girlfriend, who has filed a temporary restraining order against Andrew.

10. If Andrew was not arrested on a warrant, when will he be able to file a plea of guilty, not guilty, or no contest?
    A. At arraignment
    B. At trial
    C. At a preliminary conference
    D. At indictment

11. If Andrew is released from custody without a payment of money on the promise that he will appear for all hearings and for trial, the judge has released Andrew
    A. on his own recognizance
    B. with time served
    C. after a concurrent term
    D. on exculpatory evidence

12. In the alternative, if the judge sets bail for Andrew's release, he or she does so with the intent of
    A. punishing Andrew
    B. ensuring Andrew will appear for trial and all pre-trial hearings for which he must be present
    C. setting a fine dependent on the type of crime alleged
    D. releasing Andrew into the custody of his responsible brother, Jason

13. Which of the following should NOT be a factor a judge may use in deciding the amount of Andrew's bail?
    A. The risk of Andrew's fleeing
    B. The type of crime Andrew is alleged to have committed
    C. Andrew's age, race, and sex
    D. The safety of the community

14. During Andrew's initial appearance, the judge explains to Andrew that he has a right to a trial by jury.
    If Andrew does not want a trial by jury, what type of trial will he receive?
    A. An expedited trial
    B. A bench trial
    C. A summation
    D. An information

15. Andrew pleads no contest to the charges in his initial appearance.
    Andrew is effectively
    A. not admitting guilt or disputing the charge alleged
    B. admitting guilt
    C. denying the charge but admitting he will pay any fines incurred
    D. deferring his plea until a later date

Questions 16-19.

DIRECTIONS: Questions 16 through 19 are to be answered on the basis of the following fact pattern.

Jameson and Avery are neighbors. Jameson moved and purchased a home in the lot next to Avery's lot three months ago. Avery is suing Jameson for building a fence on Avery's property. Jameson attests the fence is actually being built on his own property and there is no boundary dispute. Jameson and Avery are both represented by counsel. A number of motions are filed by each party and discovery has been a lengthy process thus far.

16. Both parties serve each other requests to answer questions in writing under oath. Avery's attorney demands Jameson answer questions about the purchase of his home and dealings with the contractors building the fence. Jameson demands Avery answer questions about the property line dividing their property.
    This type of discovery is called
    A. interrogatories
    B. demands
    C. summons
    D. written decision

17. Avery's attorney would like to depose the property surveyor, Abe.
    Can Jameson and/or Jameson's attorney attend Abe's deposition?
    A. No, because Abe will be Avery's witness
    B. No, because Avery can share the information with Jameson's counsel at a later date
    C. No, because Abe's testimony may not be inadmissible in court so Jameson's presence would be futile
    D. Yes

18. Which of the following will NOT occur at the pre-trial conference between the parties?
    A. A deadline for discovery will be set.
    B. A trial date will be set.
    C. The judge will encourage stipulations between the parties.
    D. The judge will ask for oral arguments.

19. During discovery, both parties ascertain that Jameson built the fence on his side of the property line. Jameson's attorney asks the court to dismiss the case because there is no longer a legally sound basis to proceed.
    This request to the court is a motion to
    A. relinquish   B. dismiss   C. vacate   D. suppress

20. Which type of evidence suggests a fact by implication or inference?
    A. Exculpatory   B. Demandable
    C. Circumstantial   D. Ascertainable

21. Sam sued David civilly last September. Sam prevailed in the original suit. David has appealed. David is now the _____ and Sam is the _____.
    A. petitionery; respondent   B. appellant; appellee
    C. appellant; petitioner   D. respondent; appellee

22. If an appellate court remands a case back to the lower trial court, which of the following instructions may be imposed on the trial court.
    A. A new trial be held
    B. The trial court's judgment be modified or corrected
    C. The trial court reconsider the facts and/or the evidence presented
    D. All of the above

23. Which of the following motions may only be filed after all of the evidence has been presented?
    A. Motion in limine   B. Motion for directed verdict
    C. Motion for summary judgment   D. Motion for admission

24. When is it permissible for parties to settle a suit?
    A. Before the trial begins   B. During the trial
    c. While the jury is deliberating D. All of the above

25. Summations are typically a part of _____ and discuss the evidence and the inferences that can be drawn from that evidence.   25.____
    A. closing arguments
    B. indictments
    C. hearings on the merits
    D. ex-parte communications

KEY (CORRECT ANSWERS)

1. C
2. A
3. B
4. A
5. D

6. B
7. B
8. D
9. D
10. A

11. A
12. B
13. C
14. B
15. A

16. A
17. D
18. D
19. B
20. C

21. B
22. D
23. B
24. D
25. A

TEST 3

DIRECTIONS: Each question or incomplete statement is followed by several suggested answers or completions. Select the one that BEST answers the question or completes the statement. *PRINT THE LETTER OF THE CORRECT ANSWER IN THE SPACE AT THE RIGHT.*

Questions 1-4.

DIRECTIONS: Questions 1 through 4 are to be answered on the basis of the following fact pattern.

Steven is on trial for embezzlement. The case is complex; there are eight witnesses for the prosecution and twelve witnesses for the defense, including character witnesses. Steven has filed a cross-claim against his former employer, and plaintiff, ABC Corp., Inc. for defamation of character. Steven maintains that he never stole a dime from ABC Corp., Inc. and wants ABC Corp., Inc. to issue him a public apology when the trial is over.

1. The BEST place to refer back to the testimony of one witness is 1.____
   A. the docket
   B. the judge's notes
   C. the stenographer's transcript
   D. clerk notes

2. Steven's attorney presents evidence that his client was not working on the 2.____
   days the theft from ABC Corp. allegedly occurred.
   What kind of evidence is Steven's counsel presenting to the court?
   A. Alibi
   B. Exculpatory
   C. Exclusionary
   D. Exemplary

3. Alexandra, a friend of Steven, testifies for the prosecution in Steven's case. 3.____
   Alexandra testifies that Steven told her that he embezzled money from ABC Corp. Steven's attorney objects to Alexandra's testimony because it is
   A. exculpatory   B. hearsay   C. untrue   D. impeachment

4. At the close of Steven's trial, oral arguments are made by _____ to the 4.____
   court, summarizing their position on the evidence that has been presented and their theories on the case in its entirety.
   A. jurors   B. plaintiffs   C. attorneys   D. defense

Questions 5-8.

DIRECTIONS: Questions 5 through 8 are to be answered on the basis of the following fact pattern.

April 16 is turning out to be a very busy day at the courthouse. In the morning, three cases were withdrawn by the plaintiff without a hearing, six cases were dismissed without prejudice by the judge, and two cases were settled out of court.

5. How many were decided by the judge on April 16? 5.____
   A. 0   B. 2   C. 6   D. 3

2 (#3)

6. How many cases were heard before the judge?   6.____
   A. 3   B. 6   C. 2   D. 8

7. How many cases would the court reporter need to be present for?   7.____
   A. 6   B. 3   C. 2   D. 8

8. How many of the cases were awarded damages?   8.____
   A. 2   B. 6   C. 3   D. 0

Questions 9-12.

DIRECTIONS: Questions 9 through 12 are to be answered on the basis of the following fact pattern.

Miranda has initiated a lawsuit against her former friend, Anne, for breach of contract. Miranda referred Anne's interior design services to Miranda's boss. Anne went to Miranda's boss' house for an initial consultation and, even though Anne agreed to design three rooms in the house, she never followed through with the contract. Miranda is incredibly embarrassed by the entire situation. Anne, however, maintains that she has a reasonable excuse for not finishing the work.

9. In addition to money damages, Miranda would also like the court to compel   9.____
   Anne to execute the contract or, in other words, actually design the rooms.
   This remedy is deemed
   A. compulsion under order   B. specific performance
   C. remedy at law   D. joint and several liability

10. Miranda alleges that she suffered pain and suffering from Anne's inability to   10.____
    execute the contract.
    What type of damages are pain and suffering categorized as?
    A. Punitive   B. Special   C. Specific   D. Compensatory

11. Miranda lives in New York. Anne lives in New Jersey. Miranda's boss   11.____
    lives in Connecticut. When Miranda files suit in New York, the judge initially
    indicates that she does not have
    A. authority   B. jurisdiction   C. venue   D. domicile

12. The contract that is alleged to have been breached exists between Anne and   12.____
    Miranda's boss, not Miranda. Therefore, there is no legal cause of action for
    the case to proceed. Miranda's boss is free to file the claim against Anne at a
    later date if she so chooses.
    The court will
    A. dismiss the action without prejudice
    B. deny the action without prejudice
    C. sustain the action
    D. abdicate as necessary

13. Nominal damages are
    A. damages awarded in name only, indicating no substantial harm was done
    B. damages to recompense the injured for the infliction of emotional distress
    C. damages to recompense the initiator of the lawsuit
    D. a reimbursement of filing fees, awarded to the person who can prove they are injured

14. The type of recovery being sought by the plaintiff is known as the
    A. order   B. punishment   C. remedy   D. issue

15. Robert approaches the clerk's desk in a panic. He says that he filed a lawsuit against his cousin, Mike, but neglected to add his cousin's friend, Roy, to the suit.
    What action is Robert attempting to take?
    A. Amending the complaint
    B. Adding an addendum to the summons
    C. Re-issuing a summons
    D. Redacting the answer

Questions 16-20.

DIRECTIONS: Questions 16 through 20 are to be answered on the basis of the following fact pattern.

Daniel and Patrick sue one another civilly. Daniel sues Patrick for intentional infliction of emotional distress and Patrick countersues Daniel for assault. Both causes of action stem from a physical altercation which took place at a youth hockey game where Daniel's and Patrick's sons played against one another. At trial, the judge found that Daniel started the fight and attacked Patrick and found, by extension, that Patrick was not a contributor in the altercation.
Daniel appealed the decision to an appellate court. Daniel's attorney argued that the trial court erred, as a matter of law, in finding that Daniel was the sole initiator of the altercation and ignored evidence to the contrary. Appellate courts generally render decisions by a panel. The panel in Daniel's appeal was comprised of three justices. The appellate court agreed with the trial court's finding of fault.

16. The ultimate disposition of this case was the appellate court
    A. affirmed the lower court's decision
    B. remanded the lower court's decision
    C. reversed the lower court's decision
    D. acquitted Daniel of all charges

17. An opinion from the entire panel of justices is known as a
    A. per curiam decision   B. affirmative decision
    C. stare decisis   D. en banc order

18. One of the judges agrees with the decision of the court, but disagrees with the reasoning of the conclusion. This judge decides to write his own opinion. This is deemed a
    A. dissenting opinion
    B. remedial decision
    C. concurring opinion
    D. recurrent opinion

    18.____

19. Suppose that one of the judges disagrees entirely with the ruling. How will the judgment be altered because of the disagreement? The judgment
    A. is unaffected because the majority voted in agreement with the trial court
    B. is unaffected because this judge did not author a dissenting opinion
    C. is unaffected because oral arguments were not made before the panel
    D. will be overturned

    19.____

20. The appellate court still requires _____, even if it is established by the trial court, known as original _____.
    A. domicile; venue
    B. venue; jurisdiction
    C. jurisdiction; jurisdiction
    D. jurisdiction; domicile

    20.____

21. The legal theory upon which a case is based is called a
    A. basis
    B. decisis
    C. cause of action
    D. precedent

    21.____

Questions 22-25.

DIRECTIONS: Questions 22 through 25 are to be answered on the basis of the following fact pattern.

Last July, Sarah stole Alexis's car and took it for a joyride along Main Street. After a long joyride, Sarah decided to pick up Ashley at Ashley's apartment. Although Ashley asked when Sarah bought a new car, Sarah lied and told Ashley that it was her aunt's car that she borrowed with permission. Sarah and Ashley went on another joyride, this time driving up to 90 miles per hour on the highways around town. After three hours, Ashley asked to go home and Sarah obliged. After Sarah dropped Ashley back off at her apartment, Sarah sped through a busy intersection and crashed the car. The car was totaled.
Alexis has filed a lawsuit against both Sarah and Ashley.

22. Alexis is determined to sue both Sarah and Ashley for conversion, or the wrongful act of dominion or control over another person's property. However, after meeting with her attorney, Alexis decided she may not be able to prove each _____ of the alleged crime against Ashley.
    A. stage   B. element   C. circumstance   D. remedy

    22.____

23. After Alexis initiated her lawsuit against Sarah and Ashley, Ashley requested the court remove her from the lawsuit altogether. She attested that she could not have participated in a crime if she did not know the car was stolen. Her request to the court will come in the form of a(n)
    A. notice   B. motion   C. termination   D. demand

    23.____

24. Ashley's attorney asks the judge to instruct the jury that it can consider mitigating factors in rendering a verdict against Ashley.
An example of a mitigating factor in this scenario would MOST likely be
    A. Ashley does not known Alexis
    B. Sarah is no longer friends with Alexis
    C. Ashley asked Sarah about the origins of the car and Sarah's reply was untruthful
    D. Ashley and Sarah were working in cahoots to steal Alexis's car

25. During the time of the crime Sarah was a minor. A minor is legally defined as
    A. someone who cannot think for themselves
    B. anyone under 21
    C. a legally emancipated individual
    D. an infant or individual under the age of legal competence

KEY (CORRECT ANSWERS)

1.	C	11.	B
2.	B	12.	A
3.	B	13.	A
4.	C	14.	C
5.	C	15.	A
6.	B	16.	A
7.	A	17.	A
8.	D	18.	C
9.	B	19.	A
10.	D	20.	C

21.	C
22.	B
23.	B
24.	C
25.	D

TEST 4

DIRECTIONS: Each question or incomplete statement is followed by several suggested answers or completions. Select the one that BEST answers the question or completes the statement. *PRINT THE LETTER OF THE CORRECT ANSWER IN THE SPACE AT THE RIGHT.*

Questions 1-4.

DIRECTIONS: Questions 1 through 4 are to be answered on the basis of the following fact pattern.

A complex civil litigation suit is set to begin between ABC Insurance Corp. and DEF Indemnity Corp. Adam represents ABC Insurance and Jane represents DEF Indemnity Corp. Multiple extensions have been granted to either side to conduct more extensive discovery. At the last conference scheduled before trial, the presiding judge is notably frustrated at the requested delays from both Adam and Jane. The presiding judge would like both parties to stipulate to as many points as possible.

1. Adam and Jane appear in the permanent record as _____ unless either are withdrawn or are otherwise removed from the case.
   A. attorneys in time
   B. attorneys of record
   C. attorneys of the case
   D. permanent attorneys

   1._____

2. The judge asks whether the parties have attempted to settle this matter in another forum, such as binding _____.
   A. decision-making
   B. arbitration
   C. neutral court
   D. judgment arena

   2._____

3. While the judge would like the parties to settle, he quickly realizes that it is not a possibility between these two parties. Adam and Jane continue to argue about various issues including expert witnesses. Adam argues that Jane's expert witness, who will testify about financial crimes, is a quack. In response, Jane offers that her witness be _____, or testify under oath at a date prior to trial.
   A. sworn in   B. indemnified   C. deposed   D. saddled

   3._____

4. Which of the following is the LEAST appropriate behavior of the judge during a pre-trial conference?
   A. Providing advice on Adam or Jane's legal strategy for trial
   B. Asking the parties to stipulate to the facts
   C. Remaining indifferent about the witnesses each party plans to call at trial
   D. Setting a date for trial more than three months away

   4._____

5. A lawsuit with a single cause of action being breach of contract will be classified as what type of suit?
   A. Criminal   B. Divisional   C. Situational   D. Civil

   5._____

6. Sheila's mother passed away last week. She comes to the courthouse and asks about the probate process. You inform her that probate may not be necessary if she is the person named in the will as the individual who will administer her mother's estate. This individual is otherwise known as the
   A. administrator   B. guarantor   C. creditor   D. executor

7. Brandy would like her juvenile record expunged. What is she seeking to do? She is requesting
   A. her record, or a portion of her record, be removed
   B. her record be sealed
   C. her record be unsealed
   D. to make her record unavailable to creditors

8. Having never met Jamie, a pro se litigant, Judge Smith strikes up a friendly conversation about the recent political climate in the elevator with him on the way to the courtroom. In the courtroom that afternoon, Jamie enters his appearance and says, "You and I are clearly already on the same page, Judge" in open court. Jamie's adversary, Courtney, requests that the judge recuses himself from the case. Why?
   A. Jamie and Judge Smith's political affiliations are unsavory.
   B. Judge Smith is clearly biased as evidenced by Jamie's comment.
   C. Judge Smith and Jamie have partaken in en banc communications.
   D. Judicial discrimination is appropriate if a conflict of interest would affect a judge's ruling.

9. Emily appears at court with a crumbled notice in her hands. She has a complaint in her hands and indicates that she never answered or responded to the complaint, hoping it would go away or resolve itself.
   Emily is currently
   A. in default   B. owes restitution
   C. in declaratory judgment   D. subsidiary

10. A conditional release from incarceration is known as
    A. an expungement   B. a restitution
    C. parole   D. reduced sentence

11. Tom paid a contractor to cut down a large pine tree in front of his house. The tree had grown so tall that it has started to interfere with the power lines running parallel to the street. As the contractor cut down the tree, a large gust of wind blew and the tree crashed down on top of his neighbor, Dane's, roof. Dane is suing Tom for failure to exercise the degree of care that a reasonable person would have exercised in the same circumstance.
    Dane is suing Tom for
    A. lack of judgment   B. breach of contract
    C. negligence   D. conversion

12. Lawyers are generally prohibited from asking _____ questions of their own witnesses because they are suggestive, or prompt, the witness to answer in a certain way.
    A. leading   B. direct   C. cross   D. sustainable

13. One process that is generally private, and not heard in open court, is(are)
    A. testimony of expert witnesses
    B. swearing in of jurors
    C. objections
    D. plea bargaining

14. The burden of proof in a civil case is _____ stringent than that in a criminal case.
    A. less   B. more   C. equally   D. substantially

15. May jurors consider arguments made during an attorney's opening or closing arguments as evidence or fact?
    A. Yes, but only if compelling
    B. Yes, but only under the circumstances explained by the judge
    C. Yes, unconditionally
    D. No

16. In reviewing the court transcript, which of the following is the attorney LEAST likely to find?
    A. The judge's opinions on the case
    B. Testimony of the petitioner
    C. Attorneys of record
    D. Names of the expert witnesses

17. A mandatory injunction has the effect of
    A. requiring a party to do a particular act
    B. providing the option of a party to do a particular act
    C. requiring a party to report their actions
    D. providing the party an option to report their actions

18. James approaches the clerk's desk and asks how, generally, judges make their decisions on legal matters.
    The MOST correct answer would be: Based on
    A. case law, or the body of all court decisions which govern or provide precedent on the same legal issue before the judge
    B. case law, personal opinion, and oral arguments by attorneys
    C. case law, oral arguments by attorneys, and the defendant's rap sheet
    D. "stare decisis" or that which has already been decided

19. Which of the following individuals is LEAST likely to serve on a jury?
    A. Susan, who has been called numerous times but never served on a jury
    B. Bill, a supporter of labor unions and freelance political columnist
    C. Gary, who served on a murder trial 10 years ago
    D. Amy, a 16-year-old genius who just finished her junior year of college

20. If a grand jury decides there is enough evidence to move forward with criminal charges against a group or individual, they return a(n)
    A. information   B. indictment   C. warrant   D. seizure

21. When an attorney attempts to reduce the credibility of the other side's witness, they are said to be trying to _____ the witness.
    A. objectify B. anger C. impeach D. frustrate

21.____

22. During a lengthy murder trial, it is discovered that two of the jurors have been romantically involved. They have conspired with one another to enter votes of "not guilty" and attempt to sway other jurors in their favor in an attempt to close out deliberations early.
    What is the likely outcome of the trial?
    A. Hung jury   B. Mistrial
    C. Acquittal   D. Defensive charge

22.____

23. The judge's charge to the jury is also known as
    A. voir dire   B. en banc
    C. jury instructions   D. sua sponte

23.____

24. Who is MOST likely to deliver the sentence to the convicted?
    A. Bailiff   B. Jury
    C. Judge   D. Jury foreperson

24.____

25. A motion for directed verdict is made
    A. without the jury present
    B. with only the jury foreperson present
    C. with the entire jury present
    D. with only the alternate jurors present

25.____

KEY (CORRECT ANSWERS)

1.	B		11.	C
2.	B		12.	A
3.	C		13.	D
4.	A		14.	A
5.	D		15.	D
6.	D		16.	A
7.	A		17.	A
8.	D		18.	A
9.	A		19.	D
10.	C		20.	B

21. C
22. B
23. C
24. C
25. A

EXAMINATION SECTION
TEST 1

DIRECTIONS: Each question or incomplete statement is followed by several suggested answers or completions. Select the one that BEST answers the question or completes the statement. *PRINT THE LETTER OF THE CORRECT ANSWER IN THE SPACE AT THE RIGHT.*

1. While waiting for jury selection, one of the prospective jurors asks you how long a typical trial lasts.
   Which of the following is the MOST appropriate response?
   A. Trials can be lengthy.
   B. The length of trials varies widely, but every aspect of it is important.
   C. Civil trials typically last three to five days, while criminal trials are generally five to ten days.
   D. Decline to respond for fear of appearing biased.

   1.____

2. One of the jurors appears faint and starts to wobble while seated in the jury box.
   How should you handle the situation?
   A. Let one of the other jurors come to the ailing juror's aid first.
   B. Alert the court officer of what you see and ask that the trial be held indefinitely.
   C. Politely interject the trial proceedings and ask the juror if he or she is feeling well.
   D. Alert the court officer who may or may not escort the juror out of the courtroom.

   2.____

3. During trial, you believe that you see the defendant winking at one of the jurors. No one else seems to notice their interaction, including the judge.
   Which of the following actions would you take?
   A. Alert the judge in chambers
   B. Tell the court officer during a break in trial
   C. Interrupt the trial to make all parties aware of the behavior
   D. Confirm with the juror in question that the defendant is winking at her to determine if the feeling is mutual

   3.____

4. During a recess in the trial, the defendant's expert witness is seen chatting with one of the alternate jurors outside the courthouse. While it is unclear what they are talking about, it seems to be a friendly exchange of information.
   What should you do before the court is called back to order?
   A. Tell the juror she must disclose her conversation with the expert witness in open court
   B. Tell the expert witness he must disclose the conversation with the juror in open court
   C. Inform the plaintiff's attorney about the conversation
   D. Inform the judge about the conversation

   4.____

Questions 5-7.

DIRECTIONS: Questions 5 through 7 are to be answered on the basis of the following fact pattern.

After a TRO is issued to the plaintiff, the ex-wife of the defendant, both parties are free to go. The defendant appeared in court and rigorously opposed his ex-wife's request. His ex-wife already has sole custody of their three children and he seems incredibly distraught by the judge's grant of her request.

5. In a follow-up hearing, where the plaintiff is requesting to extend a TRO, the defendant does not show up. Instead, the defendant's brother appears at the hearing on his behalf. Is the defendant's brother permitted to voice his concerns about extending the TRO?
The defendant's brother
 A. is not a party to the action and must wait outside of the courtroom during proceedings.
 B. is welcome to testify on his brother's behalf
 C. can testify on his brother's behalf as long as he remains calm while doing so
 D. can testify on his brother's behalf so long as the plaintiff's sister can testify on her behalf

5._____

6. A TRO is a _____ restraining order, while a QDRO is a qualified _____ order.
 A. temporary; domicile relations   B. territorial; domicile relations
 C. temporary; domestic revision   D. temporary; domestic relations

6._____

7. How many alternate jurors are typically sworn in for trial?
 A. Up to 12   B. Up to 14   C. Up to 10   D. Up to 6

7._____

Questions 8-10.

DIRECTIONS: Questions 8 through 10 are to be answered on the basis of the following fact pattern.

While those waiting for the court to open file into the hallway, an argument breaks out between two women and one man. When you intervene between the parties, you discover the two women are arguing over custody of a child – who is standing nearby – and the man is one of their attorneys. Barbara is the biological mother of the child. Tina raised the child from birth. Tina and her attorney, Bill, came with the child to court today.

8. Which party should stay with the child?
 A. The biological mother, Barbara, of the child should stay with the child while they await for court to begin.
 B. Tina and Bill should stay with the child since she raised the child from birth.

8._____

C. The parties should separate and the child should come with you to a sequestered part of the courthouse.
D. Tina and Bill should stay with the child as petitioners of the court, Barbara should wait in a separate area away from all three and refrain from contact.

9. Which of the following are Barbara and her attorney MOST likely to request in court? 9.____
   A. An order of protection
   B. Order to expunge
   C. Order to impeach
   D. Deposition

10. Should you tell the judge about the behavior of the parties during the hearing? 10.____
    A. You can inform the judge if asked, but not during the hearing itself.
    B. You can inform the judge if asked, but should wait until a hearing is not in session.
    C. Before the hearing is set to begin, you should inform the judge of your encounter with the parties and let the judge decide how to best confront the situation between all involved.
    D. No.

Questions 11-14.

DIRECTIONS: Questions 11 through 14 are to be answered on the basis of the following fact pattern.

At district court, a trial of a group of alleged rapists has drawn a huge crowd of spectators at each day of the hearings. Two of the defendants are locals of Nassau County, while the other is a local of Richmond County. The trial date has been set and moved multiple times.

11. Which of the following will the defendants MOST likely be charged with? 11.____
    A. An information
    B. A felony
    C. A misdemeanor
    D. An indictment

12. In reading the charge, which of the following is LEAST likely to appear? 12.____
    A. The name of the attorneys of record
    B. The names of the victims
    C. The number of counts of each crime
    D. The name of the judge hearing the case

13. There are likely to be multiples of which during this trial? 13.____
    A. Multiple court officers
    B. Multiple attorneys
    C. Multiple charges
    D. All of the above

14. The venue of the trial is MOST likely to be 14.____
    A. Nassau County
    B. Richmond County
    C. Determined by the jury
    D. Determined by the judge

Questions 15-17.

DIRECTIONS: Questions 15 through 17 are to be answered on the basis of the following fact pattern.

In the Supreme Court Foreclosure Part, a variety of parties are awaiting for hearings to begin. Homeowners, attorneys, creditors, and trustees anxiously talk amongst themselves. Based on your knowledge of foreclosure procedures, answer the following questions.

15. As you approach the foreclosure part, a woman rushes toward you. She is incredibly upset and begins to cry as soon as she begins speaking. She tells you that she cannot wait any longer for her hearing to begin because her mother just had an accident and she must rush to the hospital.
If she misses her court date, what should she be MOST concerned with as it relates to her foreclosure case?
    A. Having to reschedule her court date to defend herself
    B. Defaulting and, therefore, her creditor(s) prevailing against her
    C. Answering a motion to show cause from the bank
    D. Answering a complaint from the bank

15.____

16. One of the most frequent questions you are asked is whether a bank can accelerate the mortgage loan against a homeowner/borrower after the homeowner has made a few late payments.
Acceleration is
    A. requiring a borrower to immediately pay off the balance of the loan
    B. the amount of money owed on the mortgage
    C. the document showing the ownership of a mortgage or deed of trust
    D. the basic repayment plan the homeowner/borrower initially agreed to when purchasing the home

16.____

17. Homeowners in foreclosure sometimes file simultaneously for bankruptcy. The automatic stay is a function unique to bankruptcy.
An automatic stay is defined as
    A. a large lump sum payment due as the last payment on a loan
    B. an injunction automatically issued by the bankruptcy court when someone files for bankruptcy
    C. an optional injunction that requires creditors to call the debtor and seek a settlement
    D. another term meaning "to stay a motion" or to hold a request from the court temporarily

17.____

18. Dave approaches the clerk's desk and asks how, generally, judges make their decisions on legal matters. The MOST correct answer would be based on
    A. case law, or the body of all court decisions which govern or provide precedent on the same legal issue before the judge
    B. case law, personal opinion and oral arguments by attorneys
    C. case law, oral arguments by attorneys, and the defendant's rap sheet
    D. "stare decisis" or that which has already been decided

18.____

19. Which hearing below will MOST likely be heard in the Commercial Division of the Suffolk County Supreme courthouse?
    A. Divorce petition between Bill and Amy
    B. A custody dispute between Jim and John
    C. A business dispute between ABC Corp. and XYZ, Inc.
    D. A petition for expungement of a stockbroker's record

19.____

20. Richard may face criminal charges for allegedly embezzling thousands of dollars from his company's business account.
    If a grand jury decides there is enough evidence to move forward with criminal charges against Richard, they
    A. return an information
    B. return an indictment
    C. issue a warrant
    D. issue a seizure

20.____

21. At trial, the prosecutor asks many pointed questions at Richard. The prosecutor believes Richard is lying on the stand.
    When an attorney attempts to reduce the credibility of the other side's witness, they are said to be trying to _____ the witness on the stand.
    A. objectify   B. anger   C. impeach   D. frustrate

21.____

22. During a lengthy trial, four jurors conspire with one another to enter votes of "not guilty" and hatch a plan to sway other jurors in their favor in an attempt to close out deliberations early.
    What is the likely outcome of the trial?
    A. Hung jury
    B. Mistrial
    C. Acquittal
    D. Defensive charge

22.____

23. The judge's charge to the jury is also known as
    A. closing statements
    B. quid pro quo
    C. jury instructions
    D. sua sponte

23.____

24. Who is the only party responsible for delivering the sentence to the convicted?
    A. Bailiff
    B. Jury
    C. Judge
    D. Jury foreperson

24.____

25. A motion for directed verdict is made
    A. without the jury present
    B. with only the jury foreperson present
    C. with the entire jury present
    D. with only the alternate jurors present

25.____

KEY (CORRECT ANSWERS)

1.	C	11.	B
2.	D	12.	B
3.	A	13.	D
4.	D	14.	D
5.	A	15.	B
6.	D	16.	A
7.	D	17.	B
8.	D	18.	A
9.	A	19.	C
10.	C	20.	B

21. C
22. B
23. C
24. C
25. A

TEST 2

DIRECTIONS: Each question or incomplete statement is followed by several suggested answers or completions. Select the one that BEST answers the question or completes the statement. *PRINT THE LETTER OF THE CORRECT ANSWER IN THE SPACE AT THE RIGHT.*

1. Juror #12 is a close friend of your brother's, Tom. Tom starts to strike up a conversation with you outside of the courtroom.
   How should you respond?
   A. Politely decline to engage, unless he or she is asking for directions
   B. Politely decline to engage, unless he or she would like to talk about the case
   C. Politely decline to engage, unless he or she knows you personally
   D. Engage in the conversation remaining mindful of the appearance of bias and immediately ceasing the conversation if the trial at hand comes up

   1._____

2. A charge of attempted murder is LEAST likely to accompany a charge of
   A. murder   B. burglary   C. robbery   D. assault

   2._____

Questions 3-4.

DIRECTIONS: Questions 3 and 4 are to be answered on the basis of the following fact pattern.

   Mary approaches you inside the Albany County Supreme Court and says that she has been served with a lawsuit. She is confused about the entire lawsuit process and is confused as to what area of the courthouse she should be in. She believes, but is not entirely sure, that her sister may be suing her over money she lent her then subsequently lost gambling in the casino.

3. Which of the following is the MOST appropriate response you can provide Mary with regard to her being served?
   She should have a copy of the _____ with her and refer to it, which will tell her where she would report within the courthouse.
   A. answer   B. complaint   C. summons   D. information

   3._____

4. Mary produces the document and asks you if there is anything she can do to respond to the lawsuit.
   What is the MOST appropriate answer?
   She should
   A. file an answer, and perhaps seek legal counsel
   B. seek legal counsel
   C. check in at the Preliminary Conference desk
   D. file an injunction, and perhaps seek legal counsel

   4._____

5. Who decides whether the jurors are allowed to take notes during the trial?
   A. The judge
   B. The plaintiff's attorney, since they are bringing the case to court
   C. Jurors are always allowed to take notes during trials
   D. Jurors are never allowed to take notes during trials.

   5._____

6. During a trial, one of the jurors writes a question for one of the witnesses on a piece of paper and hands it to the court officer.
   What is the CORRECT procedure?
   The court officer
   A. may, but is not required to, pass the written question to the judge
   B. must pass the written question to the judge, who may or may not ask the witness the question posed
   C. must decline receipt of the written message
   D. passes the written question to the court assistant who may or may not read the question aloud

7. If questions arise during the jury deliberation process, what is the role of the court officer?
   A. To deliver the written question from the jury foreperson to the judge
   B. To repeat the question orally as told to the court officer by the jury foreperson to the judge
   C. To read the written question in open court with all parties present other than the defendant
   D. To record the written question in the docket

8. A juror has informed you that she accidentally read information about the case she is serving on while she was at the supermarket last night.
   How should you respond to her?
   A. Berate her for not being more diligent in seeking out information about the case
   B. Inform the court officer that the juror should be replaced
   C. Remove the juror from the jury box and replace him or her with an alternate juror yourself
   D. Inform the judge immediately

9. Which court proceeding takes place CLOSEST in time to an arrest?
   A. Arraignment   B. Sentencing
   C. Trial   D. Jury selection

10. Which of the following is LEAST likely to occur at the conclusion of a trial?
    A. Sentencing   B. Appeal
    C. Reversal   D. Plea bargaining

11. You overhear two jurors talking about the case in the hallway during recess. From their conversation, it appears that they are related to one another.
    You should
    A. do nothing as it's none of your business
    B. make sure no one else hears them
    C. simply tell them not to discuss the case between themselves
    D. tell the judge

12. How many jurors typically serve on a criminal trial?
    A. 12 B. 18 C. 16 D. 6

13. During jury selection, the judge has already excused 25 prospective jurors for cause. How many more jurors can be excused for cause before reaching the excusal limit?
    A. 5
    B. 10
    C. The judge has reached the limit
    D. There is no excusal limit "for cause"

    13.____

14. Which of the following is the jury usually prohibited from doing during a trial on which they are serving?
    A. Visiting the scene of the alleged crime
    B. Read or listen to news about the trial from outside sources
    C. Research case law that applies to the trial
    D. All of the above

    14.____

15. In New York City, jury trials are conducted at which of the following courts?
    A. Supreme Court   B. New York City Civil Court
    C. New York City Criminal Court   D. All of the above

    15.____

16. A trial involving an alleged assault and battery is MOST likely to occur at which New York City court?
    A. Town and Village Court   B. New York City Civil Court
    C. New York City Criminal Court   D. County Court

    16.____

17. In vacating a default, which must the petitioner file FIRST?
    A. Notice of motion   B. Emergency affidavit
    C. Legal back   D. Injunction

    17.____

18. Order the steps of a typical trial from first to last.
    I. Opening statements   II. Jury selection
    III. Deliberations   IV. Oath and preliminary instructions
    The CORRECT answer is:
    A. I, II, III, IV   B. IV, III, II, I   C. I, II, IV, III   D. II, IV, I, III

    18.____

19. On appeal, three justices hear a case that was already decided in the lower courts. The issue before them is a complicated issue involving a determination of legal guardian.
    An opinion from the entire panel of justices is known as a(n)
    A. per curiam decision   B. affirmative decision
    C. stare decisis   D. en banc order

    19.____

20. One of the judges agrees with the decision of the court, but disagrees with the reasoning of the conclusion. This judge decides to write his own opinion. This is deemed a
    A. dissenting opinion   B. remedial decision
    C. concurring opinion   D. recurrent opinion

    20.____

21. Suppose that one of the judges disagrees entirely with the ruling. How will the judgment be altered because of the disagreement?
The judgment
   A. is unaffected because the majority voted in agreement with the trial court
   B. is unaffected because this judge did not author a dissenting opinion
   C. is unaffected because oral arguments were not made before the panel
   D. will be overturned

22. The appellate court still requires _____, even if it is established by the trial court, known as original _____.
   A. domicile; venue
   B. venue; jurisdiction
   C. jurisdiction; jurisdiction
   D. jurisdiction; domicile

23. The legal theory upon which a case is based is called a
   A. basis
   B. decisis
   C. cause of action
   D. precedent

24. Sarah and her friend, Ashley, burglarized a number of homes in Kings County over the summer. They were only apprehended after one of their other friends overheard them talking about their crimes. At the time, both Sarah and Ashley were 18 and legally minors.
A minor is legally defined as:
   A. In New York, a minor is anyone under the age of 18
   B. Anyone under 18
   C. A legally emancipated individual
   D. An infant or individual under the age of legal competence

25. The BEST place to refer back to the testimony of one witness is
   A. the docket
   B. the judge's notes which can be obtained freely from chambers
   C. the stenographer's transcript
   D. clerk notes which, in some instances, are available online

KEY (CORRECT ANSWERS)

1.	D	11.	D
2.	A	12.	A
3.	B	13.	D
4.	B	14.	D
5.	A	15.	D
6.	B	16.	C
7.	A	17.	A
8.	D	18.	D
9.	A	19.	A
10.	D	20.	C

21.	A
22.	C
23.	C
24.	D
25.	C

TEST 3

DIRECTIONS: Each question or incomplete statement is followed by several suggested answers or completions. Select the one that BEST answers the question or completes the statement. *PRINT THE LETTER OF THE CORRECT ANSWER IN THE SPACE AT THE RIGHT.*

1. The pre-trial hearing is MOST likely to take place after _____, but before _____.
   A. arraignment; jury selection
   B. deliberations; closing statements
   C. assignment; adjudication
   D. plea bargain; opening statement

   1._____

2. During a court recess, you see one of the jurors walking into the judge's chambers. You immediately
   A. halt the juror and demand he or she return to the deliberation room
   B. allow the juror to proceed, but ask the judge about the incident later
   C. allow the juror to proceed and assume they know one another personally
   D. allow the juror to proceed, but inform the court officer of the incident

   2._____

3. When reading an indictment in court, each charge represents a(n)
   A. allegation of a crime
   B. proven criminal act
   C. evidentiary plea
   D. legal certainty

   3._____

4. After a defendant has been acquitted, he or she will likely be
   A. free to leave the courthouse
   B. remanded to federal prison
   C. detained until further notice
   D. formally sentenced

   4._____

5. Jeremiah, a defense attorney, has approached you in the hallways of the New York Civil Court. He is concerned that his client, Dave, may become violent during court proceedings.
   How do you handle Jeremiah's request to closely supervise Dave while court is in session?
   A. Inform the judge of Jeremiah's request and allow proceedings to continue as normal
   B. Ask that a court officer be present during court proceedings
   C. Request the judge to sequester the jury while Dave is present
   D. Ignore Jeremiah's request for now, until you see how Dave behaves yourself

   5._____

6. Jury sequestration is
   A. extremely common given the complex nature of most criminal trials
   B. becoming increasingly common
   C. more common in civil cases than in criminal trials
   D. rare

   6._____

7. At arraignment, the defendant is MOST likely to
   A. state his case
   B. convince the judge of his or her innocence
   C. enter a plea
   D. gather information on his or her case from the State's attorney

   7._____

8. A warrant can be issued for an individual's arrest or for
   A. search of premises outlined in the warrant itself
   B. testimony
   C. deposition of the arrested individual
   D. evidence found at the scene

8._____

9. The responsibility to record notes for the judge and listen to issues of law that may need to be researched later are reserved for the
   A. court officer
   B. stenographer
   C. judge's clerk
   D. jury

9._____

10. Information about the charges against the defendant, as well as the parties involved in the case, can MOST likely be found in the
    A. judge's notes
    B. docket
    C. information
    D. discovery report

10._____

11. The opening statements in a trial are delivered by the
    A. defendant
    B. plaintiff
    C. attorneys
    D. judge

11._____

12. When the judge sustains the objection of an attorney who is asking a question of the witness on the stand, the witness must
    A. answer the question as asked
    B. wait for counsel to re-phrase the question in a proper form or ask another question before answering
    C. refuse to answer the question
    D. the witness may step down

12._____

13. An expert is permitted to
    A. review the plaintiff's evidence, draw a reasonable conclusion and give testimony to that effect
    B. review the defendant's evidence, draw a reasonable conclusion and submit his or her opinion in writing to the judge
    C. give his or her opinion based on the facts in evidence and provide the reasoning for that opinion
    D. provide an opinion in open court

13._____

14. Prosecutor and defense counsel have both made closing arguments in the trial of Samuel Smith Jones. Mr. Jones is being tried for capital murder for the alleged murder of his mother and sister.
    Which party is entitled to a rebuttal in closing arguments?
    A. The prosecutor
    B. The defense
    C. The defense, but only after the plaintiff has given their closing argument
    D. The defense, but only if the plaintiff waives their right to make a closing argument

14._____

15. When a jury cannot agree on a verdict, a(n) _____ occurs and the result is a _____.
    A. mistrial; acquittal
    B. mistrial; hung jury
    C. hung jury; mistrial
    D. acquittal; mistrial

15.____

16. Nominal damages are
    A. damages awarded in name only, indicating no substantial harm was done
    B. damages to recompense the injured for the infliction of emotional distress
    C. damages to recompense the initiator of the lawsuit
    D. a reimbursement of filing fees, awarded to the person who can prove they are injured

16.____

17. The type of recovery being sought by the plaintiff is known as the
    A. order
    B. punishment
    C. remedy
    D. issue

17.____

18. Robert approaches the clerk's desk in a panic. He says that he filed a lawsuit last week against his cousin, Mike, but neglected to add his cousin's friend, Rory, to the suit.
    Robert must _____ the compliant.
    A. amend   B. refile   C. re-serve   D. redact

18.____

19. In a foreclosure action, which of the following will the borrower MOST likely be asked about in terms of securing a second or third mortgage?
    A. Business terms
    B. Collateral
    C. Damages
    D. Remedy

19.____

20. Maya has asked you about Article 7A proceedings.
    Article 7A hearings allow
    A. tenants being foreclosed upon to file a class action against the landlord
    B. at least 1/3 of tenants to ask the court to appoint an administrator to run the building in select circumstances
    C. tenants to forego paying the rent when living conditions in the building become inhabitable
    D. tenants to book their landlord from collecting rent when living conditions in the building become inhabitable

20.____

21. The Housing Court, sometimes referred to as Landlord and Tenant Court, is held at the
    A. Town and Village Court
    B. New York City Civil Court
    C. New York City Criminal Court
    D. County Court

21.____

22. Without an attorney, how much money can one sue for in Town or Village Courts, outside of New York City?
    A. Up to $3,000
    B. Up to $5,000
    C. Up to $2,500
    D. Up to $2,000

22.____

23. Judith wants to sue her neighbor, Samantha, in small claims court after Samantha borrowed Judith's lawnmower and refused to return it. Judith has begun a petition in small claims court for recovery of the lawnmower. How will the case proceed?
    A. The case will not go forward, because only money damages can be sought in small claims court.
    B. The case will not go forward, because small claims court cannot compel Samantha to return the lawnmower.
    C. The case will not go forward, because the lawnmower exceeds the small claims court limit.
    D. Judith will likely prevail.

24. Daniel wants to file for probate of his father's estate. The filing fee is based on
    A. Daniel's assets
    B. Daniel's age
    C. The size of the estate
    D. The age at which Daniel's father passed

25. Family court will hear each of the following cases EXCEPT
    A. custody and visitation
    B. adoption
    C. juvenile delinquency
    D. estate

KEY (CORRECT ANSWERS)

1.	A		11.	C
2.	A		12.	B
3.	A		13.	C
4.	A		14.	A
5.	B		15.	C
6.	D		16.	A
7.	C		17.	C
8.	A		18.	A
9.	C		19.	B
10.	B		20.	B

21. B
22. A
23. A
24. C
25. D

TEST 4

DIRECTIONS: Each question or incomplete statement is followed by several suggested answers or completions. Select the one that BEST answers the question or completes the statement. *PRINT THE LETTER OF THE CORRECT ANSWER IN THE SPACE AT THE RIGHT.*

1. Jason is currently a student at SUNY Buffalo. He is worried that his recent conviction will affect his financial aid package with the college.
   How will Jason's conviction of drug possession affect his financial aid?
   It will
   A. remain unaffected
   B. remain unaffected as long as Jason is represented by counsel
   C. automatically be cancelled for a period of time
   D. be cancelled indefinitely

   1.____

2. Who is responsible for drafting the Pre-Sentence report that judges use in sentencing convicted defendants?
   A. Defendant's attorney
   B. Probation officer
   C. Court assistant
   D. Judge's law clerk

   2.____

3. Restitution cannot be made for
   A. breach of contract
   B. assault and battery
   C. lost wages
   D. future losses

   3.____

4. In a bench trial, the _____ serves as the ultimate fact finder.
   A. jury   B. judge   C. bailiff   D. law clerk

   4.____

5. The role of the bankruptcy trustee is to represent the
   A. interest of the bankruptcy estate and the creditors of the debtor
   B. debtor against all creditors
   C. largest creditor of the debtor
   D. smallest creditor of the debtor

   5.____

6. The bankruptcy estate typically includes _____ at the time of the filing.
   A. all property of the debtor, including interests in property
   B. the home where the debtor resides
   C. the home and personal vehicle of the debtor
   D. all personal property, but not real property, of the debtor

   6.____

7. When a party to a lawsuit cannot afford the cost of the lawsuit, the Court
   A. may permit that party to proceed without being required to pay for court costs
   B. disallows payment for foreclosure proceeds
   C. does not require that party to pay for filing fees
   D. requires that party to settle the matter in ADR

   7.____

8. An answer is a formal response to which document?
   A. indictment   B. discovery   C. complaint   D. summons

9. Ishmael sued his former employer, Igor, for loss of wages. Igor lost the case and now wishes to appeal the ruling.
   When Igor appeals the case, he becomes an
   A. appellee   B. appellant   C. respondent   D. defendant

10. Damiano has been sentenced to six years for armed robbery and ten years for grand larceny. He is sentenced to serve his prison terms concurrently. What is the MAXIMUM amount of time he will spend behind bars?
    A. Six years
    B. Sixteen years
    C. Ten years
    D. Four years

11. What does the exclusionary rule exclude in a criminal trial?
    A. Testimony that is deemed hearsay by a judge in a court of competent jurisdiction
    B. Evidence obtained in violation of a defendant's constitutional or statutory rights
    C. Depositions that are unsworn or not notarized
    D. Affidavits that are unsworn or not notarized

12. David is being arraigned and needs to enter a plea for the crime he allegedly committed while he was with his friend, Robert. Robert pleads guilty during his arraignment yesterday, but David has been advised by his attorney to plead no contest, also known as
    A. nolo contendere   B. pro se   C. quid pro quo   D. qui tam

13. Adoptions can be heard in which two courts?
    A. Family court and surrogate court
    B. Foreclosure court and family court
    C. Family court and commercial court
    D. Family court and court of claims

14. Which party may NOT file a paternity petition?
    A. The child's mother
    B. The man who believes he may be the father of the child
    C. The child or the child's guardian
    D. The child's teacher or other close associate

15. Amy was married to Bob at the time her child was born. John believes he is the father of Amy's baby.
    Who is presumed to be the father of Amy's child?
    A. Bob
    B. John
    C. Neither can be presumed; a DNA test must be administered in this circumstance
    D. Neither can be presumed; each has to petition the court separately

16. Parties that represent themselves during court hearings are referred to as _____ litigants.
    A. qui tam   B. pro se   C. en banc   D. quid quo pro

17. Normally, guardianship petitions must be filed in _____ court.
    A. family   B. surrogates   C. probate   D. civil

18. At what age can a child's own preference be taken under consideration in guardianship or custody hearings?
    A. 12   B. 14   C. 17   D. 16

19. Civil litigation claims against the State of New York or other State-related agencies are heard exclusively in the
    A. Civil Court
    B. Criminal Court
    C. Court of Claims
    D. Surrogate Court

20. Preliminary conferences are automatically scheduled by the Court within _____ days after a Request for Judicial Intervention (RJI).
    A. 30   B. 45   C. 50   D. 55

21. There are two junior attorneys that have been sent to cover the preliminary conference of their case *Abe v. Gabe* in part 22 of the court. Both attorneys approach the clerk's desk to ask what the "return date" on a motion refers to. The return date is the date the
    A. motion will be conferenced and/or orally argued at the discretion of the court
    B. attorneys must return for more information
    C. attorneys must return with the clients
    D. attorneys must return to complete discovery

22. Decisions made on motions and pro se litigants must be
    A. mailed or a copy provided of the decision
    B. made available for photocopy or fax
    C. made available for scan, but not photocopied or faxed
    D. uploaded to the court website so it can be easily accessed online

23. A stipulation of settlement represents a formal agreement between the
    A. judge and the parties resolving the case
    B. litigants and their attorneys resolving the dispute
    C. clerk and the litigants representing a near end to the dispute at issue
    D. judge and the clerk representing a notation of the resolution

24. A motion to vacate a default in foreclosure part represents an attempt by the homeowner or borrower to
    A. reverse the court's finding of default
    B. reverse the court's finding of dereliction
    C. obtain a new hearing
    D. reschedule a hearing due to a missed court date

25. The Personal Appearance Part in the Civil Court is where which types of cases are heard?
    Cases where
    A. one or both parties are self-represented
    B. the plaintiff is self-represented
    C. the defendant is self-represented
    D. clerk is the fact finder

25.____

KEY (CORRECT ANSWERS)

1.	C	11.	B
2.	B	12.	A
3.	D	13.	A
4.	B	14.	D
5.	A	15.	A
6.	A	16.	B
7.	A	17.	A
8.	C	18.	B
9.	B	19.	C
10.	C	20.	B

21. A
22. A
23. B
24. A
25. A

EXAMINATION SECTION

TEST 1

DIRECTIONS: Each question or incomplete statement is followed by several suggested answers or completions. Select the one that BEST answers the question or completes the statement. *PRINT THE LETTER OF THE CORRECT ANSWER IN THE SPACE AT THE RIGHT.*

Questions 1-5.

DIRECTIONS: Questions 1 through 5 are to be answered on the basis of the following fact pattern.

Astrid's son, Carlos, attends the local high school. Carlos and another student, Manny, have been bullying another student both on and off school premises. The high school principal has notified the New York Police Department School Safety Unit of the issue. The principal has also been in touch with Astrid and Manny's mother, Mary. Mary believes Carlos is a bad influence to her son, Manny. After obtaining Astrid's phone number, Mary called Astrid and made threats towards her and Carlos. She indicated that if Carlos did not stay away from her son, Manny, she would have them both killed. The next day after school, Carlos is jumped by a group of teenagers and his leg is broken in the brawl. Astrid sues Manny, Mary, and the school district. Mary intends to countersue.

1. Who is the complainant?
    A. Manny   B. Mary   C. Astrid   D. Carlos

2. Which of the following is NOT a possible cause of action?
    A. Harassment   B. Assault
    C. Negligence   D. Breach of Contract

3. What key information is missing from the complaint?
    A. The name of the bullied student
    B. The location where Carlos was jumped
    C. The name of the high school principal
    D. The name of the police officer at the NYPD School Safety Unit who was originally notified on the issue

4. Is Mary obligated to countersue because she or her son, Manny, may have been involved in the assault against Carlos?
    A. Yes; she must answer the suit and countersue as required
    B. Yes; she must countersue to clear her son's name
    C. No; Mary is not obligated to countersue and can simply answer to the claims as alleged
    D. No; Mary is not obligated to countersue but she is obligated to countersue on Manny's behalf

5. Assume that Carlos and Manny are minors.
   What effect, if any, would this fact have on the lawsuit that is filed?
   A. The legal guardians of Carlos and Manny will need to file, and answer, the lawsuit on their behalf.
   B. Carlos and Manny do not need to appear in court.
   C. Minors cannot sue other people.
   D. The lawsuit is unaffected by their age.

6.
Mary Williams	Mary S. Williams	Mary S. Williams
1 Court Way	1 Court Way	1 Court Way
Smithtown, NY 10170	Smithtown, NY 10170	Smith Town, NY 10170

   Which selection below accurately describes the addresses as listed above?
   A. All three addresses are the same.
   B. The first and the third address are the same.
   C. None of the addresses are the same.
   D. The second and third address are the same.

Questions 7-9.

DIRECTIONS: Questions 7 through 9 are to be answered on the basis of the following table.

Schedule – Judge Presser		
Petitioner	**Respondent**	**Status**
Williams	Smith	Dismissed with prejudice
Jones	Johnson	Continued
Adams	Doe	Dismissed with prejudice
Ash	Link	Adjourned
Lam	Garcia	Settled

7. How many cases were adjourned?
   A. 3   B. 1   C. 4   D. 5

8. In how many cases were money damages awarded by the judge?
   A. 0   B. 3   C. 4   D. 5

9. How many cases will be heard again?
   A. 2   B. 1   C. 3   D. 5

10. A warrant for the arrest of Benjamin Lang. Lang lives in Suffolk County, New York. What is recorded on the warrant?
    Lang's
    A. venue
    B. domicile
    C. jurisdiction
    D. subject matter jurisdiction

Questions 11-13.

DIRECTIONS: Questions 11 through 13 are to be answered on the basis of the following table.

455888912	455888812	455888912	455888812
Civil Court	Civil Court	Civil Court	Civil Court
Contract	Contract	Contract	Contract
Pam L. Williams	Pam Williams	Pam Williams	Pam L. Williams

11. Which selection below accurately describes the case captions as listed above?
    A. All of the captions are the same.
    B. Caption 1 and Caption 3 are the same.
    C. Caption 2 and Caption 4 are the same.
    D. None of the captions are the same.

12. Which digit above is dissimilar in two of the above captions?
    A. The seventh digit
    B. The fifth digit
    C. The sixth digit
    D. The eighth digit

13. The notation "contract" in each caption above describes the _____ of the case.
    A. Cause of action
    B. Remedy at issue
    C. Order of the court
    D. Disposition

14. Melinda was seen stealing money from a car on Atlantic Avenue in Brooklyn. Samuel witnessed the crime from his apartment and called the police. Officer Tang recorded the call in the police log. Samuel does not own a car and reported the crime anonymously. Later that same evening, Jeremy returned his car and found the passenger window had been broken and $500 was stolen from the glove compartment. Jeremy called the police to report the crime.
    In the judge's docket, the petitioner of the case against Melinda is MOST likely
    A. Jeremy
    B. Samuel
    C. Officer Tang
    D. The petitioner is anonymous

15. Judge Oswald hears cases in the Surrogate Court.
    Which of the following would NOT be in Judge Oswald's court calendar?
    A. Adoption
    B. Wills
    C. Estate and Probation
    D. Negligence

Questions 16-19.

DIRECTIONS: Questions 16 through 19 are to be answered on the basis of the following fact pattern.

Judge Laredo, Smith and Ora hear no-fault cases in the 10th Judicial District throughout the week. Judge Laredo hears cases the first Monday of each month. Judge Smith hears cases with amounts in dispute over $10,000 on Tuesday, Wednesday, and Friday. Judge Ora hears cases without amounts in dispute below $25,000 on Tuesdays only.

16. Geico and ABC Chiropractic are parties to a no-fault dispute with an amount in dispute of $8,500.
    If Judge Laredo is unavailable, what day can the case be heard?
    A. Wednesday   B. Friday   C. Monday   D. Tuesday

    16._____

17. Blue Health Medical and Progressive Insurance are parties to a no-fault dispute which is scheduled to be heard February 18th. Blue Health demands Progressive reimburse the provider $5,000 for the primary surgeon fees and $12,000 in assistant surgeon fees.
    Which judge will hear the matter and on which day?
    A. Judge Smith on Friday
    B. Judge Smith on Tuesday
    C. Judge Smith on Wednesday
    D. Judge Ora on Tuesday

    17._____

18. A no-fault dispute is being heard on Monday, June 10th.
    Which statement below must be TRUE?
    A. The amount in dispute is above $10,000.
    B. The amount in dispute is less than $25,000.
    C. The amount in dispute is less than $10,000.
    D. Judge Laredo is hearing the case.

    18._____

19. What information must be obtained in order to properly schedule the court calendar?
    A. The amount in dispute for each case
    B. The parties in each case
    C. Verification the dispute is "no-fault in nature"
    D. All of the above

    19._____

20. A victim impact statement is an oral or _____ statement that may be read in court.
    A. recorded   B. transcribed   C. written   D. visualized

    20._____

21. The clerk in the Surrogates Court will need to have access to what information in the preparation of adoption hearings?
    A. Personal information of a child's current or prior legal guardian
    B. Emancipation petition documentation
    C. Deed or will
    D. Probate documentation

    21._____

Questions 22-25.

DIRECTIONS: Questions 22 through 25 are to be answered on the basis of the following table.

Schedule – Judge Orlando			
Complainant/Plaintiff	**Defendant**	**Case Type**	**Money Awarded**
Williams	Smith	Civil	$5,000
Jones	Johnson	Criminal	No
Adams	Doe	Criminal	$10,000
Ash	Link	Civil	$15,000
Lam	Garcia	Civil	$25,000

22. What is the total amount of money damages from civil disputes? 22.____
    A. $45,000 B. $40,000 C. $5,000 D. 0

23. Which complainant/plaintiff was awarded less than $20,000? 23.____
    A. Williams, Adams, and Ash   B. Jones, Adams, and Ash
    C. Lam, Williams, and Jones   D. Jones, Adams, and Lam

24. How many criminal cases were heard by Judge Orlando? 24.____
    A. 4 B. 5 C. 2 D. 3

25. Which defendants are responsible for paying more than $10,000? 25.____
    A. Doe and Link   B. Link and Garcia
    C. John and Doe   D. Smith and Garcia

KEY (CORRECT ANSWERS)

1. C		11. D	
2. D		12. A	
3. B		13. A	
4. C		14. A	
5. A		15. D	
6. C		16. D	
7. B		17. D	
8. A		18. D	
9. A		19. D	
10. B		20. C	

21. A
22. A
23. A
24. C
25. B

TEST 2

DIRECTIONS: Each question or incomplete statement is followed by several suggested answers or completions. Select the one that BEST answers the question or completes the statement. *PRINT THE LETTER OF THE CORRECT ANSWER IN THE SPACE AT THE RIGHT.*

Questions 1-4.

DIRECTIONS: Questions 1 through 4 are to be answered on the basis of the following text.

After a lengthy trial with multiple ___1___, Jim was acquitted of armed robbery and conspiracy. On the other hand, his alleged partner, Bob, was ___2___ of armed robbery. The conspiracy charge was dropped against Bob since the 12-person ___3___ found he acted alone. Jim's attorney ___4___.

1. Fill in the blank for #1:   1.____
   A. witnesses   B. evidence   C. discretionary   D. turbulent

2. Fill in the blank for #2:   2.____
   A. guilty   B. convicted   C. indicted   D. surmised

3. Fill in the blank for #3:   3.____
   A. judge   B. spectator   C. jury   D. bailiff

4. Fill in the blank for #4:   4.____
   A. appealed   B. remanded   C. reversed   D. rescinded

Questions 5-10.

DIRECTIONS: Questions 5 through 10 are to be answered on the basis of the following table.

Court Schedule - Tuesday			
Judge	Total Cases	Cases Dismissed	Cases with Money Awarded
Presser	10	2	X
O'Dell	5	5	
Williams	6	6	
Sasha	8	7	X

5. How many cases were awarded money damages from Judge Presser's calendar?   5.____
   A. 2   B. 8   C. 6   D. 10

6. How many cases were awarded money damages from Judge Sasha's calendar?   6.____
   A. 8   B. 7   C. 1   D. 0

7. How many cases were dismissed on Tuesday? 7.____
   A. 11 B. 20 C. 7 D. 10

8. How many cases were awarded money damages on Tuesday? 8.____
   A. 9 B. 8 C. 1 D. 10

9. Which judge heard the MOST cases on Tuesday? 9.____
   A. Presser B. O'Dell C. Williams D. Sasha

10. Which judge heard the LEAST cases on Tuesday? 10.____
    A. Presser B. O'Dell C. WilIliams D. Sasha

Questions 11-15.

DIRECTIONS: Questions 11 through 15 are to be answered on the basis of the following text.

Judge Smith hears adoption cases on Fridays. Judge Clark hears criminal cases every weekday except Tuesday in the New York City Criminal Court. Judge Clark hears felony criminal cases on Tuesday in Supreme Court. Judge Amy hears felony criminal cases on Thursday in Supreme Court.

11. Daniel is being charged with the murder of his cousin, Jerrell. 11.____
    Which judge can hear the case and on what day?
    A. Judge Smith on Friday   B. Judge Clark on Monday
    C. Judge Amy on Tuesday   D. Judge Clark on Tuesday

12. Jamal lives in Staten Island with his sister, Tisha, and Tisha's boyfriend, 12.____
    Hunter. Hunter and Jamal do not get along and one day last January, Hunter
    and Jamal were involved in a physical altercation. Hunter and Jamal both
    allege that the other assault and battered the other.
    Which judge can hear the case and on what day?
    A. Judge Clark on Tuesday   B. Judge Amy on Thursday
    C. Judge Smith on Friday   D. Judge Clark on Monday

13. Assuming the crime of assault and battery are not felonies, in which court 13.____
    will Jamal and Hunter's dispute be heard?
    A. Supreme Court   B. Surrogates Court
    C. New York City Criminal Court D. Small Claims Court

14. Assume that Tisha and Hunter have a six-year-old daughter. 14.____
    If Hunter is incarcerated for his role in the physical altercation with Jamal,
    which court would have jurisdiction over Hunter's trial?
    A. Surrogates Court   B. New York City Criminal Court
    C. Bronx Housing Court   D. Richmond County Civil Court

15. What day of the week are the MOST cases heard between all three judges? 15.____
    A. Monday B. Thursday C. Tuesday D. Friday

Questions 16-19.

DIRECTIONS: Questions 16 through 19 are to be answered on the basis of the following table.

Caption #1	Caption #2	Caption #3	Caption #4
Case 12-908	Case 12-909	Case 12-910	Case 12-911
Bronx Housing Court	Civil Court	Civil Court	Surrogates Court
Landlord/Tenant	Assault	Breach of Contract	Guardianship
ABC Property Mgmt v. Sam Smith	Jim Jones v. Sam Hunt	Terrell Williams v. Daniel Tang	In re: Jane Doe

16. Which caption above contains an INCORRECT cause of action?
    A. 1   B. 2   C. 3   D. 4

17. When were the cases in each of the captions above initiated?
    A. 2015
    B. 2016
    C. 2012
    D. Unable to determine based on the information provided

18. Which case caption above corresponds to a matter that will NOT have monetary damages awarded?
    A. 1   B. 2   C. 3   D. 4

19. Which case caption has a matter involving an institutional, rather than an individual, petitioner?
    A. 1   B. 2   C. 3   D. 4

20. A pro se litigant wants to initiate a lawsuit against his intrusive neighbor. Assuming the pro se litigant prevails, which form should be served against the neighbor after the judgment is entered?
    A. Notice of entry
    B. Notice of appeal
    C. Remand service
    D. Process discovery

21. A(n) _____ is a hearing for the purpose of determining the amount of damages sue on a claim. The clerk can enter the request on the judge's calendar after the opposing party has defaulted.
    A. imposition   B. inquest   C. tardy notice   D. reversal

22. After a judgment is entered, it becomes enforceable for a period of time. For real property, a transcript of _____ is filed with the County Clerk which makes the judgment enforceable for a period of ten years.
    A. enforcement
    B. judgment
    C. engagement
    D. affidavit

23. Sensitive information must be _____ before it becomes public record.
    A. retained   B. reposed   C. redacted   D. recanted

4 (#2)

24. Service of process can be filed upon the individual or upon the _____. The affidavit of service will state the party that received the service. 24.____
    A. secretary of state
    B. guardian
    C. ad litem
    D. second most suitable person

25. A warrant can be issued to a sheriff or a marshal. The warrant clerk is responsible for reviewing the paperwork and ensuring that all is in order, including 25.____
    A. the names of the parties
    B. address of the premises
    C. the index number
    D. all of the above

KEY (CORRECT ANSWERS)

1.	A	11.	D
2.	B	12.	D
3.	C	13.	C
4.	A	14.	B
5.	B	15.	D
6.	C	16.	B
7.	B	17.	C
8.	A	18.	D
9.	A	19.	A
10.	B	20.	A

21.	B
22.	B
23.	C
24.	A
25.	D

TEST 3

DIRECTIONS: Each question or incomplete statement is followed by several suggested answers or completions. Select the one that BEST answers the question or completes the statement. *PRINT THE LETTER OF THE CORRECT ANSWER IN THE SPACE AT THE RIGHT.*

1. Supreme Court clerks need to be on notice when a(n) _____ is filed as a judge is not assigned until one that parties files this document and pays the filing fee. A case will never go to trial if this document is never filed.
    A. request for maintenance
    B. request for judicial intervention
    C. remediation
    D. arbitration

1._____

Questions 2-4.

DIRECTIONS: Questions 1 through 5 are to be answered on the basis of the following chart.

Row	Case Type	Court
1	Divorce	Supreme Court
2	Custody/Visitation	Family Court
3	Child Support	Family Court
4	Paternity	Family Court
5	When Someone Dies	Surrogates Court
6	Guardianship	Surrogate's Court
7	Name Change	Supreme Court
8	Housing	New York City Housing Court

2. Assume that you are advising a pro se litigant on the proper forms to file when representing him or herself. Where would John file a small estate affidavit?
    A. Family Court
    B. Supreme Court
    C. Surrogates Court
    D. New York Civil Court

2._____

3. Where would Tom's sister, Emmanuela, file a name change?
    A. Supreme Court
    B. Family Court
    C. Surrogates Court
    D. New York City Civil Court

3._____

4. Tara and her husband, Cassidy, share custody of their twin sons, Drake and Austin. Cassidy would like to petition the court for sole custody. Where would Cassidy file his petition?
    A. New York City Housing Court
    B. Supreme Court
    C. Family Court
    D. Surrogates Court

4._____

5. Richard is representing himself in a lawsuit against his landlord. Richard does not have the financial means to hire an attorney and would like to request a reduction in the court filing fees. Richard must file a request for a _____ which is made by filing a _____ and sworn _____ which explains his finances to the court.
   A. fee waiver; notice of motion; affirmation
   B. fee waiver, notice of motion, affidavit
   C. affidavit, notice of motion, fee waiver
   D. affidavit, fee waiver, notice of motion

Questions 6-10.

DIRECTIONS: Questions 6 through 10 are to be answered on the basis of the following text.

Daniel walks into this local supermarket after lunch and falls in one of the store aisles. Daniel lies on the floor – which is nearly empty – until one of the store managers finds him, helps him up, and offers to pay for his groceries. Daniel leaves the store bruised, but not seriously injured. Two days later, Daniel falls at another grocery store. This time, Daniel threatens to sue the grocery store. The second grocery store has heard about Daniel and is concerned that he is falsifying his injuries to gain sympathy and money. The second grocery store sues Daniel to get ahead of Daniel suing them.

6. Who is the plaintiff in the case?
   A. The first grocery store   B. The second grocery store
   C. The grocery store manager   D. Daniel

7. Which of the following is the MOST likely cause of action in a suit that Daniel initiates against the grocery store?
   A. Breach of contract   B. Discrimination
   C. Negligence   D. Assault

8. After the lawsuit has commenced, which party would respond or file an answer to the complaint?
   A. Daniel   B. The first grocery store
   C. The second grocery store   D. The grocery store manager

9. Which party is eligible to countersue?
   A. The first grocery store   B. The second grocery store
   C. The grocery store manager   D. Daniel

10. The lawsuit will likely be dismissed. Why?
    A. Daniel is clearly not exaggerating his injuries.
    B. Daniel has not sued either grocery store.
    C. The store manager did not take a report of Daniel's injuries.
    D. The first grocery store must sue Daniel first.

11. A settlement between parties is not a final and binding legal agreement until the _____ of settlement is signed by both parties.
    A. amendment   B. agreement   C. stipulation   D. simulation

12. Which of the following are appropriate reasons for filing an Order to Show Cause?
    A. Changing the terms of a court order
    B. Requesting the court to dismiss a case
    C. Bringing the case back to court for any reason
    D. All of the above

    12.____

13. Which of the following is NOT an appropriate reason for filing an Order to Show Case?
    A. Asking for more time to do something previously agreed upon by court order
    B. Explaining why either party missed a court date
    C. Submitting financial information for a landlord/tenant dispute
    D. Fixing errors in a stipulation

    13.____

Questions 14-17.

DIRECTIONS: Questions 14 through 17 are to be answered on the basis of the following text.

Judge Chin hears child neglect and abuse cases in Family Court on Mondays and Tuesdays. Judge Amy hears divorce cases on Mondays, Wednesdays, and Fridays. Judge Snell hears child support and visitation cases every day of the week except Thursday. Termination of parental rights, foster care placement, and other child support cases are scheduled on Thursdays only with any of the three judges.

14. Tim and Sarah would like to adjust their visitation schedule for their eight-year-old daughter, Samantha. They would like the courts to assist them with this issue as they have been unable to come to an agreement on their own.
    Which judge will hear the case and on what day?
    A. Judge Snell on Thursday   B. Judge Snell on Monday
    C. Judge Chin on Monday   D. Judge Chin on Friday

    14.____

15. Amanda would like to file for emancipation from her parents.
    Which judge is MOST likely to hear her case?
    A. Judge Chin
    B. Judge Amy
    C. Judge Snell'
    D. Any of the judges can hear Amanda's case

    15.____

16. Jimmy and Eva are legally separating. Which judge will hear their case and on what day?
    A. Judge Chin on Monday   B. Judge Snell on Monday
    C. Judge Amy on Monday   D. Judge Chin on Tuesday

    16.____

4 (#3)

17. The State of New York intends to file a case against Eric for the abuses and neglect of his daughter, Clare. Eric, however, is not Clare's legal guardian. Clare's legal guardian is her grandmother, Allison. Even though it is not clear that Clare has been neglected, the courts have found that Clare should be placed into foster care until it can be determined who the ultimate caregiver should be.
Which judge will MOST likely hear this case?
A. Judge Amy
B. Judge Chin
C. Judge Snell
D. Any of the judges can hear this case

17._____

Questions 18-25.

DIRECTIONS: Questions 18 through 25 are to be answered on the basis of the following chart.

Item	Fee
Obtaining an index number	$210
RJI	$95
Note of Issue	$30
Motion or Cross-Motion	$45
Demand for Jury Trial	$65
Voluntary Discontinuance	$35
Notice of Appeal	$65

18. What is the final cost to obtain an index number, demand a jury trial, and file a notice of appeal?
A. $210   B. $35   C. $65   D. $310

18._____

19. What is the final cost to obtain an RJI and note of issue?
A. $125   B. $95   C. $30   D. $65

19._____

20. Which of the following is MOST likely to be filed with an RJI?
A. Demand for jury trial
B. Notice of appeal
C. Voluntary discontinuance
D. Obtaining an index number

20._____

21. Which of the following is the MOST likely outcome of filing a voluntary discontinuance?
The case
A. is automatically appealed
B. is dismissed
C. is rescheduled
D. will be remanded

21._____

22. What is the final cost of filing a notice of appeal?
A. $35   B. $65   C. $95   D. $120

22._____

23. What is the final cost of all items prior to filing a motion or cross-motion?
A. $210   B. $95   C. $45   D. $335

23._____

5 (#3)

24. Jamal would like to petition the court to compel discovery from his adversary and former friend, Bob. He would also like to speed up the date of trial by filing a demand for jury trial and RJI.
What is the final cost to do so?
A. $160	B. $95	C. $65	D. $205

24.____

25. What is the LEAST costly court document filing fee?
A. Notice of motion	B. Demand for jury trial
C. Note of issue	D. RJI

25.____

KEY (CORRECT ANSWERS)

1. B
2. C
3. A
4. C
5. B

6. B
7. C
8. A
9. D
10. B

11. C
12. D
13. C
14. B
15. D

16. C
17. D
18. D
19. A
20. D

21. B
22. B
23. D
24. D
25. C

TEST 4

DIRECTIONS: Each question or incomplete statement is followed by several suggested answers or completions. Select the one that BEST answers the question or completes the statement. *PRINT THE LETTER OF THE CORRECT ANSWER IN THE SPACE AT THE RIGHT.*

1. A lawsuit for money damages amounting to more than $25,000 can be heard in which court?
    A. Surrogates Court
    B. Supreme Court
    C. New York City Civil Court
    D. New York City Criminal Court

    1._____

2. Which of the following will NOT be on a Notice of Entry?
    A. Name of plaintiff
    B. Name of defendant
    C. Index number
    D. Social Security number

    2._____

3. Court clerks are prohibited from which of the following?
    A. Predicting the judgment of the court
    B. Explaining available options for a case or problem
    C. Providing past rulings
    D. Providing citations or copies of the law

    3._____

4. Court clerks are permitted to do all of the following EXCEPT
    A. provide forms with instructions
    B. instruct an individual on how to make a complaint
    C. analyze the law based on the specifics of a case
    D. describe court records and their availability

    4._____

5. Mary would like to sue her neighbor, Jacob, for money damages. Mary claims Jacob ran his car into Mary's garage door while it was down and caused $5,000 in damages. For claims below $1,000, the filing fee is $15, while the filing fee is $5 more for claims above $1,000.
    How much is Mary's filing fee?
    A. $15   B. $10   C. $20   D. $25

    5._____

Questions 6-10.

DIRECTIONS: Questions 6 through 10 are to be answered on the basis of the following table.

Schedule – Judge O'Neill		
Wednesday	**Thursday**	**Friday**
Continued	Dismissed with prejudice	Dismissed with prejudice
Continued	Adjourned	Continued
Settled	Dismissed with prejudice	Dismissed without prejudice
Settled	Continued	Settled
Settled	Continued	Settled

6. How many cases were adjourned this week?
    A. 5   B. 6   C. 1   D. 2

    6._____

67

7. How many cases settled this week?
   A. 5   B. 4   C. 3   D. 8

8. How many cases were dismissed this week?
   A. 6   B. 4   C. 5   D. 7

9. How many cases will likely be heard again or, in other words, how many cases can be re-filed or are otherwise continued?
   A. 6   B. 5   C. 7   D. 8

10. Which day was Judge O'Neill the LEAST busy?
    A. Thursday
    B. Friday
    C. Wednesday
    D. Each day was equally busy

Questions 11-15.

DIRECTIONS: Questions 11 through 15 are to be answered on the basis of the following text.

At Alex's arraignment, he pled ___1___ to the charge of driving under the influence and vehicular manslaughter. At trial, the prosecutor presented evidence from several ___2___ that testified Alex had a drinking problem. While Alex's defense attorneys ___3___ to that testimony and argued it was hearsay, the judge overruled those objections and allowed the testimony to be entered in the record as originally spoken. At the conclusion of the trial, Alex was found ___4___ and sentenced to community service.

11. Fill in the blank for #1:
    A. nolo   B. contendere   C. not guilty   D. guilty

12. Fill in the blank for #2:
    A. witnesses   B. evidence   C. testimony   D. bearer

13. Fill in the blank for #3:
    A. disagreed   B. objected   C. qualified   D. disclaimed

14. Fill in the blank for #4:
    A. arraigned   B. protested   C. remanded   D. guilty

15. An acquittal can also be recorded in court documentation as a finding of
    A. reversal   B. recusal   C. not guilty   D. remand

16. Evidence must be found _____ before it can be marked and evaluated by the fact finder, either a judge or jury, in civil and criminal cases.
    A. relevant   B. redacted   C. qualified   D. admissible

17. The party who seeks an appeal from a decision of a court is deemed a(n) _____ and is recorded in court documentation as such.
    A. petitioner   B. respondent   C. appellant   D. re-respondent

3 (#4)

18. How would a condominium be recorded in a bankruptcy proceeding? 18.____
    A. Real property   B. Personal property
    C. Intangible asset   D. chattel

19. Which of the following is LEAST likely to be recorded as a written statement 19.____
    describing one's legal and factual arguments?
    A. Attorney's brief   B. Motion
    C. Summons   D. Complaint

20. A lawsuit where one or more members of a large group of individuals sues 20.____
    on behalf of the other individuals in the large group is recorded as a _____
    lawsuit.
    A. introductory   B. class action   C. municipality   D. winning

21. Jamal has filed for bankruptcy. After the trustee has reviewed Jamal's 21.____
    assets, the trustee proposes a plan to the court where Jamal promises property
    that he already owns to satisfy the major of his debt.
    The property Jamal owns that will satisfy the debt is recorded as
    A. demerits   B. collateral   C. debris   D. probate

22. Judge Presser has rendered Emilio's sentence for the charges of armed 22.____
    robbery and kidnapping. Emilio will serve 10 years for armed robbery and 12
    years for kidnapping.
    If Emilio's total time in prison is 12 years, his sentence is recorded as
    A. consecutive   B. demonstrative
    C. concurrent   D. rebated

23. Assume the same facts as the previous question, but assume Emilio serves 23.____
    22 years in prison.
    In this instance, his sentence is recorded as
    A. consecutive   B. demonstrative
    C. concurrent   D. rebated

24. A conviction can also be recorded in court records as a judgment of 24.____
    _____ against a defendant.
    A. guilt   B. remorse   C. retaliation   D. acquittal

25. In bankruptcy, Jamal sells his house to his mother for $5 in an effort to 25.____
    hide it from creditors who will require that he sell it to satisfy his debts.
    This sale is recorded as a
    A. fraudulent transfer   B. falsified sale
    C. remarkable trade   D. clawback trade

KEY (CORRECT ANSWERS)

1.	B		11.	C
2.	D		12.	A
3.	A		13.	B
4.	C		14.	D
5.	C		15.	C
6.	C		16.	D
7.	A		17.	C
8.	B		18.	A
9.	A		19.	C
10.	C		20.	B

21.	B
22.	C
23.	A
24.	A
25.	A

EXAMINATION SECTION
TEST 1

DIRECTIONS: Each question or incomplete statement is followed by several suggested answers or completions. Select the one that BEST answers the question or completes the statement. *PRINT THE LETTER OF THE CORRECT ANSWER IN THE SPACE AT THE RIGHT.*

Questions 1-6.

DIRECTIONS: Questions 1 through 6 consist of descriptions of material to which a filing designation must be assigned.

Assume that the matters and cases described in the questions were referred for handling to a government legal office which has its files set up according to these file designations. The file designation consists of a number of characters and punctuation marks as described below.

The first character refers to agencies whose legal work is handled by this office. These agencies are numbered consecutively in the order in which they first submit a matter for attention, and are identified in an alphabetical card index. To date numbers have been assigned to agencies as follows:

Department of Correction	1
Police Department	2
Department of Traffic	3
Department of Consumer Affairs	4
Commission on Human Rights	5
Board of Elections	6
Department of Personnel	7
Board of Estimate	8

The second character is separated from the first character by a dash. The second character is the last digit of the year in which a particular lawsuit or matter is referred to the legal office.

The third character is separated from the second character by a colon and may consist of either of the following:

I. A sub-number assigned to each lawsuit to which the agency is a party. Lawsuits are numbered consecutively regardless of year. (Lawsuits are brought by or against agency heads rather than agencies themselves, but references are made to agencies for the purpose of simplification.)

or II. A capital letter assigned to each matter other than a lawsuit according to subject, the subject being identified in an alphabetical index. To date, letters have been assigned to subjects as follows:

Citizenship	A	Housing	E
Discrimination	B	Gambling	F
Residence Requirements	C	Freedom of Religion	G
Civil Service Examinations	D		

These referrals are numbered consecutively regardless of year. The first referral by a particular agency on citizenship, for example, would be designated A1, followed by A2, A3, etc.

If no reference is made in a question as to how many letters involving a certain subject or how many lawsuits have been referred by an agency, assume that it is the first.

For each question, choose the file designation which is MOST appropriate for filing the material described in the question.

1. In January 2010, two candidates in a 2009 civil service examination for positions with the Department of Correction filed a suit against the Department of Personnel seeking to set aside an educational requirement for the title.
   The Department of Personnel immediately referred the lawsuit to the legal office for handling.

   A. 1-9:1   B. 1-0:D1   C. 7-9:D1   D. 7-0:1

2. In 2014, the Police Department made its sixth request for an opinion on whether an employee assignment proposed for 2015 could be considered discriminatory.

   A. 2-5:1-B6   B. 2-4:6   C. 2-4:1-B6   D. 2-4:B6

3. In 2015, a lawsuit was brought by the Bay Island Action Committee against the Board of Estimate in which the plaintiff sought withdrawal of approval of housing for the elderly in the Bay Island area given by the Board in 2015.

   A. 8-3:1   B. 8-5:1   C. 8-3:B1   D. 8-5:E1

4. In December 2014, community leaders asked the Police Department to ban outdoor meetings of a religious group on the grounds that the meetings were disrupting the area. Such meetings had been held from time to time during 2014. On January 31, 2015, the Police Department asked the government legal office for an opinion on whether granting this request would violate the worshippers' right to freedom of religion.

   A. 2-4:G-1   B. 2-5:G1   C. 2-5:B-1   D. 2-4:B1

5. In 2014, a woman filed suit against the Board of Elections. She alleged that she had not been permitted to vote at her usual polling place in the 2013 election and had been told she was not registered there. She claimed that she had always voted there and that her record card had been lost. This was the fourth case of its type for this agency.

   A. 6-4:4   B. 6-3:C4   C. 3-4:6   D. 6-3:4

6. A lawsuit was brought in 2011 by the Ace Pinball Machine Company against the Commissioner of Consumer Affairs. The lawsuit contested an ordinance which banned the use of pinball machines on the ground that they are gambling devices.
   This was the third lawsuit to which the Department of Consumer Affairs was a party.

   A. 4-1:1   B. 4-3:F1   C. 4-1:3   D. 3F-4:1

7. You are instructed by your supervisor to type a statement that must be signed by the person making the statement and by three witnesses to the signature. The typed statement will take two pages and will leave no room for signatures if the normal margin is maintained at the bottom of the second page.
In this situation, the PREFERRED method is to type

   A. the signature lines below the normal margin on the second page
   B. nothing further and have the witnesses sign without a typed signature line
   C. the signature lines on a third page
   D. some of the text and the signature lines on a third page

8. Certain legal documents always begin with a statement of venue - that is, the county and state in which the document is executed. This is usually boxed with a parentheses or colons.
The one of the following documents that ALWAYS bears a statement of venue in a prominent position at its head is a(n)

   A. affidavit   B. memorandum of law
   C. contract of sale   D. will

9. A court stenographer is to take stenographic notes and transcribe the statements of a person under oath. The person has a heavy accent and speaks in ungrammatical and broken English.
When he or she is transcribing the testimony, of the following, the BEST thing for them to do is to

   A. transcribe the testimony exactly as spoken, making no grammatical changes
   B. make only the grammatical changes which would clarify the client's statements
   C. make all grammatical changes so that the testimony is in standard English form
   D. ask the client's permission before making any grammatical changes

10. When the material typed on a printed form does not fill the space provided, a Z-ruling is frequently drawn to fill up the unused space.
The MAIN purpose of this practice is to

    A. make the document more pleasing to the eye
    B. indicate that the preceding material is correct
    C. insure that the document is not altered
    D. show that the lawyer has read it

11. After you had typed an original and five copies of a certain document, some changes were made in ink on the original and were initialed by all the parties. The original was signed by all the parties, and the signatures were notarized.
Which of the following should *generally* be typed on the copies BEFORE filing the original and the copies? The inked changes

    A. but not the signatures, initials, or notarial data
    B. the signatures and the initials but not the notarial data
    C. and the notarial data but not the signatures or initials
    D. the signatures, the initials, and the notarial data

12. The first paragraph of a noncourt agreement *generally* contains all of the following EXCEPT the

    A. specific terms of the agreement
    B. date of the agreement
    C. purpose of the agreement
    D. names of the parties involved

13. When typing an answer in a court proceeding, the place where the word ANSWER should be typed on the first page of the document is

    A. at the upper left-hand corner
    B. below the index number and to the right of the box containing the names of the parties to the action
    C. above the index number and to the right of the box containing the names of the parties to the action
    D. to the left of the names of the attorneys for the defendant

14. Which one of the following statements BEST describes the legal document called an acknowledgment?
    It is

    A. an answer to an affidavit
    B. a receipt issued by the court when a document is filed
    C. proof of service of a summons
    D. a declaration that a signature is valid

15. Suppose you typed the original and three copies of a legal document which was dictated by an attorney in your office. He has already signed the original copy, and corrections have been made on all copies.
    Regarding the copies, which one of the following procedures is the PROPER one to follow?

    A. Leave the signature line blank on the copies
    B. Ask the attorney to sign the copies
    C. Print or type the attorney's name on the signature line on the copies
    D. Sign your name to the copies followed by the attorney's initials

16. Suppose your office is defending a particular person in a court action. This person comes to the office and asks to see some of the lawyer's working papers in his file. The lawyer assigned to the case is out of the office at the time.
    You SHOULD

    A. permit him to examine his entire file as long as he does not remove any materials from it
    B. make an appointment for the caller to come back later when the lawyer will be there
    C. ask him what working papers he wants to see and show him only those papers
    D. tell him that he needs written permission from the lawyer in order to see any records

17. Suppose that you receive a phone call from an official who is annoyed about a letter from your office which she just received. The lawyer who dictated the letter is not in the office at the moment.
    Of the following, the BEST action for you to take is to

    A. explain that the lawyer is out but that you will ask the lawyer to return her call when he returns
    B. take down all of the details of her complaint and tell her that you will get back to her with an explanation
    C. refer to the proper file so that you can give her an explanation of the reasons for the letter over the phone
    D. make an appointment for her to stop by the office to speak with the lawyer

18. Suppose that you have taken dictation for an interoffice memorandum. You are asked to prepare it for distribution to four lawyers in your department whose names are given to you. You will type an original and make four copies. Which one of the following is CORRECT with regard to the typing of the lawyers' names?
    The names of all of the lawyers should appear

    A. *only* on the original
    B. on the original and each copy should have the name of one lawyer
    C. on each of the copies but not on the original
    D. on the original and on all of the copies

19. Regarding the correct typing of punctuation, the GENERALLY accepted practice is that there should be

    A. two spaces after a semi-colon
    B. one space before an apostrophe used in the body of a word
    C. no space between parentheses and the matter enclosed
    D. one space before and after a hyphen

20. Suppose you have just completed typing an original and two copies of a letter requesting information. The original is to be signed by a lawyer in your office. The first copy is for the files, and the second is to be used as a reminder to follow up.
    The PROPER time to file the file copy of the letter is

    A. after the letter has been signed and corrections have been made on the copies
    B. before you take the letter to the lawyer for his signature
    C. after a follow-up letter has been sent
    D. after a response to the letter has been received

21. A secretary in a legal office has just typed a letter. She has typed the copy distribution notation on the copies to indicate *blind copy distribution*. This *blind copy* notation shows that

    A. copies of the letter are being sent to persons that the addressee does not know
    B. copies of the letter are being sent to other persons without the addressee's knowledge
    C. a copy of the letter will be enlarged for a legally blind person
    D. a copy of the letter is being given as an extra copy to the addressee

22. Suppose that one of the attorneys in your office dictates material to you without indicating punctuation. He has asked that you give him, as soon as possible, a single copy of a rough draft to be triple-spaced so that he can make corrections.
Of the following, what is the BEST thing for you to do in this situation?

 A. Assume that no punctuation is desired in the material
 B. Insert the punctuation as you type the rough draft
 C. Transcribe the material exactly as dictated, but attach a note to the attorney stating your suggested changes
 D. Before you start to type the draft, tell the attorney you want to read back your notes so that he can indicate punctuation

23. When it is necessary to type a mailing notation such as CERTIFIED, REGISTERED, or FEDEX on an envelope, the GENERALLY accepted place to type it is

 A. directly above the address
 B. in the area below where the stamp will be affixed
 C. in the lower left-hand corner
 D. in the upper left-hand corner

24. When taking a citation of a case in shorthand, which of the following should you write FIRST if you are having difficulty keeping up with the dictation?

 A. Volume and page number   B. Title of volume
 C. Name of plaintiff   D. Name of defendant

25. All of the following abbreviations and their meanings are correctly paired EXCEPT

 A. viz. - namely   B. ibid. - refer
 C. n.b. - note well   D. q.v. - which see

KEY (CORRECT ANSWERS)

1. D	11. D
2. D	12. A
3. B	13. B
4. B	14. D
5. A	15. C
6. C	16. B
7. D	17. A
8. A	18. D
9. A	19. C
10. C	20. A

21. B
22. B
23. B
24. A
25. B

EXAMINATION SECTION
TEST 1

DIRECTIONS: Each question or incomplete statement is followed by several suggested answers or completions. Select the one that BEST answers the question or completes the statement. *PRINT THE LETTER OF THE CORRECT ANSWER IN THE SPACE AT THE RIGHT.*

Questions 1-9.

DIRECTIONS: Questions 1 through 9 consist of sentences which may or may not be examples of good English usage. Consider grammar, punctuation, spelling, capitalization, awkwardness, etc. Examine each sentence, and then choose the correct statement about it from the four choices below it. If the English usage in the sentence given is better than it would be with any of the changes suggested in options B, C, and D, choose option A. Do not choose an option that will change the meaning of the sentence.

1. According to Judge Frank, the grocer's sons found guilty of assault and sentenced last Thursday.   1.____

    A. This is an example of acceptable writing.
    B. A comma should be placed after the word *sentenced*.
    C. The word *were* should be placed after *sons*
    D. The apostrophe in *grocer's* should be placed after the *s*.

2. The department heads assistant said that the stenographers should type duplicate copies of all contracts, leases, and bills.   2.____

    A. This is an example of acceptable writing.
    B. A comma should be placed before the word *contracts*.
    C. An apostrophe should be placed before the *s* in *heads*.
    D. Quotation marks should be placed before *the stenographers* and after *bills*.

3. The lawyers questioned the men to determine who was the true property owner?   3.____

    A. This is an example of acceptable writing.
    B. The phrase *questioned the men* should be changed to *asked the men questions*.
    C. The word *was* should be changed to *were*.
    D. The question mark should be changed to a period.

4. The terms stated in the present contract are more specific than those stated in the previous contract.   4.____

    A. This is an example of acceptable writing.
    B. The word *are* should be changed to *is*.
    C. The word *than* should be changed to *then*.
    D. The word *specific* should be changed to *specified*.

5. Of the lawyers considered, the one who argued more skillful was chosen for the job.   5.____

    A. This is an example of acceptable writing.
    B. The word *more* should be replaced by the word *most*.
    C. The word *skillful* should be replaced by the word *skillfully*,
    D. The word *chosen* should be replaced by the word *selected*.

77

6. Each of the states has a court of appeals; some states have circuit courts.   6.____

   A. This is an example of acceptable writing.
   B. The semi-colon should be changed to a comma.
   C. The word *has* should be changed to *have*.
   D. The word *some* should be capitalized.

7. The court trial has greatly effected the child's mental condition.   7.____

   A. This is an example of acceptable writing.
   B. The word *effected* should be changed to *affected*.
   C. The word *greatly* should be placed after *effected*.
   D. The apostrophe in *child's* should be placed after the *s*.

8. Last week, the petition signed by all the officers was sent to the Better Business Bureau.   8.____

   A. This is an example of acceptable writing.
   B. The phrase *last week* should be placed after *officers*.
   C. A comma should be placed after *petition*.
   D. The word *was* should be changed to *were*.

9. Mr. Farrell claims that he requested form A-12, and three booklets describing court procedures.   9.____

   A. This is an example of acceptable writing.
   B. The word *that* should be eliminated.
   C. A colon should be placed after *requested*.
   D. The comma after *A-12* should be eliminated.

Questions 10-21.

DIRECTIONS: Questions 10 through 21 contain a word in capital letters followed by four suggested meanings of the word. For each question, choose the BEST meaning for the word in capital letters.

10. SIGNATORY - A   10.____

    A. lawyer who draws up a legal document
    B. document that must be signed by a judge
    C. person who signs a document
    D. true copy of a signature

11. RETAINER - A   11.____

    A. fee paid to a lawyer for his services
    B. document held by a third party
    C. court decision to send a prisoner back to custody pending trial
    D. legal requirement to keep certain types of files

12. BEQUEATH - To   12.____

    A. receive assistance from a charitable organization
    B. give personal property by will to another
    C. transfer real property from one person to another
    D. receive an inheritance upon the death of a relative

13. RATIFY - To 13.____

    A. approve and sanction   B. forego
    C. produce evidence   D. summarize

14. CODICIL - A 14.____

    A. document introduced in evidence in a civil action
    B. subsection of a law
    C. type of legal action that can be brought by a plaintiff
    D. supplement or an addition to a will

15. ALIAS 15.____

    A. Assumed name   B. In favor of
    C. Against   D. A writ

16. PROXY - A(n) 16.____

    A. phony document in a real estate transaction
    B. opinion by a judge of a civil court
    C. document containing appointment of an agent
    D. summons in a lawsuit

17. ALLEGED 17.____

    A. Innocent   B. Asserted
    C. Guilty   D. Called upon

18. EXECUTE - To 18.____

    A. complete a legal document by signing it
    B. set requirements
    C. render services to a duly elected executive of a municipality
    D. initiate legal action such as a lawsuit

19. NOTARY PUBLIC - A 19.____

    A. lawyer who is running for public office
    B. judge who hears minor cases
    C. public officer, one of whose functions is to administer oaths
    D. lawyer who gives free legal services to persons unable to pay

20. WAIVE - To 20.____

    A. disturb a calm state of affairs
    B. knowingly renounce a right or claim
    C. pardon someone for a minor fault
    D. purposely mislead a person during an investigation

21. ARRAIGN - To 21.____

    A. prevent an escape   B. defend a prisoner
    C. verify a document   D. accuse in a court of law

Questions 22-40.

DIRECTIONS: Questions 22 through 40 each consist of four words which may or may not be spelled correctly. If you find an error in
only one word, mark your answer A;
any two words, mark your answer B;
any three words, mark your answer C;
none of these words, mark your answer D.

22.	occurrence	Febuary	privilege	similiar	22._____
23.	separate	transferring	analyze	column	23._____
24.	develop	license	bankrupcy	abreviate	24._____
25.	subpoena	arguement	dissolution	foreclosure	25._____
26.	exaggerate	fundamental	significance	warrant	26._____
27.	citizen	endorsed	marraige	appraissal	27._____
28.	precedant	univercity	observence	preliminary	28._____
29.	stipulate	negligence	judgment	prominent	29._____
30.	judisial	whereas	release	guardian	30._____
31.	appeal	larcenny	transcrip	jurist	31._____
32.	petition	tenancy	agenda	insurance	32._____
33.	superfical	premise	morgaged	maintainance	33._____
34.	testamony	publically	installment	possessed	34._____
35.	escrow	decree	eviction	miscelaneous	35._____
36.	securitys	abeyance	adhere	corporate	36._____
37.	kaleidoscope	anesthesia	vermilion	tafetta	37._____
38.	congruant	barrenness	plebescite	vigilance	38._____
39.	picnicing	promisory	resevoir	omission	39._____
40.	supersede	banister	wholly	seize	40._____

KEY (CORRECT ANSWERS)

1. C	11. A	21. D	31. B
2. C	12. B	22. B	32. D
3. D	13. A	23. D	33. C
4. A	14. D	24. B	34. B
5. C	15. A	25. A	35. A
6. A	16. C	26. D	36. A
7. B	17. B	27. B	37. A
8. A	18. A	28. C	38. B
9. D	19. C	29. D	39. C
10. C	20. B	30. A	40. D

DOCUMENTS AND FORMS
PREPARING WRITTEN MATERIALS
EXAMINATION SECTION
TEST 1

DIRECTIONS: Each question or incomplete statement is followed by several suggested answers or completions. Select the one that BEST answers the question or completes the statement. *PRINT THE LETTER OF THE CORRECT ANSWER IN THE SPACE AT THE RIGHT.*

1. Of the following types of documents, it is MOST important to retain and file
    A. working drafts of reports that have been submitted in final form
    B. copies of letters of good will which conveyed a message that could not be handled by phone
    C. interoffice orders for materials which have been received and verified
    D. interoffice memoranda regarding the routine of standard forms

2. The MAXIMUM number of 2¾" x 4¼" size forms which may be obtained from one ream of 17" x 22" paper is
    A. 4,000   B. 8,000   C. 12,000   D. 16,000

3. On a general organization chart, staff positions NORMALLY should be pictured
    A. directly above the line positions to which they report
    B. to the sides of the main flow lines
    C. within the box of the highest level subordinate positions pictured
    D. directly below the line positions which report to them

4. When an administrator is diagramming an office layout, of the following, his PRIMARY job generally should be to indicate the
    A. lighting intensities that will be required by each operator
    B. noise level that will be produced by the various equipment employed in the office
    C. direction of the work flow and the distance involved in each transfer
    D. durability of major pieces of office equipment currently in use or to be utilized

5. One common guideline or rule-of-thumb ratio for evaluating the efficiency of files is the number of records requested divided by the number of records filed. Generally, if this ratio is very low, it would point MOST directly to the need for
    A. improving the indexing and coding systems
    B. improving the charge-out procedures
    C. exploring the need for transferring records from active storage to the archives
    D. exploring the need to encourage employees to keep more records in their private files

6. The GREATEST percentage of money spent on preparing and keeping the usual records in an office generally is expended for which one of the following?
    A. Renting space in which to place the record-keeping equipment
    B. Paying salaries of record-preparing and record-keeping personnel
    C. Depreciation of purchased record-preparation and record-keeping machines
    D. Paper and forms upon which to place the records

6.____

7. In a certain office, file folders are constantly being removed from the files for use by administrators. At the same time, new material is coming in to be filed in some of these folders.
Of the following, the BEST way to avoid delays in filing of the new material and to keep track of the removed folders is to
    A. keep a sheet listing all folders removed from the file, who has them, and a follow-update to check on their return; attach to this list new material received for filing
    B. put an "out" slip in the place of any file folder removed, telling what folder is missing, date removed, and who has it; file new material received at front of files
    C. put a temporary "out" folder in place of the one removed, giving title or subject, date removed, and who has it; put into this temporary folder any new material received
    D. keep a list of all folders removed and who has them; forward any new material received for filing while a folder is out to the person who has it

7.____

8. Folders labeled "Miscellaneous" should be used in an alphabetic filing system MAINLY to
    A. provide quick access to recent material
    B. avoid setting up individual folders for infrequent correspondence
    C. provide temporary storage for less important documents
    D. temporarily hold papers which will not fit into already crowded individual folders

8.____

9. Out-of-date and seldom-used records should be removed periodically from the files because
    A. overall responsibility for records will be transferred to the person in charge of the central storage files
    B. duplicate copies of every record are not needed
    C. valuable filing space will be regained and the time needed to find a current record will be cut down
    D. worthwhile suggestions on improving the filing system will result whenever this is done

9.____

10. Of the following, the BEST reason for discarding certain material from office files would be that the
    A. files are crowded
    B. material in the files is old
    C. material duplicates information obtainable from other sources in the files
    D. material is referred to most often by employees in an adjoining office

10.____

11. Of the following, the MAIN factor contributing to the expense of maintaining an office procedure manual would be the
    A. infrequent use of the manual
    B. need to revise it regularly
    C. cost of loose-leaf binders
    D. high cost of printing

11.____

12. The suggestion that memos or directives which circulate among subordinates be initialed by each employee is a
    A. *poor* one, because, with modern copying machines, it would be possible to supply every subordinate with a copy of each message for his personal use
    B. *good* one, because it relieves the supervisor of blame for the action of subordinates who have read and initialed the messages
    C. *poor* one, because initialing the memo or directive is no guarantee that the subordinate has read the material
    D. *good* one, because it can be used as a record by the supervisor to show that his subordinates have received the message and were responsible for reading it

12.____

13. Of the following, the MOST important reason for microfilming office records is to
    A. save storage space needed to keep records
    B. make it easier to get records when needed
    C. speed up the classification of information
    D. shorten the time which records must be kept

13.____

14. Your office filing cabinets have become so overcrowded that it is difficult to use the files.
    Of the following, the MOST desirable step for you to take FIRST to relieve this situation would be to
    A. assign your assistant to spend some time each day reviewing the material in the files and to give you his recommendations as to what material may be discarded
    B. discard all material which has been in the files more than a given number of years
    C. submit a request for additional filing cabinets in your next budget request
    D. transfer enough material to the central storage room of your agency to give you the amount of additional filing space needed

14.____

15. In indexing names of business firms and other organizations, one of the rules to be followed is:
    A. The word "and" is considered an indexing unit
    B. When a firm name includes the full name of a person who is not well known, the person's first name is considered as the first indexing unit
    C. Usually, the units in a firm name are indexed in the order in which they are written
    D. When a firm's name is made up of single letters (such as ABC Corp.), the letters taken together are considered as more than one indexing unit

15.____

16. Assume that your unit processes confidential forms which are submitted by persons seeking financial assistance. An individual comes to your office, gives you his name, and states that he would like to look over a form which he sent in about a week ago because he believes he omitted some important information.
Of the following, the BEST thing for you to do FIRST is to
    A. locate the proper form
    B. call the individual's home telephone number to verify his identity
    C. ask the individual if he has proof of his identity
    D. call the security office

16.____

17. An employee has been assigned to open her division head's mail and place it on his desk. One day, the employee opens a letter which she then notices is marked "Personal."
Of the following, the BEST action for her to take is to
    A. write "Personal" on the letter and staple the envelope to the back of the letter
    B. ignore the matter and treat the letter the same way as the others
    C. give it to another division head to hold until her own division head comes into the office
    D. leave the letter in the envelope and write "Sorry-opened by mistake" on the envelope, and initial it

17.____

18. The MOST important reason for having a filing system is to
    A. get papers out of the way
    B. have a record of everything that has happened
    C. retain information to justify your actions
    D. enable rapid retrieval of information

18.____

19. The system of filing which is used MOST frequently is called _____ filing.
    A. alphabetic   B. alphanumeric
    C. geographic   D. numeric

19.____

20. In judging the adequacy of a standard office form, which of the following is LEAST important?
    A. Date of the form   B. Legibility of the form
    C. Size of the form   D. Design of the form

20.____

21. Assume that the letters and reports which are dictated to you fall into a few distinct subject-matter areas.
The practice of trying to familiarize yourself with the terminology in these areas is
    A. *good*, because you will have a basis for commenting on the dictated material
    B. *good*, because it will be easier to take the dictation at the rate at which it is given
    C. *poor*, because the functions and policies of an office are not of your concern
    D. *poor*, because it will take too much time away from your assigned work

21.____

22. A letter was dictated on June 9 and was ready to be typed on June 12. The letter was typed on June 13, signed on June 14, and mailed on June 14. The date that, ORDINARILY, should have appeared on the letter is June
    A. 9
    B. 12
    C. 13
    D. 14

23. Of the following, the BEST reason for putting the "key point" at the beginning of a letter is that it
    A. may save time for the reader
    B. is standard practice in writing letters
    C. will more likely to be typed correctly
    D. cannot logically be placed elsewhere

24. As a supervisor, you have been asked to attend committee meetings and take the minutes.
    The body of such minutes GENERALLY consists of
    A. the date and place of the meeting and the list of persons present
    B. an exact verbatim report of everything that was said by each person who spoke
    C. a clear description of each matter discussed and the action decided on
    D. the agenda of the meeting

25. When typing a rough draft from a recorded transcription, a stenographer under your supervision reaches a spot on the recording that is virtually inaudible.
    Of the following, the MOST advisable action that you should recommend to her is to
    A. guess what the dictator intended to say based on what he said in the parts that are clear
    B. ask the dictator to listen to his unsatisfactory recording
    C. leave an appropriate amount of space for that portion that is inaudible
    D. stop typing the draft and send a note to the dictator identifying the item that could not be completed

KEY (CORRECT ANSWERS)

1.	D	11.	B
2.	D	12.	D
3.	B	13.	A
4.	C	14.	A
5.	C	15.	C
6.	B	16.	C
7.	C	17.	D
8.	B	18.	D
9.	C	19.	A
10.	C	20.	A

21.	B
22.	D
23.	A
24.	C
25.	C

TEST 2

DIRECTIONS: Each question or incomplete statement is followed by several suggested answers or completions. Select the one that BEST answers the question or completes the statement. *PRINT THE LETTER OF THE CORRECT ANSWER IN THE SPACE AT THE RIGHT.*

1. To tell a newly employed clerk to fill a top drawer of a four-drawer cabinet with heavy binders which will be often used and to keep lower drawers only partly filled is
   A. *good*, because a tall person would have to bend unnecessarily if he had to use a lower drawer
   B. *bad*, because the file cabinet may tip over when the top drawer is opened
   C. *good*, because it is the most easily reachable drawer for the average person
   D. *bad*, because a person bending down at another drawer may accidentally bang his head on the bottom of the drawer when he straightens up

1.____

2. If you have requisitioned a "ream" of paper in order to duplicate a single page office announcement, how many announcements can be printed from the one package of paper?
   A. 200   B. 500   C. 700   D. 1,000

2.____

3. In the operations of a government agency, a voucher is ORDINARILY used to
   A. refer someone to the agency for a position or assignment
   B. certify that an agency's records of financial transactions are accurate
   C. order payment from agency funds of a stated amount to an individual
   D. enter a statement of official opinion in the records of the agency

3.____

4. Of the following types of cards used in filing systems, the one which is generally MOST helpful in locating records which might be filed under more than one subject is the _____ card.
   A. out
   B. tickler
   C. cross-reference
   D. visible index

4.____

5. The type of filing system in which one does NOT need to refer to a card index in order to find the folder is called
   A. alphabetic   B. geographic   C. subject   D. locational

5.____

6. Of the following, records management is LEAST concerned with
   A. the development of the best method for retrieving important information
   B. deciding what records should be kept
   C. deciding the number of appointments a client will need
   D. determining the types of folders to be used

6.____

7. If records are continually removed from a set of files without "charging" them to the borrower, the filing system will soon become ineffective.
Of the following terms, the one which is NOT applied to a form used in the charge-out system is a
   A. requisition card
   B. out-folder
   C. record retrieval form
   D. substitution card

8. A new clerk has been told to put 500 cards in alphabetical order. Another clerk suggests that she divide the cards into four groups, such as A to F, G to L, M to R, and S to Z, and then alphabetize these four smaller groups.
The suggested method is
   A. *poor*, because the clerk will have to handle the sheets more than once and will waste time
   B. *good*, because it saves time, is more accurate, and is less tiring
   C. *good*, because she will not have to concentrate on it so much when it is in smaller groups
   D. *poor*, because this method is much more tiring than straight alphabetizing

9. In Microsoft Excel, data and records are entered into
   A. pages
   B. forms
   C. cells
   D. contracts

10. Suppose a clerk has been given pads of pre-printed forms to use when taking phone messages for others in her office. The clerk is then observed using scraps of paper and not the forms for writing her messages.
It should be explained that the BEST reason for using the forms is that
   A. they act as a checklist to make sure that the important information is taken
   B. she is expected to do her work in the same way as others in the office
   C. they make sure that unassigned paper is not wasted on phone messages
   D. learning to use these forms will help train her to use more difficult forms

11. The high-speed printing process used for producing large quantities of superior quality copy and cost efficiency is called
   A. photocopying
   B. laser printing
   C. inkjet printing
   D. word processing

12. Of the following, the MAIN reason a stock clerk keeps a perpetual inventory of supplies in the storeroom is that such an inventory will
   A. eliminate the need for a physical inventory
   B. provide a continuous record of supplies on hand
   C. indicate whether a shipment of supplies is satisfactory
   D. dictate the terms of the purchase order

13. As a supervisor, you may be required to handle different types of correspondence.
Of the following types of letters, it would be MOST important to promptly seal which kind of letter?
    A. One marked "confidential"
    B. Those containing enclosures
    C. Any letter to be sent airmail
    D. Those in which copies will be sent along with the original

14. While opening incoming mail, you notice that one letter indicates that an enclosure was to be included but, even after careful inspection, you are not able to find the information to which this refers.
Of the following, the thing that you should do FIRST is
    A. replace the letter in its envelope and return it to the sender
    B. file the letter until the sender's office mails the missing information
    C. type out a letter to the sender informing him of his error
    D. make a notation in the margin of the letter that the enclosure was omitted

15. You have been given a checklist and assigned the responsibility of inspecting certain equipment in the various offices of your agency.
Which of the following is the GREATEST advantage of the checklist?
    A. It indicates which equipment is in greatest demand.
    B. Each piece of equipment on the checklist will be checked only once.
    C. It helps to insure that the equipment listed will not be overlooked.
    D. The equipment listed suggests other equipment you should look for.

16. The BEST way to evaluate the overall state of completion of a construction project is to check the progress estimate against the
    A. inspection worksheet   B. construction schedule
    C. inspector's checklist   D. equipment maintenance schedule

17. The usual contract for agency work includes a section entitled "Instructions to Bidders," which states that the
    A. contractor agrees that he has made his own examination and will make no claim for damages on account of errors or omissions
    B. contractor shall not make claims for damages of any discrepancy, error, or omission in any plans
    C. estimates of quantities and calculations are guaranteed by the agency to be correct and are deemed to be a representation of the conditions affecting the work
    D. plans, measurements, dimensions, and conditions under which the work is to be performed are guaranteed by the agency

18. In order to avoid disputes over payments for extra work in a contract for construction, the BEST procedure to follow would be to
    A. have contractor submit work progress reports daily
    B. insert a special clause in the contract specifications
    C. have a representative on the job at all times to verify conditions
    D. allocate a certain percentage of the cost of the job to cover such expenses

19. Prior to the installation of equipment called for in the specifications, the contractor is USUALLY required to submit for approval
    A. sets of shop drawings
    B. a set of revised specifications
    C. a detailed description of the methods of work to be used
    D. a complete list of skilled and unskilled tradesmen he proposes to use

20. During the actual construction work, the CHIEF value of a construction schedule is to
    A. insure that the work will be done on time
    B. reveal whether production is falling behind
    C. show how much equipment and material is required for the project
    D. furnish data as to the methods and techniques of construction operations

KEY (CORRECT ANSWERS)

1.	B	11.	B
2.	B	12.	B
3.	C	13.	A
4.	C	14.	D
5.	A	15.	C
6.	C	16.	B
7.	C	17.	A
8.	B	18.	C
9.	C	19.	A
10.	A	20.	B

PREPARING WRITTEN MATERIALS
EXAMINATION SECTION
TEST 1

DIRECTIONS: Each question consists of a sentence which may be classified appropriately under one of the following four categories:
A. Incorrect because of faulty grammar or sentence structure.
B. Incorrect because of faulty punctuation.
C. Incorrect because of faulty spelling or capitalization.
D. Correct

Examine each sentence carefully. Then, in the space at the right, print the capital letter preceding the option which is the BEST of the four suggested above. All incorrect sentences contain only one type of error. Consider a sentence correct if it contains none of the types of errors mentioned, although there may be other correct ways of expressing the same thought.

1. The fire apparently started in the storeroom, which is usually locked. 1.____
2. On approaching the victim two bruises were noticed by this officer. 2.____
3. The officer, who was there examined the report with great care. 3.____
4. Each employee in the office had a separate desk. 4.____
5. The suggested procedure is similar to the one now in use. 5.____
6. No one was more pleased with the new procedure than the chauffeur. 6.____
7. He tried to pursuade her to change the procedure. 7.____
8. The total of the expenses charged to petty cash were high. 8.____
9. An understanding between him and I was finally reached. 9.____
10. It was at the supervisor's request that the clerk agreed to postpone his vacation. 10.____
11. We do not believe that it is necessary for both he and the clerk to attend the conference. 11.____
12. All employees, who display perseverance, will be given adequate recognition. 12.____
13. He regrets that some of us employees are dissatisfied with our new assignments. 13.____

14. "Do you think that the raise was merited," asked the supervisor? 14._____

15. The new manual of procedure is a valuable supplament to our rules and regulation. 15._____

16. The typist admitted that she had attempted to pursuade the other employees to assist her in her work. 16._____

17. The supervisor asked that all amendments to the regulations be handled by you and I. 17._____

18. They told both he and I that the prisoner had escaped. 18._____

19. Any superior officer, who, disregards the just complaints of his subordinates, is remiss in the performance of his duty. 19._____

20. Only those members of the national organization who resided in the Middle west attended the conference in Chicago. 20._____

21. We told him to give the investigation assignment to whoever was available. 21._____

22. Please do not disappoint and embarass us by not appearing in court. 22._____

23. Despite the efforts of the Supervising mechanic, the elevator could not be started. 23._____

24. The U.S. Weather Bureau, weather record for the accident date was checked. 24._____

KEY (CORRECT ANSWERS)

1. D
2. A
3. B
4. D
5. D

6. D
7. C
8. A
9. A
10. D

11. A
12. B
13. D
14. B
15. C

16. C
17. A
18. A
19. B
20. C

21. D
22. C
23. C
24. B

TEST 2

DIRECTIONS: Each question consists of a sentence. Some of the sentences contain errors in English grammar or usage, punctuation, spelling, or capitalization. A sentence does not contain an error simply because it could be written in a different manner. Choose answer:
- A. If the sentence contains an error in English grammar or usage.
- B. if the sentence contains an error in punctuation.
- C. If the sentence contains an error in spelling or capitalization
- D. If the sentence does not contain any errors.

1. The severity of the sentence prescribed by contemporary statutes—including both the former and the revised New York Penal Laws—do not depend on what crime was intended by the offender.   1._____

2. It is generally recognized that two defects in the early law of attempt played a part in the birth of burglary: (1) immunity from prosecution for conduct short of the last act before completion of the crime, and (2) the relatively minor penalty imposed for an attempt (it being a common law misdemeanor) vis-à-vis the completed offense.   2._____

3. The first sentence of the statute is applicable to employees who enter their place of employment, invited guests, and all other persons who have an express or implied license or privilege to enter the premises.   3._____

4. Contemporary criminal codes in the United States generally divide burglary into various degrees, differentiating the categories according to place, time and other attendent circumstances.   4._____

5. The assignment was completed in record time but the payroll for it has not yet been prepaid.   5._____

6. The operator, on the other hand, is willing to learn me how to use the mimeograph.   6._____

7. She is the prettiest of the three sisters.   7._____

8. She doesn't know; if the mail has arrived.   8._____

9. The doorknob of the office door is broke.   9._____

10. Although the department's supply of scratch pads and stationery have diminished considerably, the allotment for our division has not been reduced.   10._____

11. You have not told us whom you wish to designate as your secretary.   11._____

12. Upon reading the minutes of the last meeting, the new proposal was taken up for consideration.   12._____

13. Before beginning the discussion, we locked the door as a precautionery measure. 13.____

14. The supervisor remarked, "Only those clerks, who perform routine work, are permitted to take a rest period." 14.____

15. Not only will this duplicating machine make accurate copies, but it will also produce a quantity of work equal to fifteen transcribing typists. 15.____

16. "Mr. Jones," said the supervisor, "we regret our inability to grant you an extention of your leave of absence." 16.____

17. Although the employees find the work monotonous and fatigueing, they rarely complain. 17.____

18. We completed the tabulation of the receipts on time despite the fact that Miss Smith our fastest operator was absent for over a week. 18.____

19. The reaction of the employees who attended the meeting, as well as the reaction of those who did not attend, indicates clearly that the schedule is satisfactory to everyone concerned. 19.____

20. Of the two employees, the one in our office is the most efficient. 20.____

21. No one can apply or even understand, the new rules and regulations. 21.____

22. A large amount of supplies were stored in the empty office. 22.____

23. If an employee is occassionally asked to work overtime, he should do so willingly. 23.____

24. It is true that the new procedures are difficult to use but, we are certain that you will learn them quickly. 24.____

25. The office manager said that he did not know who would be given a large allotment under the new plan. 25.____

KEY (CORRECT ANSWERS)

1.	A	11.	D
2.	D	12.	A
3.	D	13.	C
4.	C	14.	B
5.	C	15.	A
6.	A	16.	C
7.	D	17.	C
8.	B	18.	B
9.	A	19.	D
10.	A	20.	A

21.	B
22.	A
23.	C
24.	B
25.	D

TEST 3

DIRECTIONS: Each of the following sentences may be classified MOST appropriately under one of the following categories:
  A. Faulty because of incorrect grammar
  B. Faulty because of incorrect punctuation
  C. Faulty because of incorrect capitalization
  D. Correct

Examine each sentence carefully. Then, in the space at the right, print the capital letter preceding the option which is the BEST of the four suggested above. All incorrect sentence contain but one type of error. Consider a sentence correct if it contains none of the types of errors mentioned, even though there may be other correct ways of expressing the same thought.

1. The desk, as well as the chairs, were moved out of the office. 1.____

2. The clerk whose production was greatest for the month won a day's vacation as first prize. 2.____

3. Upon entering the room, the employees were found hard at work at their desks. 3.____

4. John Smith our new employee always arrives at work on time. 4.____

5. Punish whoever is guilty of stealing the money. 5.____

6. Intelligent and persistent effort lead to success no matter what the job may be. 6.____

7. The secretary asked, "can you call again at three o'clock?" 7.____

8. He told us, that if the report was not accepted at the next meeting, it would have to be rewritten. 8.____

9. He would not have sent the letter if he had known that it would cause so much excitement. 9.____

10. We all looked forward to him coming to visit us. 10.____

11. If you find that you are unable to complete the assignment please notify me as soon as possible. 11.____

12. Every girl in the office went home on time but me; there was still some work for me to finish. 12.____

13. He wanted to know who the letter was addressed to, Mr. Brown or Mr. Smith. 13.____

14. "Mr. Jones, he said, please answer this letter as soon as possible." 14.____

15. The new clerk had an unusual accent inasmuch as he was born and educated in the south. 15.____

16. Although he is younger than her, he earns a higher salary. 16.____

17. Neither of the two administrators are going to attend the conference being held in Washington, D.C. 17.____

18. Since Miss Smith and Miss Jones have more experience than us, they have been given more responsible duties. 18.____

19. Mr. Shaw the supervisor of the stock room maintains an inventory of stationery and office supplies. 19.____

20. Inasmuch as this matter affects both you and I, we should take joint action. 20.____

21. Who do you think will be able to perform this highly technical work? 21.____

22. Of the two employees, John is considered the most competent. 22.____

23. He is not coming home on tuesday; we expect him next week. 23.____

24. Stenographers, as well as typists must be able to type rapidly and accurately. 24.____

25. Having been placed in the safe we were sure that the money would not be stolen. 25.____

KEY (CORRECT ANSWERS)

1.	A	11.	B
2.	D	12.	D
3.	A	13.	A
4.	B	14.	B
5.	D	15.	C
6.	A	16.	A
7.	C	17.	A
8.	B	18.	A
9.	D	19.	B
10.	A	20.	A

21. D
22. A
23. C
24. B
25. A

TEST 4

DIRECTIONS: Each of the following sentences consist of four sentences lettered A, B, C, and D. One of the sentences in each group contains an error in grammar or punctuation. Indicate the INCORRECT sentence in each group. *PRINT THE LETTER OF THE CORRECT ANSWER IN THE SPACE AT THE RIGHT.*

1. A. Give the message to whoever is on duty.
   B. The teacher who's pupil won first prize presented the award.
   C. Between you and me, I don't expect the program to succeed.
   D. His running to catch the bus caused the accident.

   1.____

2. A. The process, which was patented only last year is already obsolete.
   B. His interest in science (which continues to the present) led him to convert his basement into a laboratory.
   C. He described the book as "verbose, repetitious, and bombastic".
   D. Our new director will need to possess three qualities: vision, patience, and fortitude.

   2.____

3. A. The length of ladder trucks varies considerably.
   B. The probationary fireman reported to the officer to who he was assigned.
   C. The lecturer emphasized the need for we firemen to be punctual.
   D. Neither the officers nor the members of the company knew about the new procedure.

   3.____

4. A. Ham and eggs is the specialty of the house.
   B. He is one of the students who are on probation.
   C. Do you think that either one of us have a chance to be nominated for president of the class?
   D. I assume that either he was to be in charge or you were.

   4.____

5. A. Its a long road that has no turn.
   B. To run is more tiring than to walk.
   C. We have been assigned three new reports: namely, the statistical summary, the narrative summary, and the budgetary summary.
   D. Had the first payment been made in January, the second would be due in April.

   5.____

6. A. Each employer has his own responsibilities.
   B. If a person speaks correctly, they make a good impression.
   C. Every one of the operators has had her vacation.
   D. Has anybody filed his report?

   6.____

7. A. The manager, with all his salesmen, was obliged to go.
   B. Who besides them is to sign the agreement?
   C. One report without the others is incomplete.
   D. Several clerks, as well as the proprietor, was injured.

   7.____

8. A. A suspension of these activities is expected.
    B. The machine is economical because first cost and upkeep are low.
    C. A knowledge of stenography and filing are required for this position.
    D. The condition in which the goods were received shows that the packing was not done properly.

8._____

9. A. There seems to be a great many reasons for disagreement.
    B. It does not seem possible that they could have failed.
    C. Have there always been too few applicants for these positions?
    D. There is no excuse for these errors.

9._____

10. A. We shall be pleased to answer your question.
    B. Shall we plan the meeting for Saturday?
    C. I will call you promptly at seven.
    D. Can I borrow your book after you have read it?

10._____

11. A. You are as capable as I.
    B. Everyone is willing to sign but him and me.
    C. As for he and his assistant, I cannot praise them too highly.
    D. Between you and me, I think he will be dismissed.

11._____

12. A. Our competitors bid above us last week.
    B. The survey which was began last year has not yet been completed.
    C. The operators had shown that they understood their instructions.
    D. We have never ridden over worse roads.

12._____

13. A. Who did they say was responsible?
    B. Whom did you suspect?
    C. Who do you suppose it was?
    D. Whom do you mean?

13._____

14. A. Of the two propositions, this is the worse.
    B. Which report do you consider the best—the one in January or the one in July?
    C. I believe this is the most practicable of the many plans submitted.
    D. He is the youngest employee in the organization.

14._____

15. A. The firm had but three orders last week.
    B. That doesn't really seem possible.
    C. After twenty years scarcely none of the old business remains.
    D. Has he done nothing about it?

15._____

KEY (CORRECT ANSWERS)

1.	B	6.	B	11.	C
2.	A	7.	D	12.	B
3.	C	8.	C	13.	A
4.	C	9.	A	14.	B
5.	A	10.	D	15.	C

PREPARING WRITTEN MATERIAL

PARAGRAPH REARRANGEMENT
COMMENTARY

The sentences that follow are in scrambled order. You are to rearrange them in proper order and indicate the letter choice containing the correct answer at the space at the right.

Each group of sentences in this section is actually a paragraph presented in scrambled order. Each sentence in the group has a place in that paragraph; no sentence is to be left out. You are to read each group of sentences and decide upon the best order in which to put the sentences so as to form a well-organized paragraph.

The questions in this section measure the ability to solve a problem when all the facts relevant to its solution are not given.

More specifically, certain positions of responsibility and authority require the employee to discover connection between events sometimes, apparently, unrelated. In order to do this, the employee will find it necessary to correctly infer that unspecified events have probably occurred or are likely to occur. This ability becomes especially important when action must be taken on incomplete information.

Accordingly, these questions require competitors to choose among several suggested alternatives, each of which presents a different sequential arrangement of the events. Competitors must choose the MOST logical of the suggested sequences.

In order to do so, they may be required to draw on general knowledge to infer missing concepts or events that are essential to sequencing the given events. Competitors should be careful to infer only what is essential to the sequence. The plausibility of the wrong alternatives will always require the inclusion of unlikely events or of additional chains of events which are NOT essential to sequencing the given events.

It's very important to remember that you are looking for the best of the four possible choices, and that the best choice of all may not even be one of the answers you're given to choose from.

There is no one right way to solve these problems. Many people have found it helpful to first write out the order of the sentences, as they would have arranged them, on their scrap paper before looking at the possible answers. If their optimum answer is there, this can save them some time. If it isn't, this method can still give insight into solving the problem. Others find it most helpful to just go through each of the possible choices, contrasting each as they go along. You should use whatever method feels comfortable and works for you.

While most of these types of questions are not that difficult, we've added a higher percentage of the difficult type, just to give you more practice. Usually there are only one or two questions on this section that contain such subtle distinctions that you're unable to answer confidently. And you then may find yourself stuck deciding between two possible choices, neither of which you're sure about.

PREPARING WRITTEN MATERIAL
EXAMINATION SECTION
TEST 1

DIRECTIONS: The following groups of sentences need to be arranged in an order that makes sense. Select the letter preceding the sequence that represents the BEST sentence order. *PRINT THE LETTER OF THE CORRECT ANSWER IN THE SPACE AT THE RIGHT.*

1. I. A large Naval station on Alameda Island, near Oakland, held many warships in port, and the War Department was worried that if the bridge were to be blown up by the enemy, passage to and from the bay would be hopelessly blocked.
    II. Though many skeptics were opposed to the idea of building such an enormous bridge, the most vocal opposition came from a surprising source: the United States War Department.
    III. The War Department's concerns led to a showdown at San Francisco City Hall between Strauss and the Secretary of War, who demanded to know what would happen if a military enemy blew up the bridge.
    IV. In 1933, by submitting a construction cost estimate of $17 million, an engineer named Joseph Strauss won the contract to build the Golden Gate Bridge of San Francisco, which would then become one of the world's largest bridges.
    V. Strauss quickly ended the debate by explaining that the Golden Gate Bridge was to be a suspension bridge, whose roadway would hang in the air from cables strung between two huge towers, and would immediately sink into three hundred feet of water if it were destroyed.
    The BEST order is:
    A. II, III, I, IV, V   B. I, II, III, V, IV   C. IV, II, I, III, V   D. IV, I, III, V, II

    1.____

2. I. Plastic surgeons have already begun to use virtual reality to map out the complex nerve and tissue structures of a particular patient's face, in order to prepare for delicate surgery.
    II. A virtual reality program responds to these movements by adjusting the images that a person sees on a screen or through goggles, thereby creating an "interactive" world in which a person can see and touch three-dimensional graphic objects.
    III. No more than a computer program that is designed to build and display graphic images, the virtual reality program takes graphic programs a step further by sensing a person's head and body movements.
    IV. The computer technology known as virtual reality, now in its very first stages of development, is already revolutionizing some aspects of contemporary life.
    V. Virtual reality computers are also being used by the space program, most recently to simulate conditions for the astronauts who were launched on a repair mission to the Hubble telescope.

    2.____

The BEST order is:
A. IV, II, I, V, III B. III, I, V, II, IV C. IV, III, II, I, V D. III, I, II, IV, V

3. I. Before you plant anything, the soil in your plant bed should be carefully raked level, a small section at a time, and any clods or rocks that can't be broken up should be removed.
   II. Your plant should be placed in a hole that will position it at the same level it was at the nursery, and a small indentation should be pressed into the soil around the plant in order to hold water near its roots.
   III. Before placing the plant in the soil, lightly separate any roots that may have been matted together in the container, cutting away any thick masses that can't be separated, so that the remaining roots will be able to grow outward.
   IV. After the bed is ready, remove your plant from its container by turning it upside down and tapping or pushing on the bottom —never remove it by pulling on the plant.
   V. When you bring home a small plant in an individual container from the nursery, there are several things to remember while preparing to plant it in your own garden.
   The BEST order is:
   A. V, IV, III, II, I B. V, II, IV, III, II C. I, IV, II, III, V D. I, IV, V, II, III

3.____

4. I. The motte and its tower were usually built first, so that sentries could use it as a lookout to warn the castle workers of any danger that might approach the castle.
   II. Though the moat and palisade offered the bailey a good deal of protection, it was linked to the motte by a set of stairs that led to a retractable drawbridge at the motte's gate, to enable people to evacuate onto the motte in case of an attack.
   III. The motte of these early castles was a fortified hill, sometimes as high as one hundred feet, on which stood a palisade and tower.
   IV. The bailey was a clear, level spot below the motte, also enclosed by a palisade, which in turn was surrounded by a large trench or moat.
   V. The earliest castles built in Europe were not the magnificent stone giants that still tower over much of the European landscape, but simpler wooden constructions called motte-and-bailey castles.
   The BEST order is:
   A. V, III, I, IV, II B. V, IV, I, II, III C. I, IV, III, II, V D. I, III, II, IV, V

4.____

5. I. If an infant is left alone or abandoned for a short while, its immediate response is to cry loudly, accompanying its screams with aggressive flailing of its legs and limbs.
   II. If a child has been abandoned for a longer period of time, it becomes completely still and quiet, as if realizing that now its only chance for survival is to shut its mouth and remain motionless.
   III. Along with their intense fear of the dark, the crying behavior of human infants offers insights into how prehistoric newborn children might have evolved instincts that would prevent them from becoming victims of predators.

5.____

IV. This behavior often surprises people who enter a hospital's maternity ward for the first time and encounter total silence from a roomful of infants.
V. This violent screaming response is quite different from an infant's cries of discomfort or hunger, and seems to serve as either the child's first line of defense against an unwanted intruder, or a desperate attempt to communicate its position to the mother.
The BEST order is:
A. III, II, IV, I, V   B. III, I, V, II, IV   C. I, V, IV, II, III   D. II, IV, I, V, III

6. I. When two cats meet who are strangers, their first actions and gestures determine who the "dominant" cat will be, at least for the time being.
II. Unlike dogs, cats are typically a solitary animal species who avoid social interaction, but they do display specific social responses to each other upon meeting.
III. This is unlikely, however; before such a point of open hostility is reached, one of the cats will usually take the "submissive" position of crouching down while looking away from the other dat.
IV. If a cat desires dominance or sees the other cat as a threat to its territory, it will stare directly at the intruder with a lowered tail.
V. If the other cat responds with a similar gesture, or with the strong defensive posture of an arched back, laid-back ears and raised tail, a fight or chase is likely if neither cat gives in.
The BEST order is:
A. IV, II, I, V, III   B. I, II, IV, V, III   C. I, IV, V, III, II   D. II, I, IV, V, III

7. I. A star or planet's gravitational force can best be explained in this way: anything passing through this "dent" in space will veer toward the star or planet as if it were rolling into a hole.
II. Objects that are massive or heavy, such as stars or planets, "sink" into this surface, creating a sort of dent or concavity in the surrounding space.
III. Black holes, the most massive objects known to exist in space, create dents so large and deep that the space surrounding them actually folds in on itself, preventing anything that falls in —even light —from ever escaping again.
IV. The sort of dent a star or planet makes depends on how massive it is; planets generally have weak gravitational pulls, but stars, which are larger and heavier, make a bigger "dent" that will attract more matter.
V. In outer space, the force of gravity works as if the surrounding space is a soft, flat surface.
The BEST order is:
A. III, V, II, I, IV   B. III, IV, I, V, II   C. V, II, I, IV, III   D. I, V, II, IV, III

8. I. Eventually, the society of Kyoto gave the world one of its first and greatest novels when Japan's most promising writer, Lady Murasaki Shikibu, wrote her chronicle of Kyoto's society, *The Tale of Genji*, which preceded the first European novels by more than 500 years.
II. The society of Kyoto was dedicated to the pleasures of art; the courtiers experimented with new and colorful methods of sculpture, painting, writing, decorative gardening, and even making clothes.

III. Japanese culture began under the powerful authority of Chinese Buddhism, which influenced every aspect of Japanese life from religion to politics and art.
IV. This new, vibrant culture was so sophisticated that all the people in Kyoto's imperial court considered themselves poets, and the line between life and art hardly existed —lovers corresponded entirely through written verses, and even government officials communicated by writing poems to each other.
V. In the eighth century, when the emperor established the town of Kyoto as the capital of the Japanese empire, Japanese society began to develop its own distinctive style.

The BEST order is:
A. V, II, IV, I, III   B. II, I, V, IV, III   C. V, III, IV, I, II   D. III, V, II, IV, I

9. I. Instead of wheels, the HSST uses two sets of magnets, one which sits on the track, and another that is carried by the train; these magnets generate an identical magnetic field which forces the two sets apart.
II. In the last few decades, railway travel has become less popular throughout the world, because it is much slower than travel by airplane, and not much less expensive.
III. The HSST's designers say that the train can take passengers from one town to another as quickly as a jet plane —while consuming less than half the energy.
IV. This repellent effect is strong enough to lift the entire train above the trackway, and the train, literally traveling on air, rockets along at speeds of up to 300 miles per hour.
V. The revolutionary technology of magnetic levitation, currently being tested by Japan's experimental HSST (High Speed Surface Transport), may yet bring passenger trains back from the dead.

The BEST order is:
A. II, V, I, IV, III   B. II, I, IV, III, V   C. V, II, III, I, IV   D. V, I, III, IV, II

10. I. When European countries first began to colonize the African continent, their impression of the African people was of a vast group of loosely organized tribal societies, without any great centralized source of power or wealth.
II. The legend of Timbuktu persisted until the nineteenth century, when a French adventurer visited Timbuktu and found that raids by neighboring tribesmen had made the city a shadow of its former self.
III. In the fifteenth century, when the stories of travelers who had traveled Africa's Sudan region began circulating around Europe, this impression began to change.
IV. In 1470, an Italian merchant named Benedetto Dei traveled to Timbuktu and confirmed these rumors, describing a thriving metropolis where rich and poor people worshipped together in the city's many ornate mosques — there was even a university in Timbuktu, much like its European counterparts, where African scholars pursued their studies in the arts and sciences.

V. The travelers' legends told of an enormous city in the western Sudan, Timbuktu, where the streets were crowded with goods brought by faraway caravans, and where there was a stone palace as large as any in Europe.

The BEST order is:

A. III, V, I, IV, II   B. I, II, IV, III, V   C. I, III, V, IV, II   D. II, I, III, IV, V

11.
I. Also, our reference points in sighting the moon make us believe that its size is changing; when the moon is rising through the trees, it seems huge, because our brains unconsciously compare the size of the moon with the size of the trees in the foreground.
II. To most people, the sky itself appears more distant at the horizon than directly overhead, and if the moon's size—which remains constant—is projected from the horizon, the apparent distance of the horizon makes the moon look bigger.
III. Up higher in the sky, the moon is set against tiny stars in the background, which will make the moon seem smaller.
IV. People often wonder why the moon becomes bigger when it approaches the horizon, but most scientists agree that this is a complicated optical illusion, produced by at least three factors.
V. The moon illusion may also be partially explained by a phenomenon that has nothing to do with errors in our perception—light that enters the earth's atmosphere is sometimes refracted, and so the atmosphere may act as a kind of magnifying glass for the moon's image.

The BEST order is:

A. IV, III, V, II, I   B. IV, II, I, III, V   C. V, II, I, III, IV   D. II, I, III, IV, V

11.____

12.
I. When the Native Americans were introduced to the horses used by white explorers, they were amazed at their new alternative—here was an animal that was strong and swift, would patiently carry a person or other loads on its back, and they later discovered, was right at home on the plains.
II. Before the arrival of European explorers to North America, the natives of the American plains used large dogs to carry their travois-long lodgepoles loaded with clothing, gear, and food.
III. These horses, it is now known, were not really strangers to North America; the very first horses originated here, on this continent, tens of thousands of years ago, and migrated into Asia across the Bering Land Bridge, a strip of land that used to link our continent with the Eastern world.
IV. At first, the natives knew so little about horses that at least one tribe tried to feed their new animals pieces of dried meat and animal fat, and were surprised when the horses turned their heads away and began to eat the grass of the prairie.
V. The American horse eventually became extinct, but its Asian cousins were reintroduced to the New World when the European explorers brought them to live among the Native Americans.

The BEST order is:

A. II, I, IV, III, V   B. II, IV, I, III, V   C. I, II, IV, III, V   D. I, III, V, II, IV

12.____

13.
   I. The dress worn by the dancer is believed to have been adorned in the past by shells which would strike each other as the dancer performed, creating a lovely sound.
   II. Today's jingle-dress is decorated with the tin lids of snuff cans, which are rolled into cones and sewn onto the dress,
   III. During the jingle-dress dance, the dancer must blend complicated footwork with a series of gentle hos that cause the cones to jingle in rhythm to a drumbeat.
   IV. When contemporary Native American tribes meet for a pow-wow, one of the most popular ceremonies to take place is the women's jingle-dress dance.
   V. Besides being more readily available than shells, the lids are thought by many dancers to create a softer, more subtle sound.
   The BEST order is:
   A. II, IV, V, I, III   B. IV, II, I, III, V   C. II, I, III, V, IV   D. IV, I, II, V, III

14.
   I. If a homeowner lives where seasonal climates are extreme, deciduous shade trees—which will drop their leaves in the winter and allow sunlight to pass through the windows—should be planted near the southern exposure in order to keep the house cool during the summer.
   II. This trajectory is shorter and lower in the sky than at any other time of year during the winter, when a house most requires heating; the northern-facing parts of a house do not receive any direct sunlight at all.
   III. In designing an energy-efficient house, especially in colder climates, it is important to remember that most of the house's windows should face south.
   IV. Though the sun always rises in the east and sets in the west, the sun of the northern hemisphere is permanently situated in the southern portion of the sky.
   V. The explanation for why so many architects and builders want this "southern exposure" is related to the path of the sun in the sky.
   The BEST order is:
   A. III, I, V, IV, II   B. III, V, IV, II, I   C. I, III, IV, II, V   D. I, II, V, IV, III

15.
   I. His journeying lasted twenty-four years and took him over an estimated 75,000 miles, a distance that would not be surpassed by anyone other than Magellan—who sailed around the world—for another six hundred years.
   II. Perhaps the most far-flung of these lesser-known travelers was Ibn Batuta, an African Moslem who left his birthplace of Tangier in the summer of 1325.
   III. Ibn Batuta traveled all over Africa and Asia, from Niger to Peking, and to the islands of Maldive and Indonesia.
   IV. However, a few explorers of the Eastern world logged enough miles and adventures to make Marco Polo's voyage look like an evening stroll.
   V. In America, the most well-known of the Old World's explorers are usually Europeans such as Marco Polo, the Italian who brought many elements of Chinese culture to the Western world.
   The BEST order is:
   A. V, IV, II, III, I   B. V, IV, III, II, I   C. III, II, I, IV, V   D. II, III, I, IV, V

16. I. In the rainforests of South America, a rare species of frog practices a reproductive method that is entirely different from this standard process.
    II. She will eventually carry each of the tadpoles up into the canopy and drop each into its own little pool, where it will be easy to locate and safe from most predators.
    III. After fertilization, the female of the species, who lives almost entirely on the forest floor, lays between 2 and 16 eggs among the leaf litter at the base of a tree, and stands watch over these eggs until they hatch.
    IV. Most frogs are pond-dwellers who are able to deposit hundreds of eggs in the water and then leave them alone, knowing that enough eggs have been laid to insure the survival of some of their offspring.
    V. Once the tadpoles emerge, the female backs in among them, and a tadpole will wriggle onto her back to be carried high into the forest canopy, where the female will deposit it in a little pool of water cupped in the leaf of a plant.
    The BEST order is:
    A. I, IV, III, II, V   B. I, III, V, II, IV   C. IV, III, II, V, I   D. IV, I, III, V, II

    16.____

17. I. Eratosthenes had heard from travelers that at exactly noon on June 21, in the ancient city of Aswan, Egypt, the sun cast no shadow in a well, which meant that the sun must be directly overhead.
    II. He knew the sun always cast a shadow in Alexandria, and so he figured that if he could measure the length of an Alexandria shadow at the time when there was no shadow in Aswan, he could calculate the angle of the sun, and therefore the circumference of the earth.
    III. The evidence for a round earth was not new in 1492; in fact, Eratosthenes, an Alexandrian geographer who lived nearly sixteen centuries before Columbus's voyage (275-195 B.C.), actually developed a method for calculating the circumference of the earth that is still in use today.
    IV. Eratosthenes's method was correct, but his result—28,700 miles—was about 15 percent too high, probably because of the inaccurate ancient methods of keeping time, and because Aswan was not due south of Alexandria, as Eratosthenes had believed.
    V. When Christopher Columbus sailed across the Atlantic Ocean for the first time in 1492, there were still some people in the world who ignored scientific evidence and believed that the earth was flat, rather than round.
    The BEST order is:
    A. I, II, V, III, IV   B. V, III, IV, I, II   C. V, III, I, II, IV   D. III, V, I, II, IV

    17.____

18. I. The first name for the child is considered a trial naming, often impersonal and neutral, such as the Ngoni name *Chabwera*, meaning "it has arrived."
    II. This sort of name is not due to any parental indifference to the child, but is a kind of silent recognition of Africa's sometimes high infant death rate; most parents ease the pain of losing a child with the belief that it is not really a person until it has been given a final name.
    III. In many tribal African societies, families often give two different names to their children, at different periods in time.
    IV. After the trial naming period has subsided and it is clear that the child will survive, the parents choose a final name for the child, an act that symbolically completes the act of birth.

    18.____

V. In fact, some African first-given names are explicitly uncomplimentary, translating as "I am dead" or "I am ugly," in order to avoid the jealousy of ancestral spirits who might wish to take a child that is especially healthy or attractive.

The BEST order is:
A. III, I, II, V, IV   B. III, IV, II, I, V   C. IV, III, I, II, V   D. IV, V, III, I, II

19.
   I. Though uncertain of the definite reasons for this behavior, scientists believe the birds digest the clay in order to counteract toxins contained in the seeds of certain fruits that are eaten by macaws.
   II. For example, all macaws flock to riverbanks at certain times of the year to eat the clay that is found in river mud.
   III. The macaws of South America are not only among the largest and most beautifully colored of the world's flying birds, but they are also one of the smartest.
   IV. It is believed that macaws are forced to resort to these toxic fruits during the dry season, when foods are more scarce.
   V. The macaw's intelligence has led to intense study by scientists, who have discovered some macaw behaviors that have not yet been explained.

   The BEST order is:
   A. III, IV, I, II, V   B. III, V, II, I, IV   C. V, II, I, IV, III   D. IV, I, II, III, V

20.
   I. Although Maggie Kuhn has since passed away, the Gray Panthers are still waging a campaign to reinstate the historical view of the elderly as people whose experience allows them to make their greatest contribution in their later years.
   II. In 1972, an elderly woman named Maggie Kuhn responded to this sort of treatment by forming a group called the Gray Panthers, an organization of both old and young adults with the common goal of creating change.
   III. This attitude is reflected strongly in the way elderly people are treated by our society; many are forced into early retirement, or are placed in rest homes in which they are isolated from their communities.
   IV. Unlike most other cultures around the world, Americans tend to look upon old age with a sense of dread and sadness.
   V. Kuhn believed that when the elderly are forced to withdraw into lives that lack purpose, society loses one of its greatest resources: people who have a lifetime of experience and wisdom to offer their communities.

   The BEST order is:
   A. IV, III, II, V, I   B. IV, II, I, III, V   C. II, IV, III, V, I   D. II, I, IV, III, V

21.
   I. The current theory among most anthropologists is that humans evolved from apes who lived in trees near the grasslands of Africa.
   II. Still, some anthropologists insist that such an invention was necessary for the survival of early humans, and point to the Kung Bushmen of central Africa as a society in which the sling is still used in this way.
   III. Two of these inventions—fire, and weapons such as spears and clubs—were obvious defenses against predators, and there is archaeological evidence to support the theory of their use.

IV. Once people had evolved enough to leave the safety of trees and walk upright, they needed the protection of several inventions in order to survive.
V. But another invention, a feather or fiber sling that allowed mothers to carry children while leaving their hands free to gather roots or berries, would certainly have decomposed and left behind no trace of itself.
The BEST order is:
A. I, II, III, V, IV B. IV, I, II, III, V C. I, IV, III, V, II D. IV, III, V, II, I

22. I. The person holding the bird should keep it in hot water up to its neck, and the person cleaning should work a mild solution of dishwashing liquid into the bird's plumage, paying close attention to the head and neck.
II. When rinsing the bird, after all the oil has been removed, the running water should be directed against the lay of its feathers, until water begins to bead off the surface of the feathers—a sign that all the detergent has been rinsed out.
III. If you have rescued a sea bird from an oil spill and want to restore it to clean and normal living, you need a large sink, a constant supply of running hot water (a little over 100°F), and regular dishwashing liquid.
IV. This cleaning with detergent solution should be repeated as many times as it takes to remove all traces of oil from the bird's feathers, sometime over a period of several days.
V. But before you begin to clean the bird, you must find a partner because cleaning an oiled bird is a two-person job.
The BEST order is:
A. III, I, II, IV, V B. III, V, I, IV, II C. III, I, IV, V, II D. III, IV, V, I, II

22.____

23. I. The most difficult time of year for the Tsaatang is the spring calving, when the reindeer leave their wintering ground and rush to their accustomed calving place, without stopping by night or by day.
II. Reindeer travel in herds, and though some animals are tamed by the Tsaatang for riding or milking, the herds are allowed to roam free.
III. This journey is hard for the Tsaatang, who carry all their possessions with them, but once it's over it proves worthwhile; the Tsaatang can immediately begin to gather milk from reindeer cows who have given birth.
IV. The Tsaatang, a small tribe who live in the far northwest corner of Mongolia, practice a lifestyle that is completely dependent on the reindeer, their main resource for food, clothing, and transport.
V. The people must follow their yearly migrations, living in portable shelters that resemble Native American tepees.
The BEST order is:
A. I, III, II, V, IV B. I, IV, II, V, III C. IV, I, III, V, II D. IV II, V, I, III

23.____

24. I. The Romans later improved this system by installing these heated pipe networks throughout walls and ceilings, supplying heat to even the uppermost floors of a building—a system that, to this day, hasn't been much improved.
II. Air-conditioning, the method by which humans control indoor temperatures, was practiced much earlier than most people think.

24.____

III. The earliest heating devices other than open fires were used in 350 B.C. by the ancient Greeks, who directed air that had been heated by underground fires into baked clay pipes that ran under the floor.
IV. Ironically, the first successful cooling system, patented in England in 1831, used fire as its main energy source—fires were lit in the attic of a building, creating an updraft of air that drew cool air into the building through ducts that had underground openings near the river Thames.
V. Cooling buildings was more of a challenge, and wasn't attempted until 1500: a water-based system, designed by Leonardo da Vinci, does not appear to have been successful, since it was never used again.

The BEST order is:
A. III, V, IV, I, II B. III, I, II, V, IV C. II, III, I, V, IV D. IV, II, III, I, V

25.
I. Cold, dry air from Canada passes over the Rocky Mountains and sweeps down onto the plains, where it collides with warm, moist air from the waters of the Gulf of Mexico, and when the two air masses meet, the resulting disturbance sometimes forms a violent funnel cloud that strikes the earth and destroys virtually everything in its path.
II. Hurricanes, storms which are generally not this violent and last much longer, are usually given names by meteorologists, but this tradition cannot be applied to tornados, which have a life span measured in minutes and disappear in the same way as they are born—unnamed.
III. A tornado funnel forms rotating columns of air whose speed reaches three hundred miles an hour—a speed that can only be estimated, because no wind-measuring devices in the direct path of a storm have ever survived.
IV. The natural phenomena known as tornados occur primarily over the Midwestern grasslands of the United States.
V. It is here, meteorologists tell us, that conditions for the formation of tornados are sometimes perfect during the spring months.

The BEST order is:
A. II, IV, V, I, III B. II, III, I, V, IV C. IV, V, I, III, II D. IV, III, I, V, II

KEY (CORRECT ANSWERS)

1.	C	11.	B
2.	C	12.	A
3.	B	13.	D
4.	A	14.	B
5.	B	15.	A
6.	D	16.	D
7.	C	17.	C
8.	D	18.	A
9.	A	19.	B
10.	C	20.	A

21. C
22. B
23. D
24. C
25. C

READING COMPREHENSION
UNDERSTANDING AND INTERPRETING WRITTEN MATERIAL
EXAMINATION SECTION
TEST 1

DIRECTIONS: Each question or incomplete statement is followed by several suggested answers or completions. Select the one that BEST answers the question or completes the statement. *PRINT THE LETTER OF THE CORRECT ANSWER IN THE SPACE AT THE RIGHT.*

Questions 1-4.

DIRECTIONS: Questions 1 through 4 are to be answered SOLELY on the basis of the following paragraph.

An annual leave allowance, which combines leaves previously given for vacation, personal business, family illness, and other reasons shall be granted members. Calculation of credits for such leave shall be on an annual basis beginning January 1st of each year. Annual leave credits shall be based on time served by members during preceding calendar year. However, when credits have been accrued and member retires during current year, additional annual leave credits shall, in this instance, be granted at accrual rate of three days for each completed month of service, excluding terminal leave. If accruals granted for completed months of service extend into following month, member shall be granted an additional three days accrual for completed month. This shall be the only condition where accruals in a current year are granted for vacation period in such year.

1. According to the above paragraph, if a fireman's wife were to become seriously ill so that he would take time off from work to be with her, such time off would be deducted from his _____ leave allowance.
   A. annual
   B. vacation
   C. personal business
   D. family illness

2. Terminal leave means leave taken
   A. at the end of the calendar year
   B. at the end of the vacation year
   C. immediately before retirement
   D. before actually earned, because of an emergency

3. A fireman appointed on July 1, 2017 will be able to take his first full or normal annual leave during the period
   A. July 1, 2017 to June 30, 2018
   B. Jan. 1, 2018 to Dec. 31, 2018
   C. July 1, 2018 to June 30, 2019
   D. Jan. 1, 2019 to Dec. 31, 2019

4. According to the above paragraph, a member who retires on July 15 of this year will be entitled to receive leave allowance based on this year of _____ days.
   A. 15
   B. 18
   C. 22
   D. 24

5. Fire alarm boxes are electromechanical devices for transmitting a coded signal. In each box, there is a trainwork of wheels. When the box is operated, a spring-activated code wheel begins to revolve. The code number of the box is etched on the circumference of the code wheel, and the latter is associated with the circuit in such a way that when it revolves it causes the circuit to open and close in a predetermined manner, thereby transmitting its particular signal to the central station. A fire alarm box is nothing more than a device for interrupting the flow of current in a circuit in such a way as to produce a coded signal that may be decoded by the dispatchers in the central office.
Based on the above, select the FALSE statement.
    A. Each standard fire alarm box has its own code wheel.
    B. The code wheel operates when the box is pulled.
    C. The code wheel is operated electrically.
    D. Only the break in the circuit by the notched wheel causes the alarm signal to be transmitted to the central office.

5.____

Questions 6-9.

DIRECTIONS: Questions 6 through 9 are to be answered SOLELY on the basis of the following paragraph.

    Ventilation, as used in firefighting operations, means opening up a building or structure in which a fire is burning to release the accumulated heat, smoke, and gases. Lack of knowledge of the principles of ventilation on the part of firemen may result in unnecessary punishment due to ventilation being neglected or improperly handled. While ventilation itself extinguishes no fires, when used in an intelligent manner, it allows firemen to get at the fire more quickly, easily, and with less danger and hardship.

6. According to the above paragraph, the MOST important result of failure to apply the principles of ventilation at a fire may be
    A. loss of public confidence   B. waste of water
    C. excessive use of equipment   D. injury to firemen

6.____

7. It may be inferred from the above paragraph that the CHIEF advantage of ventilation is that it
    A. eliminates the need for gas masks
    B. reduces smoke damage
    C. permits firemen to work closer to the fire
    D. cools the fire

7.____

8. Knowledge of the principles of ventilation, as defined in the above paragraph, would be LEAST important in a fire in a
    A. tenement house   B. grocery store
    C. ship's hold   D. lumberyard

8.____

9. We may conclude from the above paragraph that for the well-trained and equipped fireman, ventilation is
    A. a simple matter   B. rarely necessary
    C. relatively unimportant   D. a basic tool

9.____

Questions 10-13.

DIRECTIONS: Questions 10 through 13 are to be answered SOLELY on the basis of the following passage.

Fire exit drills should be established and held periodically to effectively train personnel to leave their working area promptly upon proper signal and to evacuate the building, speedily but without confusion. All fire exit drills should be carefully planned and carried out in a serious manner under rigid discipline so as to provide positive protection in the event of a real emergency. As a general rule, the local fire department should be furnished advance information regarding the exact date and time the exit drill is scheduled. When it is impossible to hold regular drills, written instructions should be distributed to all employees.

Depending upon individual circumstances, fires in warehouses vary from those of fast development that are almost instantly beyond any possibility of employee control to others of relatively slow development where a small readily attackable flame may be present for periods of time up to 15 minutes or more during which simple attack with fire extinguishers or small building hoses may prevent the fire development. In any case, it is characteristic of many warehouse fires that at a certain point in development they flash up to the top of the stack, increase heat quickly, and spread rapidly. There is a degree of inherent danger in attacking warehouse type fires, and all employees should be thoroughly trained in the use of the types of extinguishers or small hoses in the buildings and well instructed in the necessity of always staying between the fire and a direct pass to an exit.

10. Employees should be instructed that, when fighting a fire, they MUST
    A. try to control the blaze
    B. extinguish any fire in 15 minutes
    C. remain between the fire and a direct passage to the exit
    D. keep the fire between themselves and the fire exit

11. Whenever conditions are such that regular fire drills cannot be held, then which one of the following actions should be taken?
    A. The local fire department should be notified.
    B. Rigid discipline should be maintained during work hours.
    C. Personnel should be instructed to leave their working area by whatever means are available.
    D. Employees should receive fire drill procedures in writing.

12. The above passage indicates that the purpose of fire exit drills is to train employees to
    A. control a fire before it becomes uncontrollable
    B. act as firefighters
    C. leave the working area promptly
    D. be serious

13. According to the above passage, fire exit drills will prove to be of UTMOST effectiveness if
    A. employee participation is made voluntary
    B. they take place periodically
    C. the fire department actively participates
    D. they are held without advance planning

13.____

Questions 14-16.

DIRECTIONS: Questions 14 through 16 are to be answered SOLELY on the basis of the following paragraph.

The heat output from unit heaters will depend on how fast and how completely dry hot steam fills the unit core. For complete and fast air removal and rapid drainage of condensate, use a trap actuated by water or vapor (inverted bucket trap) and not a trap operated by temperature only (thermostatic or bellows trap). A temperature-actuated trap will hold back the hot condensate until it cools to a point where the thermal element opens. When this happens, the condensate backs up in the heater and reduces the heat output. With a water-actuated trap, this will not happen as the water or condensate is discharged as fast as it is formed.

14. On the basis of the information given in the above paragraph, it can be concluded that the PROPER type of trap to use for a unit heater is a(n) _____ trap.
    A. thermostatic   B bellows-type
    C. inverted bucket   D. temperature

14.____

15. According to the above paragraph, the MAIN reason for using the type of trap specified for a unit heater is to
    A. bring the condensate up to steam temperature
    B. prevent reduction in the heat output of the unit heater
    C. permit cycling of the heater
    D. maintain constant temperature of condensate in the trap

15.____

16. As used in the above paragraph, the word *actuated* means MOST NEARLY
    A. clogged   B. operated   C. cleaned   D. vented

16.____

Questions 17-25.

DIRECTIONS: Questions 17 through 25 are to be answered SOLELY on the basis of the following passage. Each question consists of a statement. You are to indicate whether the statement is TRUE (T) or FALSE (F).

MOVING AN OFFICE

An office with all its equipment is sometimes moved during working hours. This is a difficult task and must be done in an orderly manner to avoid confusion. The operation should be planned in such a way as not to interrupt the progress of work usually done in the office and to make possible the accurate placement of the furniture and records in the new location. If the office moves to a place inside the same building, the desks and files are moved with all their contents. If the movement is to another building, the contents of each desk and file are placed in boxes. Each box is marked with a letter showing the particular section in the new quarters to which it is to be moved. Also marked on each box is the number of the desk or file on which the box is to be placed. Each piece of equipment must have a numbered tag. The number of each piece of equipment is put in soft chalk on the floor in the new office to show the proper location, and several floor plans are made to show where each piece of equipment goes. When the moving is done, someone is stationed at each of the several exits of the old office to see that each box or piece of equipment has its destination clearly marked on it. At the new office, someone stands at each of the several entrances with a copy of the floor plan and directs the placing of the furniture and equipment according to the floor plan. No one should interfere at this point with the arrangements shown on the plan. Improvements in arrangement can be considered and made at a later date.

17. It is a hard job to move an office from one place to another during working hours.   17.____

18. Confusion cannot be avoided if an office is moved during working hours.   18.____

19. The work usually done in an office must be stopped for the day when the office is moved during working hours.   19.____

20. If an office is moved from one floor to another in the same building, the contents of a desk are taken out and put into boxes for moving.   20.____

21. If boxes are used to hold material from desks when moving an office, the box is numbered the same as the desk on which it is to be put.   21.____

22. Letters are marked in soft chalk on the floor at the new quarters to show where the desks should go when moved.   22.____

23. When the moving begins, a person is put at each exit of the old office to check that each box and piece of equipment has clearly marked on it where to go.   23.____

24. A person stationed at each entrance of the new quarters to direct the placing of the furniture and equipment has a copy of the floor plan of the new quarters.   24.____

25. If, while the furniture is being moved into the new office, a person helping at a doorway gets an idea of a better way to arrange the furniture, he should change the planned arrangement and make a record of the change.   25.____

KEY (CORRECT ANSWERS)

1.	A	11.	D
2.	C	12.	C
3.	D	13.	B
4.	B	14.	C
5.	C	15.	B
6.	D	16.	B
7.	C	17.	T
8.	D	18.	F
9.	D	19.	F
10.	C	20.	F

21. T
22. F
23. T
24. T
25. F

TEST 2

DIRECTIONS: Each question or incomplete statement is followed by several suggested answers or completions. Select the one that BEST answers the question or completes the statement. *PRINT THE LETTER OF THE CORRECT ANSWER IN THE SPACE AT THE RIGHT.*

Questions 1-4.

DIRECTIONS: Questions 1 through 4 are to be answered SOLELY on the basis of the following paragraph.

    In all cases of homicide, members of the Police Department who investigate will make every effort to obtain statements from dying persons. Such statements are of the greatest importance to the District Attorney. In many cases, there may be a failure to solve the crime if they are not taken. The principal element to be considered in taking the declaration of a dying person is his mental attitude. In order to be admissible in evidence, the person must have no hope of recovery. The patient will be fully interrogated on that point before a statement is taken.

1. In cases of homicide, according to the above paragraph, members of the police force will
    A. try to change the mental attitude of the dying person
    B. attempt to obtain a statement from the dying person
    C. not give the information they obtain directly to the District Attorney
    D. be careful not to injure the dying person unnecessarily

    1.____

2. The mental attitude of the person making the dying statement is of GREAT importance because it can determine, according to the above paragraph, whether the
    A. victim should be interrogated in the presence of witnesses
    B. victim will be willing to make a statement of any kind
    C. statement will tell the District Attorney who committed the crime
    D. the statement can be used as evidence

    2.____

3. District Attorneys find that statements of a dying person are important, according to the above paragraph, because
    A. it may be that the victim will recover and then refuse to testify
    B. they are important elements in determining the mental attitude of the victim
    C. they present a point of view
    D. it may be impossible to punish the criminal without such a statement

    3.____

4. A well-known gangster is found dying from a bullet wound. The patrolman first on the scene, in the presence of witnesses, tells the man that he is going to die and asks, *Who shot you?* The gangster says, *Jones shot me, but he hasn't killed me. I'll live to get him.* He then falls back dead. According to the above paragraph, this statement is
    A. *admissible* in evidence; the man was obviously speaking the truth
    B. *not admissible* in evidence; the man obviously did not believe that he was dying

    4.____

C. *admissible* in evidence; there were witnesses to the statement
D. *not admissible* in evidence; the victim did not sign any statement and the evidence is merely hearsay

Questions 5-7.

DIRECTIONS: Questions 5 through 7 are to be answered SOLELY on the basis of the following paragraph.

The factors contributing to crime and delinquency are varied and complex. The home and its immediate environment have been found to be crucial in determining the behavior patterns of the individual, and criminality can frequently be traced to faulty family relationships and a bad neighborhood. But in the search for a clearer understanding of the underlying causes of delinquent and criminal behavior, the total environment must be taken into consideration.

5. According to the above paragraph, family relationships
   A. tend to become faulty in bad neighborhoods
   B. are important in determining the actions of honest people as well as criminals
   C. are the only important element in the understanding of causes of delinquency
   D. are determined by the total environment

6. According to the above paragraph, the causes of crime and delinquency are
   A. not simple   B. not meaningless
   C. meaningless   D. simple

7. According to the above paragraph, faulty family relationships FREQUENTLY are
   A. responsible for varied and complex results
   B. caused when one or both parents have a criminal behavior pattern
   C. independent of the total environment
   D. the cause of criminal acts

Questions 8-10.

DIRECTIONS: Questions 8 through 10 are to be answered SOLELY on the basis of the following paragraph.

A change in the specific problems which confront the police and in the methods for dealing with them has taken place in the last few decades. The automobile is a two-way symbol of this change in policing. It menaces every city with a complicated traffic problem and has speeded up the process of committing a crime and making a getaway, but at the same time has increased the effectiveness of police operations. However, the major concern of police departments continues to be the antisocial or criminal actions and behavior of human beings.

8. On the basis of the above paragraph, it can be stated that, for the most part, in the past few decades the specific problems of a police force
   A. have changed but the general problems have not
   B. as well as the general problems have changed
   C. have remained the same but the general problems have changed
   D. as well as the general problems have remained the same

8.____

9. According to the above paragraph, advances in science and industry have, in general, made the police
   A. operations less effective from the overall point of view
   B. operations more effective from the overall point of view
   C. abandon older methods of solving police problems
   D. concern themselves more with the antisocial acts of human beings

9.____

10. The automobile is a *two-way symbol*, according to the above paragraph, because its use
    A. has speeded up getting to and away from the scene of a crime
    B. both helps and hurts police operations
    C. introduces a new antisocial act—traffic violation—and does away with criminals like horse thieves
    D. both increases and decreases speed by introducing traffic problems

10.____

Questions 11-14.

DIRECTIONS: Questions 11 through 14 are to be answered SOLELY on the basis of the following passage on INSTRUCTIONS TO COIN AND TOKEN CASHIERS.

INSTRUCTIONS TO COIN AND TOKEN CASHIERS

Cashiers should reset the machine registers to an even starting number before commencing the day's work. Money bags received directly from collecting agents shall be counted and receipted for on the collecting agent's form. Each cashier shall be responsible for all coin or token bags accepted by him. He must examine all bags to be used for bank deposits for cuts and holes before placing them in use. Care must be exercised so that bags are not cut in opening them. Each bag must be opened separately and verified before another bag is opened. The machine register must be cleared before starting the count of another bag. The amount shown on the machine register must be compared with the amount on the bag tag. The empty bag must be kept on the table for re-examination should there be a difference between the amount on the bag tag and the amount on the machine register.

11. A cashier should BEGIN his day's assignment by
    A. counting and accepting all money bags
    B. resetting the counting machine register
    C. examining all bags for cuts and holes
    D. verifying the contents of all money bags

11.____

12. In verifying the amount of money in the bags received from the collecting agent, it is BEST to
   A. check the amount in one bag at a time
   B. base the total on the amount on the collecting agent's form
   C. repeat the total shown on the bag tag
   D. refer to the bank deposit receipt

12.____

13. A cashier is instructed to keep each empty coin bag on his table while verifying its contents CHIEFLY because, as long as the bag is on the table
   A. it cannot be misplaced
   B. the supervisor can see how quickly the cashier works
   C. cuts and holes are easily noticed
   D. a recheck is possible in case the machine count disagrees with the bag tag total

13.____

14. The INSTRUCTIONS indicate that it is NOT proper procedure for a cashier to
   A. assume that coin bags are free of cuts and holes
   B. compare the machine register total with the total shown on the bag tag
   C. sign a form when he receives coin bags
   D. reset the machine register before starting the day's counting

14.____

Questions 15-17.

DIRECTIONS: Questions 15 through 17 are to be answered SOLELY on the basis of the following passage.

The mass media are an integral part of the daily life of virtually every American. Among these media the youngest, television, is the most pervasive. Ninety-five percent of American homes have at least one T.V. set, and on the average that set is in use for about 40 hours each week. The central place of television in American life makes this medium the focal point of a growing national concern over the effects of media portrayals of violence on the values, attitudes, and behavior of an ever-increasing audience.

In our concern about violence and its causes, it is easy to make television a scapegoat. But we emphasize the fact that there is no simple answer to the problem of violence—no single explanation of its causes, and no single prescription for its control. It should be remembered that America also experienced high levels of crime and violence in periods before the advent of television.

The problem of balance, taste and artistic merit in entertaining programs on television are complex. We cannot countenance government censorship of television. Nor would we seek to impose arbitrary limitations on programming which might jeopardize television's ability to deal in dramatic presentations with controversial social issues. Nonetheless, we are deeply troubled by television's constant portrayal of violence, not in any genuine attempt to focus artistic expression on the human condition, but rather in pandering to a public preoccupation with violence that television itself has helped to generate,

15. According to the above passage, television uses violence MAINLY
   A. to highlight the reality of everyday existence
   B. to satisfy the audience's hunger for destructive action

15.____

C. to shape the values and attitudes of the public
D. when it films documentaries concerning human conflict

16. Which one of the following statements is BEST supported by the above passage? 16.____
    A. Early American history reveals a crime pattern which is not related to television.
    B. Programs should give presentations of social issues and never portray violent acts.
    C. Television has proven that entertainment programs can easily make the balance between taste and artistic merit a simple matter.
    D. Values and behavior should be regulated by governmental censorship.

17. Of the following, which word has the same meaning as *countenance*, as used in the above passage? 17.____
    A. Approve   B. Exhibit   C. Oppose   D. Reject

Questions 18-21.

DIRECTIONS: Questions 18 through 21 are to be answered SOLELY on the basis of the following passage.

Maintenance of leased or licensed areas on public parks or land has always been a problem. A good rule to follow in the administration and maintenance of such areas is to limit the responsibility of any lessee or licensee to the maintenance of the structures and grounds essential to the efficient operation of the concession, not including areas for the general use of the public, such as picnic areas, public comfort stations, etc.; except where such facilities are leased to another public agency or where special conditions make such inclusion practicable, and where a good standard of maintenance can be assured and enforced. If local conditions and requirements are such that public use areas are included, adequate safeguards to the public should be written into contracts and enforced in their administration, to insure that maintenance by the concessionaire shall be equal to the maintenance standards for other park property.

18. According to the above passage, when an area on a public park is leased to a concessionaire, it is usually BEST to 18.____
    A. confine the responsibility of the concessionaire to operation of the facilities and leave the maintenance function to the park agency
    B. exclude areas of general public use from the maintenance obligation of the concessionaire
    C. make the concessionaire responsible for maintenance of the entire area including areas of general public use
    D. provide additional comfort station facilities for the area

19. According to the above passage, a valid reason for giving a concessionaire responsibility for maintenance of a picnic area within his leased area is that 19.____
    A. local conditions and requirements make it practicable
    B. more than half of the picnic area falls within his leased area
    C. the concessionaire has leased picnic facilities to another public agency
    D. the picnic area falls entirely within his leased area

20. According to the above passage, a precaution that should be taken when a concessionaire is made responsible for maintenance of an area of general public use in a park is
   A. making sure that another public agency has not previously been made responsible for this area
   B. providing the concessionaire with up-to-date equipment, if practicable
   C. requiring that the concessionaire take out adequate insurance for the protection of the public
   D. writing safeguards to the public into the contract

20.____

KEY (CORRECT ANSWERS)

1.	B	11.	B
2.	D	12.	A
3.	D	13.	D
4.	B	14.	A
5.	B	15.	B
6.	A	16.	A
7.	D	17.	A
8.	A	18.	B
9.	B	19.	A
10.	B	20.	D

TEST 3

DIRECTIONS: Each question or incomplete statement is followed by several suggested answers or completions. Select the one that BEST answers the question or completes the statement. *PRINT THE LETTER OF THE CORRECT ANSWER IN THE SPACE AT THE RIGHT.*

Questions 1-5.

DIRECTIONS: Questions 1 through 5 are to be answered SOLELY on the basis of the following paragraph.

    Physical inspections are an important tool for the examiner because he will have to decide the case in many instances on the basis of the inspection report. Most proceedings in a rent office are commenced by the filing of a written application or complaint by an interested party; that is, either the landlord or the tenant. Such an application or complaint must be filed in duplicate in order that the opposing party may be served with a copy of the application or complaint and thus be given an opportunity to answer and oppose it. Sometimes, a further opportunity is given the applicant to file a written rebuttal or reply to his adversary's answer. Often an examiner can make a determination or decision based on the written application, the answer, and the reply to the answer; and, of course, it would speed up operations if it were always possible to make decisions based on written documents only. Unfortunately, decisions can't always be made that way. There are numerous occasions where <u>disputed</u> issues of fact remain which cannot be <u>resolved</u> on the basis of the written statements of the parties. Typical examples are the following: The tenant claims that the refrigerator or stove or bathroom fixture is not functioning properly and the landlord denies this It is obvious that in such cases an inspection of the accommodations is almost the only means of resolving such disputed issues,

1. According to the above paragraph, 1.____
   A. physical inspections are made in all cases
   B. physical inspections are seldom made
   C. it is sometimes possible to determine the facts in a case without a physical inspection
   D. physical inspections are made when it is necessary to verify the examiner's determination

2. According to the above paragraph, in MOST cases, proceedings are started by a(n) 2.____
   A. inspector discovering a violation
   B. oral complaint by a tenant or landlord
   C. request from another agency, such as the Building Department
   D. written complaint by a tenant or landlord

3. According to the above paragraph, when a tenant files an application with the rent office, the landlord is 3.____
   A. not told about the proceeding until after the examiner makes his determination
   B. given the duplicate copy of the application

131

C. notified by means of an inspector visiting the premises
D. not told about the proceeding until after the inspector has visited the premises

4. As used in the above paragraph, the word *disputed* means MOST NEARLY 4.____
   A. unsettled   B. contested   C. definite   D. difficult

5. As used in the above paragraph, the word *resolved* means MOST NEARLY 5.____
   A. settled   B. fixed   C. helped   D. amended

Questions 6-10.

DIRECTIONS: Questions 6 through 10 are to be answered SOLELY on the basis of the following paragraph.

The examiner should order or request an inspection of the housing accommodations. His request for a physical inspection should be in writing, identify the accommodations and the landlord and the tenant, and specify precisely just what the inspector is to look for and report on. Unless this request is specific and lists in detail every item which the examiner wishes to be reported, the examiner will find that the inspection has not served its purpose and that even with the inspector's report, he is still in no position to decide the case due to loose ends which have not been completely tied up. The items that the examiner is interested in should be separately numbered on the inspection request and the same number referred to in the inspector's report. You can see what it would mean if an inspector came back with a report that did not cover everything. It may mean a tremendous waste of time and often require a re-inspection.

6. According to the above paragraph, the inspector makes an inspection on the order of 6.____
   A. the landlord
   B. the tenant
   C. the examiner
   D. both the landlord and the tenant

7. According to the above paragraph, the reason for numbering each item that an inspector reports on is so that 7.____
   A. the report is neat
   B. the report can be easily read and referred to
   C. none of the examiner's requests for information is missed
   D. the report will be specific

8. The one of the following items that is NOT necessarily included in the request for inspection is 8.____
   A. location of dwelling
   B. name of landlord
   C. item to be checked
   D. type of building

9. As used in the above paragraph, the word *precisely* means MOST NEARLY 9.____
   A. exactly   B. generally   C. usually   D. strongly

10. As used in the above paragraph, the words *in detail* mean MOST NEARLY 10.____
    A. clearly   B. item by item   C. substantially   D. completely

Questions 11-13.

DIRECTIONS: Questions 11 through 13 are to be answered SOLELY on the basis of the following passage.

The agreement under which a tenant rents property from a landlord is known as a lease. Generally speaking, leases are classified as either short-term or long-term in duration. They are further subdivided according to the method used to determine the amount of periodic rent payments. Of the following types of lease in use, the more commonly used ones are the following:
1. The straight or fixed lease is one in which rent may be paid in equal amounts throughout the duration of the lease. These are usually restricted to short-term leasing, or somewhat longer-term if clauses in the lease provide for periodic escalation of payments as the economy shifts.
2. Percentage leasing, used for short-term commercial leasing, provides the landlord with a stipulated percentage of a tenant's gross sales from goods and services sold on the premises, in addition to a fixed amount of rent.
3. The net lease, generally long-term (ten years or more), requires the tenant to pay all operating costs, including real estate taxes and insurance. In a net-net lease, the tenant further agrees to meet mortgage interest and principal payments.
4. An escalated lease, which is a long-term lease, requires rent to be of a stipulated base amount which periodically is subject to escalation in accordance with cost-of-living index scales, or in direct proportion to taxes, insurance, and operating costs.

11. Based on the information given in the passage, which type of lease is MOST likely to be advantageous to a landlord if there is a high rate of inflation? _____ lease. 11._____
   A. Fixed   B. Percentage   C. Net   D. Escalated

12. On the basis of thee above passage, which types of lease would generally be MOST suitable for a well-established textile company which requires permanent facilities for its large operations? 12._____
   _____ lease and _____ lease.
   A. Percentage; escalated
   B. Escalated; net
   C. Straight; net
   D. Straight; percentage

13. According to the above passage, the ONLY type of lease which assures the same amount of rent throughout a specified interval is the _____ lease. 13._____
   A. straight   B. percentage   C. net-net   D. escalated

Questions 14-15.

DIRECTIONS: Questions 14 and 15 are to be answered SOLELY on the basis of the following passage.

If you like people, if you seek contact with them rather than hide yourself in a corner, if you study your fellow men sympathetically, if you try consistently to contribute something to their success and happiness, if you are reasonably generous with your thought and your time, if you have a partial reserve with everyone but a seeming reserve with no one, you will get along with your superiors, your subordinates, and the human race.

By the scores of thousands, precepts and platitudes have been written for the guidance of personal conduct. The odd part of it is that, despite all of this labor, most of the frictions in modern society arise from the individual's feeling of inferiority, his false pride, his vanity, his unwillingness to yield space to any other man and his consequent urge to throw his own weight around. Goethe said that the quality which best enables a man to renew his own life, in his relation to others, is his capability of renouncing particular things at the right moment in order warmly to embrace something new in the next.

14. On the basis of the above passage, it may be INFERRED that
    A. a person should be unwilling to renounce privileges
    B. a person should realize that loss of a desirable job assignment may come at an opportune moment
    C. it is advisable for a person to maintain a considerable amount of reserve in his relationship with unfamiliar people
    D. people should be ready to contribute generously to a worthy charity

14.____

15. Of the following, the MOST valid implication made by the above passage is that
    A. a wealthy person who spends a considerable amount of money entertaining his friends is not really getting along with them
    B. if a person studies his fellow men carefully and impartially, he will tend to have good relationships with them
    C. individuals who maintain seemingly little reserve in their relationships with people have in some measure overcome their own feelings of inferiority
    D. most precepts that have been written for the guidance of personal conduct in relationships with other people are invalid

15.____

Questions 16-17.

DIRECTIONS: Questions 16 and 17 are to be answered SOLELY on the basis of the following passage.

When a design for a new bank note of the Federal Government has been prepared by the Bureau of Engraving and Printing and has been approved by the Secretary of the Treasury, the engravers begin the work of cutting the design in steel. No one engraver does all the work. Each man is a specialist. One works only on portraits, another on lettering, another on scroll work, and so on. Each engraver, with a steel tool known as a graver, and aided by a powerful magnifying glass, carefully carves his portion of the design into the steel. He knows that one false cut or a slip of his tool, or one miscalculation of width or depth of line, may destroy the merit of his work. A single mistake means that months or weeks of labor will have been in vain. The bureau is proud of the fact that no counterfeiter ever has duplicated the excellent work of its expert engravers.

16. According to the above passage, each engraver in the Bureau of Engraving and Printing
    A. must be approved by the Secretary of the Treasury before he can begin work on the design for a new bank note
    B. is responsible for engraving a complete design of a new bank note by himself
    C. designs new bank notes and submits them for approval to the Secretary of the Treasury
    D. performs sonly a specific part of the work of engraving a design for a new bank note

17. According to the above passage,
    A. an engraver's tools are not available to a counterfeiter
    B. mistakes made in engraving a design can be corrected immediately with little delay in the work of the Bureau
    C. the skilled work of the engravers has not been successfully reproduced by counterfeiter
    D. careful carving and cutting by the engraver is essential to prevent damage to equipment

Questions 18-21.

DIRECTIONS: Questions 18 through 21 are to be answered SOLELY on the basis of the following passage.

In the late fifties, the average American housewife spent $4.50 per day for a family of four on food and 5.15 hours in food preparation, if all of her food was *home prepared*; she spent $5.80 per day and 3.245 hours if all of her food was purchased *partially prepared*; and $6.70 per day and 1.64 hours if all of her food was purchased *ready-to-serve*.

Americans spent about 20 billion dollars for food products in 1941. They spent nearly 70 billion dollars in 1958. They spent 25 percent of their cash income on food in 1958. For the same kinds and quantities of food that consumers bought in 1941, they would have spent only 16% of their cash income in 1958. It is obvious that our food does cost more. Many factors contribute to this increase besides the additional cost that might be attributed to processing. Consumption of more expensive food items, higher marketing margins, and more food eaten in restaurants are other factors.

The Census of Manufacturers gives some indication of the total bill for processing. The value added by manufacturing of food and kindred products amounted to 3.5 billion of the 20 billion dollars spent for food in 1941. In the year 1958, the comparable figure had climbed to 14 billion dollars.

18. According to the above passage, the cash income of Americans in 1958 was MOST NEARLY _____ billion dollars.
    A. 11.2   B. 17.5   C. 70   D. 280

19. According to the above passage, if Americans bought the same kinds and quantities of food in 1958 as they did in 1941, they would have spent MOST NEARLY _____ billion dollars.
    A. 20   B. 45   C. 74   D. 84

20. According to the above passage, the percent increase in money spent for food in 1958 over 1941, as compared with the percentage increase in money spent for food processing in the same years,
    A. was greater
    B. was less
    C. was the same
    D. cannot be determined from the passage

    20.____

21. In 1958, an American housewife who bought all of her food ready-to-serve saved time, as compared with the housewife who prepared all of her food at home
    A. 1.6 hours daily
    B. 1.9 hours daily
    C. 3.5 hours daily
    D. an amount of time which cannot be determined from the above passage

    21.____

Questions 22-25.

DIRECTIONS: Questions 22 through 25 are to be answered SOLELY on the basis of the following passage.

Any member of the retirement system who is in city service, who files a proper application for service credit and agrees to deductions from his compensation at triple his normal rate of contribution, shall be credited with a period of city service previous to the beginning of his present membership in the retirement system. The period of service credited shall be equal to the period throughout which such triple deductions are made, but may not exceed the total of the city service the number rendered between his first day of eligibility for membership in the retirement system and the day he last became a member. After triple contributions for all of the first three years of service credit claimed, the remaining service credit may be purchased by a single payment of the sum of the remaining payments. If the total time purchasable exceeds ten years, triple contributions may be made for one-half of such time, and the remaining time purchased by a single payment of the sum of the remaining payments. Credit for service acquired in the above manner may be used only in determining the amount of any retirement benefit. Eligibility for such benefit will, in all cases, be based upon service rendered after the employee's membership last began, and will be exclusive of service credit purchased as described above.

22. According to the above passage, in order to obtain credit for city service previous to the beginning of an employee's present membership in the retirement system, the employee must
    A. apply for the service credit and consent to additional contributions to the retirement system
    B. apply for the service credit before he renews his membership in the retirement system
    C. have previous city service which does not exceed ten years
    D. make contributions to the retirement system for three years

    22.____

23. According to the information in the above passage, credit for city service previous to the beginning of an employee's present membership in the retirement system is 23.____
    A. credited up to a maximum of ten years
    B. credited to any member of the retirement system
    C. used in determining the amount of the employee's benefits
    D. used in establishing the employee's eligibility to receive benefits

24. According to the information in the above passage, a member of the retirement system may purchase service credit for 24.____
    A. the period of time between his first day of eligibility for membership in the retirement system and the date he applies for the service credit
    B. one-half of the total of his previous city service if the total time exceeds ten years
    C. the period of time throughout which triple deductions are made
    D. the period of city service between his first day of eligibility for membership in the retirement system and the day he last became a member

25. Suppose that a member of the retirement system has filed an application for service credit for five years of previous city service. 25.____
    Based on the information in the above passage, the employee may purchase credit for this previous city service by making
    A. triple contributions for three years
    B. triple contributions for one-half of the time and a single payment of the sum of the remaining payments
    C. triple contributions for three years and a single payment of the sum of the remaining payments
    D. a single payment of the sum of the payments

KEY (CORRECT ANSWERS)

1.	C	11.	D
2.	D	12.	B
3.	B	13.	A
4.	B	14.	B
5.	A	15.	C
6.	C	16.	D
7.	C	17.	C
8.	D	18.	D
9.	A	19.	B
10.	B	20.	B

21. C
22. A
23. C
24. D
25. C

CLERICAL ABILITIES
EXAMINATION SECTION
TEST 1

DIRECTIONS: Each question or incomplete statement is followed by several suggested answers or completions. Select the one that BEST answers the question or completes the statement. *PRINT THE LETTER OF THE CORRECT ANSWER IN THE SPACE AT THE RIGHT.*

Questions 1-4.

DIRECTIONS: Questions 1 through 4 are to be answered on the basis of the information given below.

The most commonly used filing system and the one that is easiest to learn is alphabetical filing. This involves putting records in an A to Z order, according to the letters of the alphabet. The name of a person is filed by using the following order: first, the surname or last name; second, the first name; third, the middle name or middle initial. For example, *Henry C. Young* is filed under *Y* and thereafter under *Young, Henry C.* The name of a company is filed in the same way. For example, *Long Cabinet Co.* is filed under *L* while *John T. Long Cabinet Co.* is filed under *L* and thereafter under *Long, John T. Cabinet Co.*

1. The one of the following which lists the names of persons in the CORRECT alphabetical order is:
   A. Mary Carrie, Helen Carrol, James Carson, John Carter
   B. James Carson, Mary Carrie, John Carter, Helen Carrol
   C. Helen Carrol, James Carson, John Carter, Mary Carrie
   D. John Carter, Helen Carrol, Mary Carrie, James Carson

1.____

2. The one of the following which lists the names of persons in the CORRECT alphabetical order is:
   A. Jones, John C.; Jones, John A.; Jones, John P.; Jones, John K.
   B. Jones, John P.; Jones, John K.; Jones, John C.; Jones, John A.
   C. Jones, John A.; Jones, John C.; Jones, John K.; Jones, John P.
   D. Jones, John K.; Jones, John C.; Jones, John A.; Jones, John P.

2.____

3. The one of the following which lists the names of the companies in the CORRECT alphabetical order is:
   A. Blane Co., Blake Co., Block Co., Blear Co.
   B. Blake Co., Blane Co., Blear Co., Block Co.
   C. Block Co., Blear Co., Blane Co., Blake Co.
   D. Blear Co., Blake Co., Blane Co., Block Co.

3.____

4. You are to return to the file an index card on *Barry C. Wayne Materials and Supplies Co.*
Of the following, the CORRECT alphabetical group that you should return the index card to is
 A. A to G   B. H to M   C. N to S   D. T to Z

4._____

Questions 5-10.

DIRECTIONS: In each of Questions 5 through 10, the names of four people are given. For each question, choose as your answer the one of the four names given which should be filed FIRST according to the usual system of alphabetical filing of names, as described in the following paragraph.

In filing names, you must start with the last name. Names are filed in order of the first letter of the last name, then the second letter, etc. Therefore, BAILY would be filed before BROWN, which would be filed before COLT. A name with fewer letters of the same type comes first, i.e., Smith before Smithe. If the last names are the same, the names are filed alphabetically by the first name. If the first name is an initial, a name with an initial would come before a first name that starts with the same letter as the initial. Therefore, I. BROWN would come before IRA BROWN. Finally, if both last name and first name are the same, the name would be filed alphabetically by the middle name, once again an initial coming before a middle name which starts with the same letter as the initial. If there is no middle name at all, the name would come before those with middle initials or names.

SAMPLE QUESTION: A. Lester Daniels
 B. William Dancer
 C. Nathan Danzig
 D. Dan Lester

The last names beginning with D are filed before the last name beginning with L. Since DANIELS, DANCER, and DANZIG all begin with the same three letters, you must look at the fourth letter of the last name to determine which name should be filed first. C comes before I or Z in the alphabet, so DANCER is filed before DANIELS or DANZIG. Therefore, the answer to the above sample question is B.

5. A. Scott Biala
 B. Mary Byala
 C. Martin Baylor
 D. Francis Bauer

5._____

6. A. Howard J. Black
 B. Howard Black
 C. J. Howard Black
 D. John H. Black

6._____

7. A. Theodora Garth Kingston
 B. Theadore Barth Kingston
 C. Thomas Kingston
 D. Thomas T. Kingston

7._____

8. A. Paulette Mary Huerta
    B. Paul M. Huerta
    C. Paulette L. Huerta
    D. Peter A. Huerta

9. A. Martha Hunt Morgan
    B. Martin Hunt Morgan
    C. Mary H. Morgan
    D. Martine H. Morgan

10. A. James T. Meerschaum
    B. James M. Mershum
    C. James F. Mearshaum
    D. James N. Meshum

Questions 11-14.

DIRECTIONS: Questions 11 through 14 are to be answered SOLELY on the basis of the following information.

You are required to file various documents in file drawers which are labeled according to the following pattern:

DOCUMENTS

MEMOS		LETTERS	
File	Subject	File	Subject
84PM1	(A-L)	84PC1	(A-L)
84PM2	(M-Z)	84PC2	(M-Z)

REPORTS		INQUIRIES	
File	Subject	File	Subject
84PR1	(A-L)	84PQ1	(A-L)
84PR2	(M-Z)	84PQ2	(M-Z)

11. A letter dealing with a burglary should be filed in the drawer labeled
    A. 84PM1   B. 84PC1   C. 84PR1   D. 84PQ2

12. A report on Statistics should be found in the drawer labeled
    A. 84PM1   B. 84PC2   C. 84PR2   D. 84PQS

13. An inquiry is received about parade permit procedures. It should be filed in the drawer labeled
    A. 84PM2   B. 84PC1   C. 84PR1   D. 84PQ2

14. A police officer has a question about a robbery report you filed. You should pull this file from the drawer labeled
    A. 84PM1   B. 84PM2   C. 84PR1   D. 84PR2

Questions 15-22.

DIRECTIONS: Each of Questions 15 through 22 consists of four or six numbered names. For each question, choose the option (A, B, C, or D) which indicates the order in which the names should be filed in accordance with the following filing instructions:
- File alphabetically according to last name, then first name, then middle initial.
- File according to each successive letter within a name.
- When comparing two names in which the letters in the longer name are identical to the corresponding letters in the shorter name, the shorter name is filed first.
- When the last names are the same, initials are always filed before names beginning with the same letter.

15.
  I. Ralph Robinson
  II. Alfred Ross
  III. Luis Robles
  IV. James Roberts

  The CORRECT filing sequence for the above names should be
  A. IV, II, I, III   B. I, IV, III, II   C. III, IV, I, II   D. IV, I, III, II

16.
  I. Irwin Goodwin
  II. Inez Gonzalez
  III. Irene Goodman
  IV. Ira S. Goodwin
  V. Ruth I. Goldstein
  VI. M.B. Goodman

  The CORRECT filing sequence for the above names should be
  A. V, II, I, IV, III, VI   B. V, II, VI, III, IV, I
  C. V, II, III, VI, IV, I   D. V, II, III, VI, I, IV

17.
  I. George Allan
  II. Gregory Allen
  III. Gary Allen
  IV. George Allen

  The CORRECT filing sequence for the above names should be
  A. IV, III, I, II   B. I, IV, II, III   C. III, IV, I, II   D. I, III, IV, II

5 (#1)

18. I. Simon Kauffman
     II. Leo Kaufman
     III. Robert Kaufmann
     IV. Paul Kauffmann

     The CORRECT filing sequence for the above names should be
     A. I, IV, II, III   B. II, IV, III, I   C. III, II, IV, I   D. I, II, III, IV

19. I. Roberta Williams
     II. Robin Wilson
     III. Roberta Wilson
     IV. Robin Williams

     The CORRECT filing sequence for the above names should be
     A. III, II, IV, I   B. I, IV, III, II   C. I, II, III, IV   D. III, I, II, IV

20. I. Lawrence Shultz
     II. Albert Schultz
     III. Theodore Schwartz
     IV. Thomas Schwarz
     V. Alvin Schultz
     VI. Leonard Shultz

     The CORRECT filing sequence for the above names should be
     A. II, V, III, IV, I, VI   B. IV, III, V, I, II, VI
     C. II, V, I, VI, III, IV   D. I, VI, II, V, III, IV

21. I. McArdle
     II. Mayer
     III. Maletz
     IV. McNiff
     V. Meyer
     VI. MacMahon

     The CORRECT filing sequence for the above names should be
     A. I, IV, VI, III, II, V   B. II, I, IV, VI, III, V
     C. VI, III, II, I, IV, V   D. VI, III, II, V, I, IV

22. I. Jack E. Johnson
     II. R.H. Jackson
     III. Bertha Jackson
     IV. J.T. Johnson
     V. Ann Johns
     VI. John Jacobs

     The CORRECT filing sequence for the above names should be
     A. II, III, VI, V, IV, I   B. III, II, VI, V, IV, I
     C. VI, II, III, I, V, IV   D. III, II, VI, IV, V, I

Questions 23-30.

DIRECTIONS: The code table below shows 10 letters with matching numbers. For each question, there are three sets of letters. Each set of letters is followed by a set of numbers which may or may not match their correct letter according to the code table. For each question, check all three sets of letters and numbers and mark your answer:
- A. if no pairs are correctly matched
- B. if only one pair is correctly matched
- C. if only two pairs are correctly matched
- D. if all three pairs are correctly matched

CODE TABLE

T	M	V	D	S	P	R	G	B	H
1	2	3	4	5	6	7	8	9	0

SAMPLE QUESTION: TMVDSP – 123456
RGBHTM – 789011
DSPRGB – 256789

In the sample question above, the first set of numbers correctly match its set of letters. But the second and third pairs contain mistakes. In the second pair, M is correctly matched with number 1. According to the code table, letter M should be correctly matched with number 2. In the third pair, the letter D is incorrectly matched with number 2. According to the code table, letter D should be correctly matched with number 4. Since only one of the pairs is correctly matched, the answer to this sample question is B.

23. RSBMRM – 759262
    GDSRVH – 845730
    VDBRTM - 349713   23.____

24. TGVSDR – 183247
    SMHRDP – 520647
    TRMHSR - 172057   24.____

25. DSPRGM – 456782
    MVDBHT – 234902
    HPMDBT - 062491   25.____

26. BVPTRD – 936184
    GDPHMB – 807029
    GMRHMV – 827032   26.____

27. MGVRSH – 283750
    TRDMBS – 174295
    SPRMGV - 567283   27.____

144

28. SGBSDM – 489542   28.____
    MGHPTM – 290612
    MPBMHT - 269301

29. TDPBHM – 146902   29.____
    VPBMRS – 369275
    GDMBHM - 842902

30. MVPTBV – 236194   30.____
    PDRTMB – 47128
    BGTMSM - 981232

KEY (CORRECT ANSWERS)

1.	A	11.	B	21.	C
2.	C	12.	C	22.	B
3.	B	13.	D	23.	B
4.	D	14.	D	24.	B
5.	D	15.	D	25.	C
6.	B	16.	C	26.	A
7.	B	17.	D	27.	D
8.	B	18.	A	28.	A
9.	A	19.	B	29.	D
10.	C	20.	A	30.	A

TEST 2

DIRECTIONS: Each question or incomplete statement is followed by several suggested answers or completions. Select the one that BEST answers the question or completes the statement. *PRINT THE LETTER OF THE CORRECT ANSWER IN THE SPACE AT THE RIGHT.*

Questions 1-10.

DIRECTIONS: Questions 1 through 10 each consists of two columns, each containing four lines of names, numbers and/or addresses. For each question, compare the lines in Column I with the lines in Column II to see if they match exactly, and mark your answer A, B, C, or D, according to the following instructions:
- A. all four lines match exactly
- B. only three lines match exactly
- C. only two lines match exactly
- D. only one line matches exactly

	COLUMN I	COLUMN II	
1.	I. Earl Hodgson II. 1409870 III. Shore Ave. IV. Macon Rd.	Earl Hodgson 1408970 Schore Ave. Macon Rd.	1.___
2.	I. 9671485 II. 470 Astor Court III. Halprin, Phillip IV. Frank D. Poliseo	9671485 470 Astor Court Halperin, Phillip Frank D. Poliseo	2.___
3.	I. Tandem Associates II. 144-17 Northern Blvd. III. Alberta Forchi IV. Kings Park, NY 10751	Tandom Associates 144-17 Northern Blvd. Albert Forchi Kings Point, NY 10751	3.___
4.	I. Bertha C. McCormack II. Clayton, MO III. 976-4242 IV. New City, NY 10951	Bertha C. McCormack Clayton, MO 976-4242 New City, NY 10951	4.___
5.	I. George C. Morill II. Columbia, SC 29201 III. Louis Ingham IV. 3406 Forest Ave.	George C. Morrill Columbia, SD 29201 Louis Ingham 3406 Forest Ave.	5.___
6.	I. 506 S. Elliott Pl. II. Herbert Hall III. 4712 Rockaway Pkway IV. 169 E. 7 St.	506 S. Elliott Pl. Hurbert Hall 4712 Rockaway Pkway 169 E. 7 St.	6.___

2 (#2)

7. I.   345 Park Ave.   345 Park Pl.   7.____
    II. Colman Oven Corp.   Coleman Oven Corp.
    III. Robert Conte   Robert Conti
    IV. 6179846   6179846

8. I.   Grigori Schierber   Grigori Schierber   8.____
    II. Des Moines, Iowa   Des Moines, Iowa
    III. Gouverneur Hospital   Gouverneur Hospital
    IV. 91-35 Cresskill Pl.   91-35 Cresskill Pl.

9. I.   Jeffery Janssen   Jeffrey Janssen   9.____
    II. 8041071   8041071
    III. 40 Rockefeller Plaza   40 Rockafeller Plaza
    IV. 407 6 St.   406 7 St.

10. I.   5971996   5871996   10.____
    II. 3113 Knickerbocker Ave.   31123 Knickerbocker Ave.
    III. 8434 Boston Post Rd.   8424 Boston Post Rd.
    IV. Penn Station   Penn Station

Questions 11-14.

DIRECTIONS: Questions 11 through 14 are to be answered by looking at the four groups of names and addresses listed below (I, II, III, and IV), and then finding out the number of groups that have their corresponding numbered lies exactly the same.

	GROUP I	GROUP II
Line 1.	Richmond General Hospital	Richman General Hospital
Line 2.	Geriatric Clinic	Geriatric Clinic
Line 3.	3975 Paerdegat St.	3975 Peardegat St.
Line 4.	Loudonville, New York 11538	Londonville, New York 11538

	GROUP III	GROUP IV
Line 1.	Richmond General Hospital	Richmend General Hospital
Line 2.	Geriatric Clinic	Geriatric Clinic
Line 3.	3795 Paerdegat St.	3975 Paerdegat St.
Line 4.	Loudonville, New York 11358	Loudonville, New York 11538

1. In how many groups is line one exactly the same?   11.____
    A. Two   B. Three   C. Four   D. None

12. In how many groups is line two exactly the same?   12.____
    A. Two   B. Three   C. Four   D. None

13. In how many groups is line three exactly the same?   13.____
    A. Two   B. Three   C. Four   D. None

14. In how many groups is line four exactly the same?　　　　　　　　　　　　　　　　　14.____
　　　A. Two　　　　　　B. Three　　　C. Four　　　D. None

Questions 15-18.

DIRECTIONS: Each of Questions 15 through 18 has two lists of names and addresses. Each list contains three sets of names and addresses. Check each of the three sets in the list on the right to see if they are the same as the corresponding set in the list on the left. Mark your answers:
　　　A. if none of the sets in the right list are the same as those in the left list
　　　B. if only one of the sets in the right list is the same as those in the left list
　　　C. if only two of the sets in the right list are the same as those in the left list
　　　D. if all three sets in the right list are the same as those in the left list

15.　Mary T. Berlinger　　　　　　　　　　Mary T. Berlinger　　　　　　　　　　　　15.____
　　　2351 Hampton St.　　　　　　　　　2351 Hampton St.
　　　Monsey, N.Y.　20117　　　　　　　Monsey, N.Y.　20117

　　　Eduardo Benes　　　　　　　　　　 Eduardo Benes
　　　483 Kingston Avenue　　　　　　　473 Kingston Avenue
　　　Central Islip, N.Y.　11734　　　　　Central Islip, N.Y.　11734

　　　Alan Carrington Fuchs　　　　　　 Alan Carrington Fuchs
　　　17 Gnarled Hollow Road　　　　　17 Gnarled Hollow Road
　　　Los Angeles, CA　91635　　　　　Los Angeles, CA　91685

16.　David John Jacobson　　　　　　　David John Jacobson　　　　　　　　　　16.____
　　　178 34 St. Apt. 4C　　　　　　　　 178 53 St. Apt. 4C
　　　New York, N.Y.　00927　　　　　　New York, N.Y.　00927

　　　Ann-Marie Calonella　　　　　　　Ann-Marie Calonella
　　　7243 South Ridge Blvd.　　　　　　7243 South Ridge Blvd.
　　　Bakersfield, CA　96714　　　　　　Bakersfield, CA　96714

　　　Pauline M. Thompson　　　　　　 Pauline M. Thomson
　　　872 Linden Ave.　　　　　　　　　872 Linden Ave.
　　　Houston, Texas　70321　　　　　 Houston, Texas　70321

17.　Chester LeRoy Masterton　　　　　Chester LeRoy Masterson　　　　　　　　17.____
　　　152 Lacy Rd.　　　　　　　　　　　152 Lacy Rd.
　　　Kankakee, Ill.　54532　　　　　　　Kankakee, Ill.　54532

　　　William Maloney　　　　　　　　　William Maloney
　　　S. LaCrosse Pla.　　　　　　　　　S. LaCross Pla.
　　　Wausau, Wisconsin　52136　　　　Wausau, Wisconsin　52146

　　　Cynthia V. Barnes　　　　　　　　Cynthia V. Barnes
　　　16 Pines Rd.　　　　　　　　　　　16 Pines Rd.
　　　Greenpoint, Miss.　20376　　　　 Greenpoint,, Miss.　20376

18. Marcel Jean Frontenac   Marcel Jean Frontenac   18.____
    8 Burton On The Water   6 Burton On The Water
    Calender, Me. 01471   Calender, Me. 01471

    J. Scott Marsden   J. Scott Marsden
    174 S. Tipton St.   174 Tipton St.
    Cleveland, Ohio   Cleveland, Ohio

    Lawrence T. Haney   Lawrence T. Haney
    171 McDonough St.   171 McDonough St.
    Decatur, Ga. 31304   Decatur, Ga. 31304

Questions 19-26.

DIRECTIONS: Each of Questions 19 through 26 has two lists of numbers. Each list contains three sets of numbers. Check each of the three sets in the list on the right to see if they are the same as the corresponding set in the list on the left. Mark your answers:
  A. if none of the sets in the right list are the same as those in the left list
  B. if only one of the sets in the right list is the same as those in the left list
  C. if only two of the sets in the right list are the same as those in the left list
  D. if all three sets in the right list are the same as those in the left lists

19. 7354183476   7354983476   19.____
    4474747744   4474747774
    5791430231   57914302311

20. 7143592185   7143892185   20.____
    8344517699   8344518699
    9178531263   9178531263

21. 2572114731   257214731   21.____
    8806835476   8806835476
    8255831246   8255831246

22. 331476853821   331476858621   22.____
    6976658532996   6976655832996
    3766042113715   3766042113745

23. 8806663315   88066633115   23.____
    74477138449   74477138449
    211756663666   211756663666

5 (#2)

24. 990006966996   99000696996   24._____
    53022219743   53022219843
    4171171117717   4171171177717

25. 24400222433004   24400222433004   25._____
    5300030055000355   5300030055500355
    20000075532002022   20000075532002022

26. 6111666406600011 16   61116664066001116   26._____
    7111300117001100733   7111300117001100733
    26666446664476518   26666446664476518

Questions 27-30.

DIRECTIONS: Questions 27 through 30 are to be answered by picking the answer which is in the correct numerical order, from the lowest number to the highest number, in each question.

27. A. 44533, 44518, 44516, 44547   27._____
    B. 44516, 44518, 44533, 44547
    C. 44547, 44533, 44518, 44516
    D. 44518, 44516, 44547, 44533

28. A. 95587, 95593, 95601, 95620   28._____
    B. 95601, 95620, 95587, 95593
    C. 95593, 95587, 95601. 95620
    D. 95620, 95601, 95593, 95587

29. A. 232212, 232208, 232232, 232223   29._____
    B. 232208, 232223, 232212, 232232
    C. 232208, 232212, 232223, 232232
    D. 232223, 232232, 232208, 232208

30. A. 113419, 113521, 113462, 113462   30._____
    B. 113588, 113462, 113521, 113419
    C. 113521, 113588, 113419, 113462
    D. 113419, 113462, 113521, 113588

KEY (CORRECT ANSWERS)

1. C	11. A	21. C
2. B	12. C	22. A
3. D	13. A	23. D
4. A	14. A	24. A
5. C	15. C	25. C
6. B	16. B	26. C
7. D	17. B	27. B
8. A	18. B	28. A
9. D	19. B	29. C
10. C	20. B	30. D

RECORD KEEPING
EXAMINATION SECTION
TEST 1

DIRECTIONS: Each question or incomplete statement is followed by several suggested answers or completions. Select the one that BEST answers the question or completes the statement. *PRINT THE LETTER OF THE CORRECT ANSWER IN THE SPACE AT THE RIGHT.*

Questions 1-15.

DIRECTIONS: Questions 1 through 15 are to be answered on the basis of the following list of company names below. Arrange a file alphabetically, word-by-word, disregarding punctuation, conjunctions, and apostrophes. Then answer the questions.

    A Bee C Reading Materials
    ABCO Parts
    A Better Course for Test Preparation
    AAA Auto Parts Co.
    A-Z Auto Parts, Inc.
    Aabar Books
    Abbey, Joanne
    Boman-Sylvan Law Firm
    BMW Autowerks
    C Q Service Company
    Chappell-Murray, Inc.
    E&E Life Insurance
    Emcrisco
    Gigi Arts
    Gordon, Jon & Associates
    SOS Plumbing
    Schmidt, J.B. Co.

1. Which of these files should appear FIRST?
 A. ABCO Parts
 B. A Bee C Reading Materials
 C. A Better Course for Test Preparation
 D. AAA Auto Parts Co.

2. Which of these files should appear SECOND?
 A. A-Z Auto Parts, Inc.
 B. A Bee C Reading Materials
 C. A Better Course for Test Preparation
 D. AAA Auto Parts Co.

3. Which of these files should appear THIRD? 3.____
   A. ABCO Parts B. A Bee C Reading Materials
   C. Aabar Books D. AAA Auto Parts Co.

4. Which of these files should appear FOURTH? 4.____
   A. Aabar Books B. ABCO Parts
   C. Abbey, Joanne D. AAA Auto Parts Co.

5. Which of these files should appear LAST? 5.____
   A. Gordon, Jon & Associates B. Gigi Arts
   C. Schmidt, J.B. Co. D. SOS Plumbing

6. Which of these files should appear between A-Z Auto Parts, Inc. and Abbey, Joanne? 6.____
   A. A Bee C Reading Materials
   B. AAA Auto Parts Co.
   C. ABCO Parts
   D. A Better Course for Test Preparation

7. Which of these files should appear between ABCO Parts and Aabar Books? 7.____
   A. A Bee C Reading Materials B. Abbey, Joanne
   C. Aabar Books D. A-Z Auto Parts

8. Which of these files should appear between Abbey, Joanne and Boman-Sylvan Law Firm? 8.____
   A. A Better Course for Test Preparation
   B. BMW Autowerks
   C. Chappell-Murray, Inc.
   D. Aabar Books

9. Which of these files should appear between Abbey, Joanne and C Q Service? 9.____
   A. A-Z Auto Parts, Inc. B. BMW Autowerks
   C. Choices A and B D. Chappell-Murray, Inc.

10. Which of these files should appear between C Q Service Company and Emcrisco? 10.____
    A. Chappell-Murray, Inc. B. E&E Life Insurance
    C. Gigi Arts D. Choices A and B

11. Which of these files should NOT appear between C Q Service Company and E&E Life Insurance? 11.____
    A. Gordon, Jon & Associates B. Emcrisco
    C. Gigi Arts D. All of the above

12. Which of these files should appear between Chappell-Murray, Inc. and Gigi Arts?
    A. C Q Service Inc., E&E Life Insurance, and Emcrisco
    B. Emcrisco, E&E Life Insurance, and Gordon, Jon & Associates
    C. E&E Life Insurance, and Emcrisco
    D. Emcrisco and Gordon, Jon & Associates

    12.____

13. Which of these files should appear between Gordon, Jon & Associates and SOS Plumbing?
    A. Gigi Arts
    B. Schmidt, J.B. Co.
    C. Choices A and B
    D. None of the above

    13.____

14. Each of the choices lists the four files in their proper alphabetical order EXCEPT
    A. E&E Life Insurance; Gigi Arts; Gordon, Jon & Associates; SOS Plumbing
    B. E&E Life Insurance; Emcrisco; Gigi Arts; SOS Plumbing
    C. Emcrisco; Gordon, Jon & Associates; SOS Plumbing; Schmidt, J.B. Co.
    D. Emcrisco; Gigi Arts; Gordon, Jon & Associates; SOS Plumbing

    14.____

15. Which of the choices lists the four files in their proper alphabetical order?
    A. Gigi Arts; Gordon, Jon & Associates; SOS Plumbing; Schmidt, J.B. Co.
    B. Gordon, Jon & Associates; Gigi Arts; Schmidt, J.B. Co.; SOS Plumbing
    C. Gordon, Jon & Associates; Gigi Arts; SOS Plumbing; Schmidt, J.B. Co.
    D. Gigi Arts; Gordon, Jon & Associates; Schmidt, J.B. Co.; SOS Plumbing

    15.____

16. The alphabetical filing order of two businesses with identical names is determined by the
    A. length of time each business has been operating
    B. addresses of the businesses
    C. last name of the company president
    D. no one of the above

    16.____

17. In an alphabetical filing system, if a business name includes a number, it should be
    A. disregarded
    B. considered a number and placed at the end of an alphabetical section
    C. treated as though it were written in words and alphabetized accordingly
    D. considered a number and placed at the beginning of an alphabetical section

    17.____

18. If a business name includes a contraction (such as *don't* or *it's*), how should that word be treated in an alphabetical system?
    A. Divide the word into its separate parts and treat it as two words
    B. Ignore the letters that come after the apostrophe
    C. Ignore the word that contains the contraction
    D. Ignore the apostrophe and consider all letters in the contraction

    18.____

19. In what order should the parts of an address be considered when using an alphabetical filing system?   19._____
    A. City or town; state; street name; house or building number
    B. State; city or town; street name; house or building number
    C. House or building number; street name; city or town; state
    D. Street name; city or town; state

20. A business record should be cross-referenced when a(n)   20._____
    A. organization is known by an abbreviated name
    B. business has a name change because of a sale, incorporation, or other reason
    C. business is known by a *coined* or common name which differs from a dictionary spelling
    D. all of the above

21. A geographical filing system is MOST effective when   21._____
    A. location is more important than name
    B. many names or titles sound alike
    C. dealing with companies who have offices all over the world
    D. filing personal and business files

Questions 22-25.

DIRECTIONS: Questions 22 through 25 are to be answered on the basis of the list of items below, which are to be filed geographically. Organize the items geographically and then answer the questions.

    I. University Press at Berkeley, U.S.
    II. Maria Sanchez, Mexico City, Mexico
    III. Great Expectations Ltd. in London, England
    IV. Justice League, Cape Town, South Africa, Africa
    V. Crown Pearls Ltd. in London, England
    VI. Joseph Prasad in London, England

22. Which of the following arrangements of the items is composed according to the policy of: *Continent, Country, City, Firm or Individual Name*?   22._____
    A. V, III, IV, VI, II, I   B. IV, V, III, VI, II, I
    C. I, IV, V, III, VI, II   D. IV, V, III, VI, I, II

23. Which of the following files is arranged according to the policy of: 23._____
    Continent, Country, City, Firm or Individual Name?
    A. South Africa; Africa; Cape Town; Justice League
    B. Mexico; Mexico City; Maria Sanchez
    C. North America; United States; Berkeley; University Press
    D. England; Europe; London; Prasad, Joseph

5 (#1)

24. Which of the following arrangements of the items is composed according to the policy of: *Country, City, Firm or Individual Name*?   24._____
    A. V, VI, III, II, IV, I   B. I, V, VI, III, II, IV
    C. VI, V, III, II, IV, I   D. V, III, VI, II, IV, I

25. Which of the following files is arranged according to a policy of: *Country, City, Firm or Individual Name*?   25._____
    A. England; London; Crown Pearls Ltd.
    B. North America; United States; Berkeley; University Press
    C. Africa; Cape Town; Justice League
    D. Mexico City; Mexico; Maria Sanchez

26. Under which of the following circumstances would a phonetic filing system be MOST effective?   26._____
    A. When the person in charge of filing can't spell very well
    B. With large files with names that sound alike
    C. With large files with names that are spelled alike
    D. All of the above

Questions 27-29.

DIRECTIONS: Questions 27 through 29 are to be answered on the basis of the following list of numerical files.

    I.   391-023-100
    II. 361-132-170
    III. 385-732-200
    IV. 381-432-150
    V.   391-632-387
    VI. 361-423-303
    VII. 391-123-271

27. Which of the following arrangements of the files follows a consecutive-digit system?   27._____
    A. II, III, IV, I   B. I, V, VII, III   C. II, IV, III, I   D. III, I, V, VII

28. Which of the following arrangements follows a terminal-digit system?   28._____
    A. I, VII, II, IV, III   B. II, I, IV, V, VII
    C. VII, VI, V, IV, III   D. I, IV, II, III, VII

29. Which of the following lists follows a middle-digit system?   29._____
    A. I, VII, II, VI, IV, V, III   B. I, II, VII, IV, VI, V, III
    C. VII, II, I, III, V, VI, IV   D. VII, I, II, IV, VI, V, III

Questions 30-31.

DIRECTIONS: Questions 30 and 31 are to be answered on the basis of the following information.

    I. Reconfirm Laura Bates appointment with James Caldecort on December 12 at 9:30 A.M.
    II. Laurence Kinder contact Julia Lucas on August 3 and set up a meeting for week of September 23 at 4 P.M.
    III. John Lutz contact Larry Waverly on August 3 and set up appointment for September 23 at 9:30 A.M.
    IV. Call for tickets for Gerry Stanton August 21 for New Jersey on September 23, flight 143 at 4:43 P.M.

30. A chronological file for the above information would be   30.____
    A. IV, III, II, I   B. III, II, IV, I   C. IV, II, III, I   D. III, I, II, IV

31. Using the above information, a chronological file for the date September 23 would be   31.____
    A. II, III, IV   B. III, I, IV   C. III, II, IV   D. IV, III, II

Questions 32-34.

DIRECTIONS: Questions 32 through 34 are to be answered on the basis of the following information.

    I. Call Roger Epstein, Ashoke Naipaul, Jon Anderson, and Sara Washingon on April 19 at 1:00 P.M. to set up meeting with Alika D'Ornay for June 6 in New York.
    II. Call Martin Ames before noon on April 19 to confirm afternoon meeting with Bob Greenwood on April 20th.
    III. Set up meeting room at noon for 2:30 P.M. meeting on April 19th.
    IV. Ashley Stanton contact Bob Greenwood at 9:00 A.M. on April 20 and set up meeting for June 6 at 8:30 A.M.
    V. Carol Guiland contact Shelby Van Ness during afternoon of April 20 and set up meeting for June 6 at 10:00 A.M.
    VI. Call airline and reserve tickets on June 6 for Roger Epstein trip to Denver on July 8.
    VII. Meeting at 2:30 P.M. on April 19th.

32. A chronological file for all of the above information would be   32.____
    A. II, I, III, VII, V, IV, VI   B. III, VII, II, I, IV, V, VI
    C. III, VII, I, II, V, IV, VI   D. II, III, I, VII, IV, V, VI

33. A chronological file for the date of April 19th would be   33.____
    A. II, III, VII, I   B. II, III, I, VII   C. VII, I, III, II   D. III, VII, I, II

34. Add the following information to the file, and then create a chronological file for April 20th: VIII. April 20: 3:00 P.M. meeting between Bob Greenwood and Martin Ames.
    A. IV, V, VIII B. IV, VIII, V C. VIII, V, IV D. V, IV, VIII

35. The PRIMARY advantage of computer records over a manual system is
    A. speed of retrieval B. accuracy
    C. cost D. potential file loss

KEY (CORRECT ANSWERS)

1. B	11. D	21. A	31. C
2. C	12. C	22. B	32. D
3. D	13. B	23. C	33. B
4. A	14. C	24. D	34. A
5. D	15. D	25. A	35. A
6. C	16. B	26. B	
7. B	17. C	27. C	
8. B	18. D	28. D	
9. C	19. A	29. A	
10. D	20. D	30. B	

ARITHMETICAL REASONING

EXAMINATION SECTION

TEST 1

DIRECTIONS: Each question or incomplete statement is followed by several suggested answers or completions. Select the one that BEST answers the question or completes the statement. *PRINT THE LETTER OF THE CORRECT ANSWER IN THE SPACE AT THE RIGHT.*

1. In 2015, a public agency spent $180 to buy pencils that cost three cents each. In 2017, the agency spent $420 to buy the same number of pencils that it had bought in 2015.
   The price per pencil that the agency paid in 2017 was _____ cents.
   A. $6 1/3$ B. $2/3$ C. 7 D. $7 3/4$

   1.____

2. A stenographer spent her 35 hour work week on taking dictation, transcribing the dictate material, and filing.
   If she spent 20% of the work week on taking dictation and ½ of the remaining time on transcribing the dictated material, the number of hours of the work week that she spent on filing was
   A. 7 B. 10.5 C. 14 D. 17.4

   2.____

3. A typist typed eight pages in two hours.
   If she typed an average of 50 lines per page and an average of 12 words per line, what was her typing speed, in words per minute?
   A. 40 B. 50 C. 60 D. 80

   3.____

4. The daily compensation to be paid to each consultant hired in a certain agency is computed by dividing his professional earnings in the previous year by 250. The maximum daily compensation they can receive is $200 each. Four consultants who were hired to work on a special project had the following professional earnings in the previous year: $37,500, $144,000, $46,500, and $61,100.
   What will be the TOTAL daily cost to the agency for these four consultants?
   A. $932 B. $824 C. $736 D. $712

   4.____

5. In a typing and stenographic pool consisting of 30 employees, 2/5 of them are typists, 1/3 of them are senior typists and senior stenographers, and the rest are stenographers.
   If there are 5 more stenographers than senior stenographers, how many senior stenographers are in the typing and stenographic pool?
   A. 3 B. 5 C. 8 D. 10

   5.____

161

6. There are 3,330 copies of a three-page report to be collated. One clerk starts collating at 9:00 A.M. and is joined 15 minutes later by two other clerks. It takes 15 minutes for each of these clerks to collate 90 copies of the report. At what time should the job be completed if all three clerks continue working at the same rate without breaks?
   A. 12:00 Noon   B. 12:15 P.M.   C. 1:00 P.M.   D. 1:15 P.M.

6.____

7. By the end of last year, membership in the blood credit program in a certain agency had increased from the year before by 500, bringing the total to 2,500. If the membership increased by the same percentage this year, the TOTAL number of members in the blood credit program for this agency by the end of this year should be
   A. 2,625   B. 3,000   C. 3,125   D. 3,250

7.____

8. During this year, an agency suggestion program put into practice suggestions from 24 employee, thereby saving the agency 40 times the amount of money it paid in awards.
   If $1/3$ of the employees were awarded $50 each, ½ of the employees were awarded $25 each, and the rest were awarded $10 each, how much money did the agency save by using the suggestions?
   A. $18,760   B. $29,600   C. $32,400   D. $46,740

8.____

9. A senior stenographer earned $20,100 a year and had 4.5% state tax withheld for the year.
   If she was paid every two weeks, the amount of state tax that was taken out of each of her paychecks, based on a 52-week year, was MOST NEARLY
   A. $31.38   B. $32.49   C. $34.77   D. $36.99

9.____

10. Two stenographers have been assigned to address 750 envelopes. One stenographer addresses twice as many envelopes per hour as the other stenographer.
    If it takes five hours for them to complete the job, the rate of the slower stenographer is _____ envelopes per hour.
    A. 35   B. 50   C. 75   D. 100

10.____

11. Suppose that the postage rate for mailing single copies of a magazine to persons not included on a subscription list is 18 cents for the first two ounces of the single copy and 3 cents for each additional ounce.
    Of 19 copies of a magazine, each of which weighs eleven ounces, are mailed to 19 different people, the TOTAL postage cost of these magazines is
    A. $3.42   B. $3.99   C. $6.18   D. $8.55

11.____

12. A senior stenographer spends about 40 hours a month taking dictation. Of that time, 44% is spent taking minutes of meetings, 38% if spent taking dictation of lengthy reports, and the rest of the time is spent taking dictation of letters and memoranda.
    How much more time is spent taking minutes of meetings than n taking dictation of letters and memoranda? 10 hours _____ minutes.
    A. 6   B. 16   C. 24   D. 40

12.____

3 (#1)

13. In one week, a stenographer typed 65 letter. Forty letters had 4 copies on colored paper. The rest had 3 copies on colored paper.
    If the stenographer had 50 sheets of colored paper on hand at the beginning of the week when she started typing the letters, how many sheets of colored paper did she have left at the end of the week?
    A. 190	B. 235	C. 265	D. 305

    13.____

14. An agency is planning to microfilm letters and other correspondence of the last five years. The number of letter-size documents that can be photographed on a 100-foot roll of microfilm is 2,995. The agency estimates that it will need 240 feet of microfilm to do all the pages of all of the letters.
    How many pages of letter-size documents can be photographed on this microfilm?
    A. 5,990	B. 6,785	C. 7,188	D. 7,985

    14.____

15. In an agency, ²/₃ of the total number of female stenographers and ½ of the total number of male stenographers attended a general staff meeting.
    If there are a total of 56 stenographers in the agency and 25% of them are male, the number of female stenographers who attended the general staff meeting is
    A. 14	B. 28	C. 36	D. 42

    15.____

16. A worker is currently earning $17,140 a year and pays $350 a month for rent. He expects to get a raise that will enable him to move into an apartment where his rent will be 25% of his new yearly salary.
    If this new apartment is going to cost him $390 a month, what is the TOTAL amount of raise that he expects to get?
    A. $480	B. $980	C. $1,580	D. $1,840

    16.____

17. The tops of five desks in an office are to be covered with a scratch-resistant material. Each desk top measures 60 inches by 36 inches.
    How many square feet of material will be needed for the five desk tops?
    A. 15	B. 75	C. 96	D. 180

    17.____

18. Three grades of bond paper are used in a central transcribing unit. The cost per ream of paper is $1.90 for Grade A, $1.70 for Grade B, and $1.60 for Grade C.
    If the central transcribing unit used 6 reams of Grade A paper, 14 reams of Grade B paper, and 20 reams of Grade C paper, the AVERAGE cost, per ream, of the bond paper used by this unit is between
    A. $1.62 and $1.66	B. $1.66 and $1.70
    C. $1.70 and $1.74	D. $1.73 and $1.80

    18.____

19. The Complaint Bureau of a city agency is composed of an investigation unit, a clerical unit, and a central transcribing unit. The sum of $264,000 has been appropriated for the operation of this bureau. Of this sum, $170,000 is to be allotted to the clerical unit.

    19.____

Of this bureau's total appropriation, the percentage that is left for the central transcribing unit is MOST NEARLY _____ if 41,200 is allotted for investigations.
A. 20%   B. 30%   C. 40%   D. 50%

20. Three typists were assigned to address a total of 2,655 postcards. Typist A addressed postcards at the rate of 170 per hour. Typist B addressed the postcards at the rate of 150 per hour. Typist C's rate is not known. After the three typists had addressed postcards for three and a half hours, Typist C was taken off this assignment. It was necessary for Typist A and Typist B to work two and a half hours more to complete this assignment. The rate per hour at which Typist C addressed the postcards was
   A. less than 150
   B. between 150 and 170
   C. more than 170 but less than 200
   D. more than 200

21. In 2015, a city agency bought 12,000 envelopes at $4.00 per hundred. In 2016, the price of envelopes purchased was 40 percent higher than the 2010 price, but only 60 percent as many envelopes were bought.
   The total cost of the envelopes purchased in 2016 was MOST NEARLY
   A. $250   B. $320   C. $400   D. $480

22. A stenographer has been assigned to place entries on 500 forms. She places entries on 25 forms by the end of half an hour, when she is joined by another stenographer. The second stenographer places entries at the rate of 45 an hour.
   Assuming both stenographers continue to work at their respective rates of speed, the TOTAL number of hours required to carry out the entire assignment is
   A. 5   B. 54   C. 64   D. 7

23. On Monday, a stenographer took dictation without interruption for 1½ hours and transcribed all the dictated material in 3½ hours. On Tuesday, she took dictation uninterruptedly for 1¾ hours and transcribed all the material in 3¾ hours. On Wednesday, she took dictation without interruption for 2¼ hours and transcribed all the material in 4½ hours.
   If she took dictation at the average rate of 90 words per minute during these three days, then her average transcription rate, in words per minute, for the same three days was MOST NEARLY
   A. 36   B. 41   C. 54   D. 58

24. In a division of clerks and stenographers, 15 people are currently employed, 20% of whom are stenographers.
   If management plans are to maintain the current number of stenographers, but to increase the clerical staff to the point where 12% of the total staff are stenographers, what is the MAXIMUM number of additional clerks that should be hired to meet these plans?
   A. 3   B. 8   C. 10   D. 12

25. In the first quarter of the year, a certain operator sent out 230 quarterly reports. 25.____
In the second quarter of that year, he sent out 310 quarterly reports.
The percent increase in the number of quarterly reports he sent out in the second quarter of the year compared to the first quarter of the year is MOST NEARLY
   A. 26%   B. 29%   C. 35%   D. 39%

KEY (CORRECT ANSWERS)

1.	C	11.	D
2.	C	12.	C
3.	A	13.	C
4.	C	14.	C
5.	A	15.	B
6.	B	16.	C
7.	C	17.	B
8.	B	18.	B
9.	C	19.	A
10.	B	20.	D

21. C
22. B
23. B
24. C
25. C

SOLUTIONS TO PROBLEMS

1. $180 ÷ .03 = 6000$ pencils bought. In 2017, the price per pencil = $420/6000 = .07 = 7$ cents

2. Number of hours on filing = $35 - (.20)(35) \cdot (½)(28) = 14$

3. Eight pages contain $(8)(50)(12) = 4800$ words. She thus typed 4800 words in 120 minutes = 40 words per minute

4. $37,500 ÷ 250 = $150; $144,000 ÷ 250 = $576; $46,500 ÷ 250 = $186; $61,100 ÷ 250 = $244.40. Since $200 = maximum compensation for any single consultant, total compensation = $150 + $200 + $186 + $200 = $736

5. Number of typists = $(2/5)(30) = 12$, number of senior typists and senior stenographers = $(^1/_3)(30) = 10$, number of stenographers = $30 - 12 - 10 = 8$. Finally, number of senior stenographers = $8 - 5 = 3$

6. At 9:15 A.M., 90 copies have been collated. The remaining 3,240 copies are being collated at the rate of $(3)(90) = 270$ every 15 minutes = 1080 per hour. Since $3240 ÷ 1080 = 3$ hours, the clerks will finish at 9:15 A.M. + 3 hours = 12:15 P.M.

7. During the last year, the membership increased from 2000 to 2500, which represents a $(500/2000)(100) = 25\%$ increase. A 25% increase during this year means the membership = $(2500)(1.25) = 3125$

8. Total awards = $(^1/_3)(24)($50) + (½)(24)($25) + (^1/_6)(24)($10) = 740. Thus, the savings = $(40)($740) = $29,600$

9. Her pay for 2 weeks = $20,100 ÷ 26 ≈ 773.08. Thus, her state tax for 2 weeks = $($773.08)(.045) ≈ 34.79. (Nearest correct answer is $34.77 in four selections.)

10. $750 ÷ 5$ hours = 150 envelopes per hour for the 2 stenographers combined. Let x = number of envelopes addressed by the slower stenographer. Then, $x + 2x = 150$. Solving, = 50

11. Total cost = $(19)[.18+(.03)(9)] = 8.55

12. $(.44)(40) - (.18)(40) = 10.4$ hours = 10 hrs. 24 min.

13. $500 - (40)(4) - (25)(3) = 265$

14. $2995 ÷ 100 = 29.95$ documents per foot of microfilm roll. Then, $(29.95)(240 ft) = 7188$ documents

15. There are $(.75)(56) = 42$ female stenographers. Then, $(^2/_3)(42) = 28$ of them attended the meeting

7 (#1)

16. ($390)(12) = $4679 new rent per year. Then, ($4680)(4) = $18,720 = his new yearly salary. His raise = $18,720 - $17,140 = $1580

17. Number of sq. ft. = (5)(60)(36) ÷ 144 = 75

18. Average cost per ream = [(1.90)(6) + ($1.70)(14) + ($1.60)(20)] /40 = $1.68, which is between $1.66 and $1.77

19. $264,000 - $170,000 - $41,200 = 52,800 = 20%

20. Let x = typist C's rate. Since Typists A and B each worked 6 hrs., while Typist C worked only 3.5 hours, we have (6)(170) + (6)(150) + 3.5x = 2655. Solving, x = 210, which is mre than 200

21. In 2016, the cost per hundred envelopes was ($4.00)(1.40) = $5.60 and (.60)(12,000) = 7200 envelopes were bought. Total cost in 2016 = (72)($5.60) = $403.20, or about $400

22. The first stenographer's rate is 50 forms per hour. After ½ hour, there are 500 – 25 = 475 forms to be done and the combined rate of the 2 stenographers is 95 forms per hr. Thus, total hours required = ½ + (475) ÷ (95) = 5½

23. Total time for dictation = 1¼ + 1¾ + 2¼ = 5¼ hrs. = 315 min. The number of words = (90)(315) = 28,350. The total transcription 3 time = 3¼ + 3¾ + 44 = 11½ hrs. = 690 min. Her average transcription rate = 28,350 ÷ 690 ≈ 41 words per min.

24. Currently, there are (.20)(15) = 3 stenographers, and thus 12 clerks. Let x = additional clerks. Then, $\frac{3}{3+12+x}$ = .12. This simplifies to 3 = (.12)(15+x). Solving, x = 10

25. Percent increase = $(\frac{80}{230})(100)$ ≈ 35%

TEST 2

DIRECTIONS: Each question or incomplete statement is followed by several suggested answers or completions. Select the one that BEST answers the question or completes the statement. *PRINT THE LETTER OF THE CORRECT ANSWER IN THE SPACE AT THE RIGHT.*

1. A school has 112 homeroom classes. There were 15 school days in February. The aggregate register of the school for the month of February was 52,920; the aggregate attendance was 43,860.
   The average class size, to the NEAREST tenth, is
   A. 35.3   B. 31.5   C. 29.2   D. 26.9

   1.____

2. As the school secretary in charge of supplies, you are asked to order the following items on a supplementary requisition for general supplies:
       5 gross of red pencils at $8.90 per dozen
       5,000 manila envelopes at $2.35 per C
       36 rulers at $187.20 per gross
       6 boxes of manila paper at $307.20 per carton (24 boxes to a carton)
       180 reams of composition paper at $27.80 per carton (20 reams to a carton)
   The TOTAL amount of the order is
   A. $957.20   B. $1,025.30   C. $916.80   D. $991.30

   2.____

3. In the high school to which you have been assigned as a school secretary, the annual allotment for general supplies, textbooks, repairs, etc. for the school year 2015-16 was $37,500. A special allotment of $10,000 was granted for textbooks ordered from the State Textbook List. The original requisition for general and vocational supplies amounted to $12,514.75; for science supplies, $6,287.75; for textbooks, including the special funds, $13,785.00; monies spent for equipment repairs and science perishables through December 31, 2015, $1,389.68.
   The balance in your supply allotment account on January 1, 2016 will be
   A. $14,913.00   B. $13,523.32   C. $17,308.32   D. $3,523.32

   3.____

4. The teacher of one of the sixth term typing classes in the high school to which you are assigned as a school secretary has agreed to have her students type attendance cards for the incoming students for the new schoolyear, commencing in September, as a work project. There are 24 students in the class; each student can complete 8 cards during a typing period. There will be 4,032 new students in September.
   The number of typing periods required to complete the task is
   A. 31   B. 21   C. 28   D. 24

   4.____

5. As a school secretary assigned to payroll duties, you are required to prepare the extra-curricular payroll report for the coaches teams in your high school. The rate of pay for these activities was increased on November 1 from $148 per session to $174.50 per session. The pay period which you are reporting is for the months of October, November, and December. Mr. Jones, the football coach, conducted 15 practice sessions in October, 20 in November, and 30 in December.

   5.____

His TOTAL gross pay on the December extra-curricular payroll report is
A. $10,547.50   B. $10,415.00   C. $10,945.00   D. $11,342.50

6. The comparative results on a uniform examination given in your school for the last three years follow:

	2014	2015	2016
Number Taking Test	501	496	485
Number Passing Test	441	437	436

The percentage of passing, to the nearest tenth of a percent, for the year in which the HIGHEST percent of students passed is
A. 89.3%   B. 88%   C. 89.9%   D. 90.3%

7. During his first seven terms in high school, a student compiled the following averages:

Term	Numbers of Majors Completed	Average
1	4	81.25%
2	4	83.75%
3	5	86.2%
4	5	85.8%
5	5	87.0%
6	5	83.4%
7	5	82.6%

In his eighth term, the student had the following final marks in major subjects: 90%, 95%, 80%, 90%, 85%. The student's average for all eight terms of high school, correct to the nearest tenth of a percent, is
A. 84.8%   B. 84.7%   C. 84.9%   D. 85.8%

8. A secretary is asked by her employer to order an office machine which lists at a price of $360, less trade discounts of 20% and 10%, terms 2/10, n/30. There is a delivery charge of $8 and an installation charge of $12.
If the machine is paid for in 10 days, the TOTAL cost of the machine will be
A. $264.80   B. $258.40   C. $266.96   D. $274.02

9. The school to which you have been assigned as school secretary has an annual allowance of 5,120 hours for all teacher aides. The principal decides to employ 5 teacher aides from 8:00 A.M. to 12:00 Noon, and 5 other teacher aides from 12:00 Noon to 4:00 P.M. daily for as many days as his allowance permits.
If a teacher aide earns $17.00 an hour, and he is present every day, his TOTAL earnings for the school year will be more than
A. $7,000 but less than $8,000   B. $8,000 but less than $9,000
C. $9,000 but less than $10,000   D. $10,000

3 (#2)

10. During examination week in a high school to which you have been assigned as school secretary, teachers are required to be in school at least 6 hours and 20 minutes daily although their arrival and departure times may vary each day. A teacher's time card that you have been asked to check shows the following entries for the week of June 17:

Date	Arrival	Departure
17	7:56 A.M.	2:18 P.M.
18	9:54 A.M.	4:22 P.M.
19	12:54 P.M.	7:03 P.M.
20	9:51 A.M.	4:15 P.M.
21	7:58 A.M.	2:11 P.M.

    During the week of June 17 to June 21, the teacher was in school for AT LEAST the minimum required time on _____ days.
    A. 2 of the 5   B. 3 of the 5   C. 4 of the 5   D. all 5

    10.____

11. As school secretary, you are asked to find the total of the following bill received in your school:
    750 yellow envelopes at $.22 per C
    2,400 white envelopes at $2.80 per M
    30 rulers at $5.04 per gross
    The TOTAL of the bill is
    A. $69.90   B $24.27   C. $18.87   D. $9.42

    11.____

12. A department in the school to which you have been assigned as school secretary has been given a textbook allowance of $5,50 for the school year. The department's textbook order is:
    75 books at $32.50 each
    45 books at $49.50 each
    25 books at $34.50 each
    The TOTAL of the department's order is _____ the allowance.
    A. $27.50 over   B. $27.50 under
    C. $72.50 under   D. $57.50 over

    12.____

13. The total receipts, including 5% city sales tax, for the G.O. store for the first week of school amounted to $489.09.
    The receipts from the G.O. store for the first week of school, excluding the 5% city sales tax, amounted to
    A. $465.89   B. $364.64   C. $464.63   D. $513.54

    13.____

14. Class sizes in the school to which you have been assigned as school secretary are as follows:

Number of Classes	Class Size
9	29
12	31
15	32
7	33
11	34

    14.____

The average class size in this school, correct to the nearest tenth, is
A. 30.8   B. 31.9   C. 31.8   D. 30.9

15. In 2013, the social security tax was 4.2% for the first $6,600 earned a year. In 2014, the social security tax was 4.4% on the first $6,600 earned a year. For a teacher aide earning $19,200 in 2013 and $20,400 in 2014, the increase in social security tax deduction in 2014 over 2013 was
A. $132.00   B. $13.20   C. $19.20   D. $20.40

15.____

16. A teacher aide earning $23,900 a year will incur automatic deductions of 3.90% for social security and .50% for Medicare, based on the first $6,600 a year earnings.
The TOTAL deduction for these two items will be
A. $274   B. $290.40   C. $525.80   D. $300.40

16.____

17. The school store turns in receipts totaling $131.25 to the school treasurer, including 5% which has been collected for sales tax.
The amount of money which the treasurer MUST set aside for sales tax is
A. $6.56   B. $6.25   C. $5.00   D. $5.25

17.____

18. One of the custodial assistants can wash all the windows in the main office in 3 hours. A second assistant can wash the windows in the main office in 2 hours.
If the two men work together, they should complete the task in _____ hour(s) _____ minutes.
A. 1; 0   B. 1.5; 0   C. 1; 12   D. 1; 15

18.____

19. A school secretary is requested by the principal to order an office machine which lists at a price of $120, less discounts of 10% and 5%.
The net price of the machine to the school will be
A. $100.50   B. $102.00   C. $102.60   D. $103.00

19.____

20. Five students are employed at school under a work-study program through which they are paid $10.00 an hour for work in school offices, but no student may earn more than $450 a month. Three days before the end of the month, you note that the student payroll totals $2,062.50.
The number of hours which each of the students may work during the remainder of the month is _____ hour(s).
A. 4   B. 2   C. 1   D. 3

20.____

21. You are asked to summarize expenditures made by the school within the budget allocation for the school year. You determine that the following expenditures have been made: educational supplies, $2,600; postage, $650; emergency repairs, $225; textbooks, $5,100; instructional equipment, $1,200. Since $10,680 has been allocated to the school, the following sum still remains available for office supplies.
A. $905   B. $1,005   C. $800   D. $755

21.____

22. In preparing the percentage of attendance for the period report, you note that the aggregate attendance is 57,585 and the aggregate register is 62,000.
   The percentage of attendance, to the nearest tenth of a percent, is
   A. 91.9%   B. 93.0%   C. 92.8%   D. 92.9%

22.____

23. You borrow $1,200 from your retirement fund which you must repay over a period of three years, with interest of $144, each payment to be divided equally among 36 total payments.
   The monthly deduction from your paycheck will be
   A. $37.33   B. $36.00   C. $33.00   D. $37.30

23.____

24. Tickets for a school dance are printed, starting with number 401 and ending with number 1650. They are to be sold for $7.50 each. The tickets remaining unsold should start with number 1569.
   The amount of cash which should be collected for the sale of tickets is
   A. $876.75   B. $937.50   C. $876.00   D. $875.25

24.____

25. Stage curtains are purchased by the school and delivered on October 3 under terms of 5/10, 2/30, net/60. The curtains are paid in full by a check for $522.50 on October 12.
   The invoice price was
   A. $533.16   B. $522.50   C. $540.00   D. $550.00

25.____

KEY (CORRECT ANSWERS)

1.	B		11.	D
2.	B		12.	A
3.	B		13.	A
4.	B		14.	C
5.	C		15.	B
6.	C		16.	B
7.	C		17.	B
8.	D		18.	C
9.	B		19.	C
10.	B		20.	D

21. A
22. D
23. A
24. C
25. D

SOLUTIONS TO PROBLEMS

1. Average class size = 52,920 ÷ 15 ÷ 112 = 31.5

2. Total amount = (5)(12)($8.90) + (50)($2.35) + (36)($187.20) ÷ 144 + (6)($307.20) ÷ 24 + (9)($27.80) = $1,025.30

3. Balance = $37,500 + $10,000 - $12,514.75 - $6,287.25 - $13,785 - $1,389.68 = $13,523.32

4. (24)(8) = 192 cards completed in one period. Then, 4032 ÷ 192 = 21 typing periods required

5. Total pay = (15)($148.00) + (20)($174.50) + (30)($174.50) = $10,945.00

6. The passing rates for 2014, 2015, and 2016 were 88.0%, 88.1%, and 89.9%, respectively. So, 89.9% was the highest

7. His 8th term average was 88.0%. His overall average for all 8 terms = [(4)(81.25%) + (4)(83.75%) + (5)(86.2%) + (5)(85.8%) + (5)(87.0%) + (5)(83.4%) + (5)(82.6%) + (5)(88.0%)] ÷ 38 = 84.9%

8. Total cost = ($360)(.80)(.90)(.98) + $8 + $12 ≈ $274.02 (Exact amount = $274.016)

9. 5120 ÷ 4 = 1280 teacher-days. Then, 1280 ÷ 20 = 128 days per teacher. A teacher's earnings for these 128 days = ($17.00)(4)(128) = $8,704, which is more than $8,000 but less than $9,000

10. The number of hours present on each of the 5 days listed was 6 hrs. 22 min., 6 hrs. 29 min., 6 hrs. 9 min., 6 hrs. 24 min., and 6 hrs. 13 min. On 3 days, he met the minimum time.

11. Total cost = (7.5)(.22) + (2.4)($2.80) + (30/144)(5.04) = $9.42

12. Textbook order = (75)($32.50) + (45)($49.50) + (25)($34.50) = $5,527.5, which is $27.50 over the allowance

13. Receipts without the tax = $489.09 ÷ 1.05 = $465.80

14. Average class size = [(9)(29) + (12)(31) + (7)(33) + (15)(32)] ÷ 54 ≈ 31.8

15. ($6,600)(.044-.042) = $13.20

16. ($6,600)(.039+.005) = $290.40

17. $131.25 = 1.05x, x = 125, $131.25 – 125.00 = 6.25

18. Let x = hours needed working together. Then, $(1/3)(x) + (1/2)(x) = 1$
    Simplifying, $2x + 3x = 6$. Solving, $x = 1\frac{1}{5}$ hrs. = 1 hr. 12 min.

19. Net price = 120 – 10% (12) = 108; 108 – 5% (5.40) = 102.60

20. ($225)(5) - $1031.25 = $93.75 remaining in the month. Since the 5 students earn $25 per hour combined, $93.75 ÷ $25 = 3.75, which must be rounded down to 3 hours

21. $10,680 - $2,600 - $650 - $225 - $5,100 - $1,200 = $905 for office supplies

22. 57,585 ÷ 62,000 ≈ .9288 ≈ 92.9%

23. Monthly deduction = $1344 ÷ 36 = $37.33. (Technically, 35 payments of $37.33 and 1 payment of $37.45)

24. (1569-401) = $876.00

25. The invoice price (which reflects the 5% discount) is $522.50 ÷ .95 = $550.00

TEST 3

DIRECTIONS: Each question or incomplete statement is followed by several suggested answers or completions. Select the one that BEST answers the question or completes the statement. *PRINT THE LETTER OF THE CORRECT ANSWER IN THE SPACE AT THE RIGHT.*

1. If an inch on an office layout drawing equals 4 feet of actual floor dimension, then a room which actually measures 9 feet by 14 feet is represented on the drawing by measurements equaling _____ inches × _____ inches.
    A. 2¼; 3½   B. 2½; 3½   C. 2¼; 3¼   D. 2½; 3¼

    1._____

2. A cooperative education intern works from 1:30 P.M. to 5 P.M. on Mondays, Wednesdays, and Fridays, and from 10 A.M. to 2:30 P.M. with no lunch hour on Tuesdays and Thursdays. He earns $13.50 an hour on this job. In addition, he has a Saturday job paying $16.00 an hour at which he works from 9 A.M. to 3 P.M. with a half hour off for lunch.
   The gross amount that the student earns each week is MOST NEARLY
    A. $321.90   B. $355.62   C. $364.02   D. $396.30

    2._____

3. Thirty-five percent of the College Discovery students who entered community college earned an associate degree. Of these students, 89% entered senior college, of which 67% went on to earn baccalaureate degrees.
   If there were 529 College Discovery students who entered community college, then the number of those who went on to finally receive a baccalaureate degree is MOST NEARLY
    A. 354   B. 315   C. 124   D. 110

    3._____

4. It takes 5 office assistants two days to type 125 letters. Each of the assistants works at an equal rate of speed.
   How many days will it take 10 office assistants to type 200 letters?
    A. 1   B. 1³/₅   C. 2   D. 2¹/₅

    4._____

5. The following are the grades and credits earned by Student X during the first two years in college.

Grade	Credits	Weight	Quality Points
A	10 ½	×4	
B	24	×3	
C	12	×2	
D	4 ½	×1	
F, FW	5	×0	

    5._____

   To compute an index number:
   I. Multiply the number of credits of each grade by the weight to get the number of quality points
   II. Add the credits
   III. Add the quality points
   IV. Divide the total quality point by the total credits and carry the division to two decimal places

On the basis of the given information, the index number for Student X is
A. 2.55　　B. 2.59　　C. 2.63　　D. 2.68

6. Typist X can type 20 forms per hour, and Typist Y can type 30 forms per hour. If there are 30 forms to be typed and both typists are put to work on the job, how son should they be expected to finish the work?
_____ minutes.
A. 32　　B. 34　　C. 36　　D. 38

7. Assume that there were 18 working days in February and that the six clerks in your unit had the following number of absences:

Clerk	Absences
F	3
G	2
H	8
I	1
J	0
K	5

The average percentage attendance for the six clerks in your unit in February was MOST NEARLY
A. 80%　　B. 82%　　C. 84%　　D. 86%

8. A certain employee is paid at the rate of $7.50 per hour, with time and a half for overtime. Hours in excess of 40 hours a week count as overtime. During the past week, the employee put in 48 working hours.
The employee's gross wages for the week are MOST NEARLY
A. $330　　B. $350　　C. $370　　D. $390

9. You are making a report on the number of inside and outside calls handled by a particular switchboard. Over a 15-day period, the total number of all inside and outside calls handled by the switchboard was 5,760. The average number of inside calls per day was 234. You cannot find one day's tally of outside calls, but the total number of outside calls for the other fourteen days was 2,065.
From this information, how many outside calls must have been reported on the missing tally?
A. 175　　B. 185　　C. 195　　D. 205

10. A floor plan has been prepared for a new building, drawn to a scale of ¾ inch = 1 foot. A certain area is drawn 1 and ½ feet long and 6 inches wide on the floor plan.
What are the ACTUAL dimensions of this area in the new building?
_____ feet long and _____ feet wide
A. 21; 8　　B. 24; 8　　C. 27; 9　　D. 30; 9

11. You are preparing a package of six books to mail to a professor who is on sabbatical. They weigh, respectively, 1 pound 11 ounces, 1 pound 6 ounces, 2 pounds 1 ounce, 2 pounds 2 ounces, 1 pound 7 ounces, and 1 pound 8 ounces. The packaging material weighs 6 ounces.
    The TOTAL weight of the package will be _____ pounds _____ ounces.
    A. 10; 3   B. 10; 9   C. 11; 5   D. 12; 5

    11._____

12. Part-time students are charged $70 per credit for courses at a particular college. In addition, they musts pay a $24.00 student activity fee if they take six credits or more and $14.00 lab fee for each laboratory course.
    If a person takes one 3-credit course and one 4-credit course and his 4-credit course is a laboratory course, the TOTAL cost to him will be
    A. $504   B. $528   C. $542   D. $552

    12._____

13. The graduating course of a certain community college consisted of 378 majors in secretarial science, 265 majors in engineering science, 57 majors in nursing, 513 majors in accounting, and 865 majors in liberal arts.
    The percent of students who major in liberal arts at this college was MOST NEARLY
    A. 24.0%   B. 41.6%   C. 52.3%   D. 71.6%

    13._____

14. Donald Smith earns $12.80 an hour for forty hours a week, with time and a half for all hours over forty. Last week, his total earnings amounted to $627.20.
    He worked _____ hours.
    A. 46   B. 47   C. 48   D. 49

    14._____

15. Mr. Jones desires to sell an article costing $28 at a gross profit of 30% of the selling price, and to allow a trade discount of 20% of the list price.
    The list price of the article should be
    A. $43.68   B. $45.50   C. $48.00   D. $50.00

    15._____

16. The gauge of an oil storage tank in an elementary school indicates 1/5 full. After a truck delivers 945 gallons of oil, the gauge indicates 4/5 full.
    The capacity of the tank is _____ gallons.
    A. 1,260   B. 1,575   C. 1,625   D. 1,890

    16._____

17. An invoice dated April 3, terms 3/10, 2/30, net/60, was paid in full with a check for $787.92 on May 1.
    The amount of the invoice was
    A. $772.16   B. $787.92   C. $804.00   D. $812.29

    17._____

18. Two pipes supply the water for the swimming pool at Blenheim High School. One pipe can fill the pool in 9 hours. The second pipe can fill the pool in 6 hours.
    If both pipes were opened simultaneously, the pool could be filled in _____ hours _____ minutes.
    A. 3; 36   B. 4; 30   C. 5; 15   D. 7; 30

    18._____

4 (#3)

19. John's father spent $24,000, which was one-fourth of his savings. He bought 19.____
    a car with three-eighths of the remainder of his savings.
    His bank balance now amounts to
       A. $30,000   B. $32,000   C. $45,000   D. $50,000

20. A clock that loses 4 minutes every 24 hours was set at 6 A.M. on October 1 20.____
    What time was indicated by the clock when the CORRECT time was 12:00
    Noon on October 6th?
       A. 11:36   B. 11:38   C. $11:39   D. 11:40

21. Unit S's production fluctuated substantially from one year to another. In 21.____
    2009, Unit s's production was 100% greater than in 2008. In 2010, production
    decreased by 25% from 2009. In 2011, Unit S's production was 10% greater
    than in 2010.
    On the basis of this information, it is CORRECT to conclude that Unit S's
    production in 2011 exceeded Unit S's production in 2008 by
       A. 65%   B. 85%   C. 95%   D. 135%

22. Agency X is moving into a new building. It has 1,500 employees presently on 22.____
    its staff and does not contemplate much variance from this level. The new
    building contains 100 available offices, each with a maximum capacity of 30
    employees. It has been decided that only 2/3 of the maximum capacity of each
    office will be utilized.
    The TOTAL number of office that will be occupied by Agency X is
       A. 30   B. 65   C. 75   D. 90

23. One typist completes a form letter every 5 minutes and another typist 23.____
    completes one every 6 minutes.
    If the two typists start together, how many minutes later will they again start
    typing new letters simultaneously and how many letters will they have
    completed by that time?
       A. 11; 30   B. 12; 24   C. 24; 12   D. 30; 1

24. During one week, a machine operator produces 10 fewer pages per hour 24.____
    of work than he usually does.
    If it ordinarily takes him six hours to produce a 300-page report, how many hour
    LONGER will that same 300-page report take him during the week when he
    produces more slowly?
       A. 1½   B. 1⅔   C. 2   D. 2¾

25. A study reveals that Miss Brown files N cards in M hours, and Miss Smith 25.____
    files the same number of cards in T hours.
    If the two employees work together, the number of hours it will take them to file
    N cards is
       A. $\dfrac{N}{\dfrac{N}{M}+\dfrac{N}{N}}$ B. $\dfrac{N}{T+M}+\dfrac{2N}{MT}$ C. $N(\dfrac{M}{N}+\dfrac{N}{T})$ D. $\dfrac{N}{NT+MN}$

KEY (CORRECT ANSWERS)

1.	A	11.	B
2.	B	12.	B
3.	D	13.	B
4.	B	14.	A
5.	A	15.	D
6.	C	16.	B
7.	B	17.	C
8.	D	18.	A
9.	B	19.	C
10.	B	20.	C

21.	A
22.	C
23.	D
24.	A
25.	A

SOLUTIONS TO PROBLEMS

1. $9/4 = 2¼"$ and $14/4 = 3½"$

2. Gross amount = $(3)($6.75)(3.5) + (2)($6.75)(4.5) + ($8.00)(5.5) = 174.624, which is closest to selection B ($177.81)

3. $(529)(.35)(.89)(.67) \approx 110$

4. 10 worker-days are needed to type 125 letters, so $(200)(10) \div 125 = 16$ worker-days are needed to type 200 letters. Finally, $16 \div 10$ workers = 1 3/5 days

5. Index number = $[(14)(10½) + (3)(24) + (2)(12) + (1)(4½) + (0)(5)] \div 56 \approx 2.54$

6. Typist X could do 30 forms in $30/20 = 1½$ hours. Let x = number of hour needed when working together with Typist Y.
   Then, $(\frac{1}{1\frac{1}{2}})(x) + (\frac{1}{1})x = 1$. Simplifying, $2x + 3x = 3$, so $x = \frac{3}{5}$ hr. = 36 min.

7. $(3+2+8+1+0+5) \div 6 = 3.1\overline{6}$. Then, $18 - 3.\overline{6} = 14.8\overline{3}$.

   Finally, $14.8\overline{3} \div 18 \approx 82\%$

8. Wages = $($7.50)(40) + ($11.25)(8) = 390

9. $(234)(15) = 3510$ inside calls. Then, $5760 - 3510 = 2259$ outside calls. Finally, $2250 - 2065 = 185$ outside calls on the missing day.

10. $18 \div ¾ - 24$ feet long and $6 \div ¾ = 8$ feet wide

11. Total weight = 1 lb. 11 oz. + 1 lb. 6 oz. + 2 lbs. 1 oz. + 2 lbs. 2 oz. + 1 lb. 7 oz. + 1 lb. 8 oz. + 6 oz = 8 lbs. 41 oz. 10 lbs. 9 oz.

12. Total cost = $($70)(7) + $24 + $14 = 528

13. $865 \div 2078 \approx 41.6\%$ liberal arts majors

14. $($12.80)(40) = 512, so he made $627.20 - $512 = 115.20 in overtime. His overtime rate = $($12.80)(1.5) = 19.20 per hour. Thus, he worked $115.20 \div $19.20 = 6$ overtime hours. Total hours worked = 46

15. Let x = list price. Selling price = .80x. Then, $.80x - (.30)(.80x) = 28. Simplifying, $.56x = 28. Solving, $x = 50.00

7 (#3)

16. 945 gallons represents $\frac{4}{5} \cdot \frac{1}{5} = \frac{3}{5}$ of the tank's capacity.

    Then, the capacity = $945 \div \frac{3}{5}$ = 1575 gallons

17. $787.92 ÷ .98 = $804.00

18. Let x = number of required hours. Then, (1/9)(x) + (1/6)(x) = 1
    Simplifying, 2x + 3x = 18. Solving, x = 3.6 hours = 3 hours 36 minutes

19. Bank balance = $96,000 - $24,000 – (3/8)($72,000) = $45,000

20. From Oct. 1, 6 A.M. to Oct. 6, Noon = 5½ days. The clock would show a loss of (4 min.)(5½) = 21 min. Thus, the clock's time would incorrectly) show 12:00 Noon – 21 min. = 11:39 A.M.

21. 2008 = x, 2009 = 200x, 2010 = 150x, 2011 = 165x
    65% more

22. (2/3)(30) = 20 employees in each office. Then, 1500 ÷ 20 = 75 offices

23. After 30 minutes, the typists will have finished a total of 6 + 5 = 11 letters

24. When he works more slowly, he will only produce 300 – (6)(10) = 240 pages in 6 hrs. His new slower rate is 40 pages per hour, so he will need 60/40 = 1½ more hours to do the remaining 60 pages.

25. Let x = required hours. Then $(\frac{1}{M})(x) + (\frac{1}{10})(x) = 1$.

    Simplifying, x(T+M) = MT. Solving, x = MT/(T+M)

    Note: The N value is immaterial. Also, choice A reduces to MT/(T+M)

SUPERVISION, ADMINISTRATION, MANAGEMENT AND ORGANIZATION
EXAMINATION SECTION
TEST 1

DIRECTIONS: Each question or incomplete statement is followed by several suggested answers or completions. Select the one that BEST answers the question or completes the statement. *PRINT THE LETTER OF THE CORRECT ANSWER IN THE SPACE AT THE RIGHT.*

1. The one of the following situations in which you as a supervisor of a group of clerks would probably be able to function MOST effectively from the viewpoint of departmental efficiency is where you are responsible DIRECTLY to
   A. a single supervisor having sole jurisdiction over you
   B. two or three supervisors having coordinate jurisdiction over you
   C. four or five supervisors having coordinate jurisdiction over you
   D. all individuals of higher rank than you in the department

2. Suppose that it is necessary to order one of the clerks under your supervision to stay overtime a few hours one evening. The work to be done is not especially difficult. It is the custom in your office to make such assignments by rotation. The particular clerk whose turn it is to work overtime requests to be excused that evening, but offers to work the next time that overtime is necessary. Hitherto, this clerk has always been very cooperative.
   Of the following, the BEST action for you to take is to
   A. grant the clerk's request, but require her to work overtime two additional nights to compensate for this concession
   B. inform the clerk that you are compelled to refuse any request for special consideration
   C. grant the clerk's request if another clerk is willing to substitute for her
   D. refuse the clerk's request outright because granting her request may encourage her to evade other responsibilities

3. When asked to comment upon the efficiency of Miss Jones, a clerk, her supervisor said, "Since she rarely makes an error, I consider her very efficient."
   Of the following, the MOST valid assumption underlying this supervisor's comment is that
   A. speed and accuracy should be considered separately in evaluating a clerk's efficiency
   B. the most accurate clerks are not necessarily the most efficient
   C. accuracy and competency are directly related
   D. accuracy is largely dependent upon the intelligence of a clerk

1.____

2.____

3.____

4. The one of the following which is the MOST accurate statement of one of the functions of a supervisor is to
   A. select scientifically the person best fitted for the specific job to be done
   B. train the clerks assigned to you in the best methods of doing the work of your office
   C. fit the job to be done to the clerks who are available
   D. assign a clerk only to those tasks for which she has the necessary experience

5. Assume that you, an experienced supervisor, are given a newly appointed clerk to assist you in performing a certain task. The new clerk presents a method of doing the task which is different from your method but which is obviously better and easy to adopt.
   Of the following you, the supervisor, should
   A. take the suggestion and try it out, even though it was offered by someone less experienced
   B. reject the idea, even though it appears an improvement, as it very likely would not work out
   C. send the new clerk away and get someone else to assist who will be more in accord with your ideas
   D. report him to the head of the office and ask that the new clerk be instructed to do things your way

6. As a supervisor, you should realize that the one of the following general abilities of a junior clerk which is probably LEAST susceptible to improvement by practice and training is
   A. intelligence
   B. speed of typing
   C. knowledge of office procedures
   D. accuracy of filing

7. As a supervisor, when training an employee, you should NOT
   A. correct errors as he makes them
   B. give him too much material to absorb at one time
   C. have him try the operation until he can do it perfectly
   D. treat any foolish question seriously

8. If a supervisor cannot check readily all the work in her unit, she should
   A. hold up the work until she can personally check it
   B. refuse to take additional work
   C. work overtime until she can personally finish it
   D. delegate part of the work to a qualified subordinate

9. The one of the following over which a unit supervisor has the LEAST control is
   A. the quality of the work done in his unit
   B. the nature of the work handled in his unit
   C. the morale of workers in his unit
   D. increasing efficiency of his unit

10. Suppose that you have received a note from an important official in your department commending the work of a unit of clerks under your supervision. Of the following, the BEST action for you to take is to
    A. withhold the note for possible use at a time when the morale of the unit appears to be declining
    B. show the note only to the better members of your staff as a reward for their good work
    C. show the note only to the poorer members of your staff as a stimulus for better work
    D. post the note conspicuously so that it can be seen by all members of your staff

11. If you find that one of your subordinates is becoming apathetic towards his work, you should
    A. prefer charges against him
    B. change the type of work
    C. request his transfer
    D. advise him to take a medical examination to check his health

12. Suppose that a new clerk has been assigned to the unit which you supervise. To give this clerk a brief picture of the functioning of your unit in the entire department would be
    A. *commendable*, because she will probably be able to perform her work with more understanding
    B. *undesirable*, because such action will probably serve only to confuse her
    C. *commendable*, because, if transferred, she would probably be able to work efficiently without additional training
    D. *undesirable*, because in-service training has been demonstrated to be less efficient than on-the-job training

13. Written instructions to a subordinate are of value because they
    A. can be kept up-to-date
    B. encourage initiative
    C. make a job seem easier
    D. are an aid in training

14. Suppose that you have assigned a task to a clerk under your supervision and have given appropriate instructions. After a reasonable period, you check her work and find that one specific aspect of her work is consistently incorrect. Of the following, the BEST action for you to take is to
    A. determine whether the clerk has correctly understood instructions concerning the aspect of the work not being done correctly
    B. assign the task to a more competent clerk
    C. wait for the clerk to commit a more flagrant error before taking up the matter with her
    D. indicate to the clerk that you are dissatisfied with her work and wait to see whether she is sufficiently intelligent to correct her own mistakes

15. If you wanted to check on the accuracy of the filing in your unit, you would   15._____
    A. check all the files thoroughly at regular intervals
    B. watch the clerks while they are filing
    C. glance through filed papers at random
    D. inspect thoroughly a small section of the files selected at random

16. In making job assignments to his subordinates, a supervisor should follow   16._____
    the principle that each individual generally is capable of
    A. performing one type of work well and less capable of performing other types well
    B. learning to perform a wide variety of different types of work
    C. performing best the type of work in which he has had least experience
    D. learning to perform any type of work in which he is given training

17. Of the following, the information that is generally considered MOST essential   17._____
    in a departmental organization survey chart is the
    A. detailed operations of the department
    B. lines of authority
    C. relations of the department to other departments
    D. names of the employees of the department

18. Suppose you are the supervisor in charge of a large unit in which all of the   18._____
    clerical staff perform similar tasks.
    In evaluating the relative accuracy of the clerks, the clerk who should be considered to be the LEAST accurate is the one
    A. whose errors result in the greatest financial loss
    B. whose errors cost the most to locate
    C. who makes the greatest percentage of errors in his work
    D. who makes the greatest number of errors in the unit

19. Aside from requirements imposed by authority, the frequency with which   19._____
    reports are submitted or the length of the interval which they cover should depend PRINCIPALLY on the
    A. availability of the data to be included in the reports
    B. amount of time required to prepare the reports
    C. extent of the variations in the data with the passage of time
    D. degree of comprehensiveness required in the reports

20. A serious error has been discovered by a critical superior in work carried on   20._____
    under your supervision.
    It is BEST to explain the situation and prevent its recurrence by
    A. claiming that you are not responsible because you do not check the work personally
    B. accepting the complaint and reporting the name of the employee responsible for the error
    C. assuring him that you hope it will not occur again
    D. assuring him that you will find out how it occurred, so that you can have the work checked with greater care in the future

21. A serious procedural problem develops in your office.
    In your solution of this problem, the very FIRST step to take is to
    A. select the personnel to help you
    B. analyze your problem
    C. devise the one best method of research
    D. develop an outline of your report

22. Your office staff consists of eight clerks, stenographers, and typists, cramped in a long narrow room. The room is very difficult to ventilate properly, and, as in so many other offices, the disagreement over the method of ventilation is marked. Two cliques are developing and the friction is carrying over into the work of the office.
    Of the following, the BEST way to proceed is to
    A. call your staff together, have the matter fully discussed giving each person an opportunity to be heard, and put the matter to a vote; then enforce the method of ventilation which has the most votes
    B. call your staff together and have the matter fully discussed. If a compromise arrangement is agreed upon, put it into effect. Otherwise, on the basis of all the facts at your disposal, make a decision as to how best to ventilate the room and enforce your decision
    C. speak to the employees individually, make a decision as to how to ventilate the room, and then enforce your decision
    D. study the layout of the office, make a decision as to how best to ventilate the room, and then enforce your decision

23. An organization consisting of six levels of authority, where eight persons are assigned to each supervisor on each level, would consist of APPROXIMATELY _____ persons.
    A. 50 B. 500 C. 5,000 D. 50,000

24. The one of the following which is considered by political scientists to be a GOOD principle of municipal government is
    A. concentration of authority and responsibility
    B. the long ballot
    C. low salaries and a narrow range in salaries
    D. short terms for elected city officials

25. Of the following, the statement concerning the organization of a department which is TRUE is:
    A. In general, no one employee should have active and constant supervision over more than ten persons.
    B. It is basically unwise to have a supervisor with only three subordinates.
    C. It is desirable that there be no personal contact between the rank and file employee and the supervisor once removed from him.
    D. There should be no more than four levels of authority between the top administrative office in a department and the rank and file employees.

26. Assuming that Dictaphones are not available, of the following, the situation in which it would be MOST desirable to establish a central stenographic unit is one in which the unit would serve
    A. ten correspondence clerks assigned to full-time positions answering correspondence of a large government department
    B. seven members of a government commission heading a large department
    C. seven heads of bureaus in a government department consisting of 250 employees
    D. fifty investigators in a large department

27. You are assigned to review the procedures in an office in order to recommend improvements to the commissioner directly. You go into an office performing seen routine operations in the processing of one type of office form.
    The question you should FIRST ask yourself in your study of any one of these operations is:
    A. Can it be simplified?
    B. Is it necessary?
    C. Is it performed in proper order or should its position in the procedure be changed?
    D. Is the equipment for doing it satisfactory?

28. You are assigned in charge of a clerical bureau performing a single operation. All five of your subordinates do exactly the same work. A fine spirit of cooperation has developed and the employees help each other and pool their completed work so that the work of any one employee is indistinguishable. Your office is very busy and all five clerks are doing a full day's work. However, reports come back to you from other offices that they are finding as much as 1% error in the work of your bureau. This is too high a percentage of error.
    Of the following, the BEST procedure for you to follow is to
    A. check all the work yourself
    B. have a sample of the work of each clerk checked by another clerk
    C. have all work done in your office checked by one of your clerks
    D. identify the work of each clerk in some way

29. You are put in charge of a small office. In order to cover the office during the lunch hour, you assign Employee A to remain in the office between the hours of 12 and 1 P.M. On your return to the office at 12:25 P.M., you note that no one is in the office and that the phone is ringing. You are forced to postpone your 12:30 P.M. luncheon appointment, and to remain in the office until 12:50 P.M. when Employee A returns to the office.
    The BEST of the following actions is:
    A. Ask Employee why he left the office
    B. Bring charges against Employee A for insubordination and neglect of duty
    C. Ignore the matter in your conversation with Employee A so as not to embarrass him
    D. Make a note to rate Employee A low on his service rating

30. You are assigned in charge of a large division. It had been the practice in that division for the employees to slip out for breakfast about 10:00 A.M. You had been successful in stopping this practice and for one week no one had gone out for breakfast. One day a stenographer comes over to you at 10:30 A.M. appearing to be ill. She states that she doesn't feel well and that she would like to go out for a cup of tea. She asks your permission to leave the office for a few minutes.
You should
    A. telephone and have a cup of tea delivered to her
    B. permit her to go out
    C. refuse her permission to go out inasmuch as this would be setting a bad example
    D. tell her she can leave for an early lunch hour

31. The following four remarks from a supervisor to a subordinate deal with different situations. One remark, however, implies a basically POOR supervisory practice.
Select this remark as your answer.
    A. "I've called the staff together primarily because I am displeased with the work which one of you is doing. John, don't you think you should be ashamed that you are spoiling the good work of the office?"
    B. "James, you have been with us for six months now. In general, I'm satisfied with your work. However, don't you think you could be more neat in your appearance? I also want you to try to be more accurate in your work."
    C. "Joe, when I assigned this job to you, I did it because it requires special care and I think you're one of our best men in this type of work, but here is a slip-up you've made that we should be especially careful to watch out for in the future."
    D. "Tim, first I'd like to tell you that, effective tomorrow, you are to be my assistant and will receive an increase in salary. Although I recommended you for this position because I felt that you are the best man for the job, there are some things about your work which could stand a bit of improvement. For instance, your manner with regard to visitors is not so polite as it could be."

32. Of the following, the BEST type of floor surface for an office is
    A. concrete   B. hardwood   C. linoleum   D. parquet

33. The GENERALLY accepted unit for the measurement of illumination at a desk or work bench is the
    A. ampere   B. foot-candle   C. volt   D. watt

34. The one of the following who is MOST closely allied with "scientific management" is
    A. Mosher   B. Probst   C. Taylor   D. White

35. Eliminating slack in work assignments is
    A. speed-up
    B. time study
    C. motion study
    D. efficient management

36. "Time studies" examine and measure
    A. past performance
    B. present performance
    C. long-run effect
    D. influence of change

37. The maximum number of subordinates who can be effectively supervised by one supervisor is BEST considered as
    A. determined by the law of "span of control"
    B. determined by the law of "span of attention"
    C. determined by the type of work supervised
    D. fixed at not more than six

38. In the theory and practice of public administration, the one of the following which is LEAST generally regarded as a staff function is
    A. budgeting
    B. firefighting
    C. purchasing
    D. research and information

39. Suppose you are part of an administrative structure in which the executive head has regularly reporting directly to him seventeen subordinates. To some of the subordinates there regularly report directly three employees, to others four employees, and to the remaining subordinates five employees.
    Called upon to make a suggestion concerning this organization, you would question FIRST the desirability of
    A. so large a variation among the number of employees regularly reporting directly to subordinates
    B. having so large a number of subordinates regularly reporting directly to the administrative head
    C. so small a variation among the number of employees regularly reporting directly to subordinates
    D. the hierarchical arrangement

40. Administration is the center but not necessarily the source of all ideas for procedural improvement.
    The MOST significant implication that this principle bears for the administrative officer is that
    A. before procedural improvements are introduced, they should be approved by a majority of the staff
    B. it is the unique function of the administrative officer to derive and introduce procedural improvements
    C. the administrative office should derive ideas and suggestions for procedural improvement from all possible sources, introducing any that promise to be effective
    D. the administrative officer should view employee grievances as the chief source of procedural improvements

41. The merit system should not end with the appointment of a candidate. In any worthy public service system there should be no dead-end jobs. If the best citizen is to be attracted to public service, there must be provided encouragement and incentive to enable such a career employee to progress in the service.
The one of the following which is the MOST accurate statement on the basis of the above statement is that
    A. merit system selection has replaced political appointment in many governmental units
    B. lack of opportunities for advancement in government employment will discourage the better qualified from applying
    C. employees who want to progress in the public service should avoid simple assignments
    D. most dead-end jobs have been eliminated from the public service

42. Frequently the importance of keeping office records is not appreciated until information which is badly needed cannot be found. Office records must be kept in convenient and legible form, and must be filed where they may be found quickly. Many clerks are required for this work in large offices and fixed standards of accomplishment often can and must be utilized to get the desired results without loss of time.
The one of the following which is the MOST accurate statement on the basis of the above statement is:
    A. In setting up a filing system, the system to be used is secondary to the purpose it is to serve.
    B. Office records to be valuable must be kept in duplicate.
    C. The application of work standards to certain clerical functions frequently leads to greater efficiency.
    D. The keeping of office records becomes increasingly important as the business transacted by an office grows.

43. The difference between the average worker and the expert in any occupation is to a large degree a matter of training, yet the difference in their output is enormous. Despite this fact, there are many offices which do not have any organized system of training.
The MOST accurate of the following statements on the basis of the above statement is that
    A. job training, to be valuable, should be a continuous process
    B. most clerks have the same general intelligence but differ only in the amount of training they have received
    C. skill in an occupation can be acquired as a result of instruction by others
    D. employees with similar training will produce similar quality and quantity of work

44. Sometimes the term "clerical work" is used synonymously with the term "office work" to indicate that the work is clerical work, whether done by a clerk in a place called "the office," by the foreman in the shop, or by an investigator in the field. The essential feature is the work itself, not who does it or where it is done. If it is clerical work in one place, it is clerical work everywhere.

Of the following, the LEAST DIRECT implication of the above statement is that
   A. many jobs have clerical aspects
   B. some clerical work is done in offices
   C. the term "clerical work" is used in place of the term "office work" to emphasize the nature of the work done rather than by whom it is done
   D. clerks are not called upon to perform other than clerical work

45. Scheduling work within a unit involves the knowledge of how long the component parts of the routine take, and the precedence which certain routines should take over others. Usually, the important functions should be attended to on a schedule, and less important work can be handled as fill-in.
The one of the following which is the VALID statement on the basis of the above statement is that
   A. only employees engaged in routine assignments should have their work scheduled
   B. the work of an employee should be so scheduled that occasional absences will not upset his routine
   C. a proper scheduling of work takes the importance of the various functions of a unit into consideration
   D. if office work is not properly scheduled, important functions will be neglected

46. A filing system is unquestionably an effective tool for the systematic executive, and it use in office practice is indispensable, but a casual examination of almost any filing drawer in any office will show that hundreds of letters and papers which have no value whatever are being preserved.
The LEAST accurate of the following statements on the basis of the above statement is that
   A. it is generally considered to be good office practice to destroy letters or papers which are of no value
   B. many files are cluttered with useless paper
   C. a filing system is a valuable aid in effective office management
   D. every office executive should personally make a thorough examination of the files at regular intervals

47. As a supervisor, you may receive requests for information which you know should not be divulged.
Of the following replies you may give to such a request received over the telephone, the BEST one is:
   A. "I regret to advise you that it is the policy of the department not to give out this information over the telephone."
   B. "If you hold on a moment, I'll have you connected with the chief of the division."
   C. "I am sorry that I cannot help you, but we are not permitted to give out any information regarding such matters."
   D. "I am sorry but I know nothing regarding this matter."

48. Training promotes cooperation and teamwork, and results in lowered unit costs of operation.
The one of the following which is the MOST valid implication of the above statement is that
   A. training is of most value to new employees
   B. training is a factor in increasing efficiency and morale
   C. the actual cost of training employees may be small
   D. training is unnecessary in offices where personnel costs cannot be reduced

48.____

49. A government employee should understand how his particular duties contribute to the achievement of the objectives of his department.
This statement means MOST NEARLY that
   A. an employee who understands the functions of his department will perform his work efficiently
   B. all employees contribute equally in carrying out the objectives of their department
   C. an employee should realize the significance of his work in relation to the aims of his department
   D. all employees should be able to assist in setting up the objectives of a department

49.____

50. Many office managers have a tendency to overuse form letters and are prone to print form letters for every occasion, regardless of the number of copies of these letters which is needed.
On the basis of this statement, it is MOST logical to state that the determination of the need for a form letter should depend upon the
   A. length of the period during which the form letter may be used
   B. number of form letters presently being used in the office
   C. frequency with which the form letter may be used
   D. number of typists who may use the form letter

50.____

KEY (CORRECT ANSWERS)

1. A	11. B	21. B	31. A	41. B
2. C	12. A	22. B	32. C	42. C
3. C	13. D	23. A	33. B	43. C
4. B	14. A	24. A	34. C	44. D
5. A	15. D	25. D	35. D	45. C
6. A	16. B	26. D	36. B	46. D
7. B	17. B	27. B	37. C	47. C
8. D	18. C	28. D	38. B	48. B
9. B	19. C	29. A	39. B	49. C
10. D	20. D	30. B	40. C	50. C

TEST 2

DIRECTIONS: Each question or incomplete statement is followed by several suggested answers or completions. Select the one that BEST answers the question or completes the statement. *PRINT THE LETTER OF THE CORRECT ANSWER IN THE SPACE AT THE RIGHT.*

1. Your bureau is assigned an important task.
   Of the following, the function that you, as an administrative officer, can LEAST reasonably be expected to perform under these circumstances is the
   A. division of the large job into individual tasks
   B. establishment of "production lines" within the bureau
   C. performance personally of a substantial share of all the work
   D. checkup to see that the work has been well done

   1.____

2. Suppose that you have broken a complex job into its smaller components before making assignments to the employees under your jurisdiction.
   Of the following, the LEAST advisable procedure to follow from that point is to
   A. give each employee a picture of the importance of his work for the success of the total job
   B. establish a definite line of work flow and responsibility
   C. post a written memorandum of the best method for performing each job
   D. teach a number of alternative methods for doing each job

   2.____

3. As an administrative officer, you are requested to draw up an organization chart of the whole department.
   Of the following, the MOST important characteristic of such a chart is that it will
   A. include all details of the organization which distinguish it from any other
   B. be a schematic representation of purely administrative functions within the department
   C. present a modification of the actual departmental organization in light of principles of scientific management
   D. present an accurate picture of the lines of authority and responsibility

   3.____

4. Of the following, the MOST important principle in respect to delegation of authority that should guide you in your work as supervisor in charge of a bureau is that you should
   A. delegate as much authority as you effectively can
   B. make certain that all administrative details clear through your desk
   C. have all decisions confirmed by you
   D. discourage the practice of consulting you on matters of basic policy

   4.____

5. Of the following, the LEAST valid criterion to be applied in evaluating the organization of the department in which you are employed as a supervisor is:
   A. Is authority for making decisions centralized?
   B. Is authority for formulating policy centralized?
   C. Is authority granted commensurate with the responsibility involved?
   D. Is each position and its relation to other positions from the standpoint of responsibility clearly defined?

   5.____

6. Functional centralization is the bringing together of employees doing the same kind of work and performing similar tasks.
   Of the following, the one which is NOT an important advantage flowing from the introduction of functional centralization in a large city department is that
   A. inter-bureau communication and traffic are reduced
   B. standardized work procedures are introduced more easily
   C. evaluation of employee performances is facilitated
   D. inequalities in working conditions are reduced

7. As a supervisor, you find that a probationary employee under your supervision is consistently below a reasonable standard of performance for the job he is assigned to do.
   Of the following, the MOST appropriate action for you to take FIRST is to
   A. give him an easier job to do
   B. advise him to transfer to another department
   C. recommend to your superior that he be discouraged at the end of his probationary period
   D. determine whether the cause for his below-standard performance can be readily remedied

8. Certain administrative functions, such as those concerned with budgetary and personnel selection activities, have been delegated to central agencies separated from the operating departments.
   Of the following, the PRINCIPAL reason for such separation is that
   A. a central agency is generally better able to secure funds for performing these functions
   B. decentralization increases executive control
   C. greater economy, efficiency, and uniformity can be obtained by establishing central staff of experts to perform these functions
   D. the problems involved in performing these functions vary significantly from one operating department to another

9. The one of the following which is LEAST valid as a guiding principle for you, in your work as supervisor, in building team spirit and teamwork in your bureau is that you should attempt to
   A. convince the personnel of the bureau that public administration is a worthwhile endeavor
   B. lead every employee to visualize the integration of his own individual function with the program of the whole bureau
   C. develop a favorable public attitude toward the work of the bureau
   D. maintain impartiality by convenient delegation of authority in controversial matters

10. Of the following, the LEAST desirable procedure for the competent supervisor to follow is to
    A. organize his work before taking responsibility for helping others with theirs
    B. avoid schedules and routines when he is busy
    C. be flexible in planning and carrying out his responsibilities
    D. secure the support of his staff in organizing the total job of the unit

11. The responsibility for making judgment about staff members which is inherent in the supervisor's position may arouse hostilities toward the supervisor.
    Of the following, the BEST suggestion to the supervisor for handling this responsibility is for the supervisor to avoid
    A. individual criticism by taking up problems directly through group meetings
    B. any personal feeling or action that would imply that the supervisor has any power over the staff
    C. making critical judgments without accompanying them with reassurance to the staff member concerned

11._____

12. To carry out MOST effectively his responsibility for holding to a standard of quantity and quality, the supervisor should
    A. demand much more from himself than he does from his staff
    B. provide a clearly defined statement of what is expected of the staff
    C. teach the staff to assume responsible attitudes
    D. help the staff out when they get into unavoidable difficulties

12._____

13. The supervisor should inspire confidence and respect.
    This objective is MOST likely to be attained by the supervisor if he endeavors always to
    A. know the answers to the workers' questions
    B. be fair and just
    C. know what is going on in the office
    D. behave like a supervisor

13._____

14. Two chief reasons for the centralization of office functions are to eliminate costly duplication and to bring about greater coordination.
    The MOST direct implication of this statement is that
    A. greater coordination of office work will result in centralization of office functions
    B. where there is no centralization of office functions, there can be no coordination of work
    C. centralization of office functions may reduce duplication of work
    D. decentralization of office functions may be a result of costly duplication

14._____

15. The efficient administrative assistant arranges a definite schedule of the regular work of his division, but assigns the occasional and emergency tasks when they arise to the employees available at the time to handle these tasks.
    The management procedure described in this statement is desirable MAINLY because it
    A. relieves the administrative assistant of the responsibility of supervising the work of his staff
    B. enables more of the staff to become experienced in handling different types of problems
    C. enables the administrative assistant to anticipate problems which may arise
    D. provides for consideration of current work load when making special assignments

15._____

4 (#2)

16. Well-organized training courses for office employees are regarded by most administrators as a fundamental and essential part of a well-balanced personnel program.
Such training of clerical employees results LEAST directly in
   A. providing a reservoir of trained employees who can carry on the duties of other clerks during the absence of these clerks
   B. reducing the individual differences in the innate ability of clerical employees to perform complex duties
   C. bringing about a standardization throughout the department of operational methods found to be highly effective in one of its units
   D. preparing clerical employees for promotion to more responsible positions

16.____

17. The average typing speed of a typist is not necessarily a true indication of her efficiency.
Of the following, the BEST justification for this statement is that
   A. the typist may not maintain her maximum typing speed at all times
   B. a rapid typist will ordinarily type more letters than a slow one
   C. a typist's assignments usually include other operations in addition to actual typing
   D. typing speed has no significant relationship to the difficulty of material being typed

17.____

18. Although the use of labor-saving machinery and the simplification of procedures tend to decrease unit clerical labor costs, there is, nevertheless, a contrary tendency in the overall cost of office work. This contrary tendency, evidenced by the increase in size of the office staffs, has developed from the increasingly extensive use of systems of analysis and methods of research.
Of the following, the MOST accurate statement on the basis of the above statement is that
   A. the tendency for the overall costs of office work to increase is bringing about a counter-tendency to decrease unit costs of office work
   B. office machines are of little value in reducing the unit costs of the work of offices in which the overall costs are increasing
   C. The increasing use of systems of analysis and methods of research is bringing about a condition which will necessitate a curtailment of the use of these techniques in the office
   D. expanded office functions tend to offset savings resulting from increased efficiency in office management

18.____

19. The most successful supervisor wins his victories through preventive rather than through curative action.
The one of the following which is the MOST accurate statement on the basis of this statement is that
   A. success in supervision may be measured more accurately in terms of errors corrected than in terms of errors prevented
   B. anticipating problems makes for better supervision than waiting until these problems arise

19.____

C. difficulties that cannot be prevented by the supervisor cannot be overcome
D. the solution of problems in supervision is best achieved by scientific methods

20. Assume that you have been requested to design an office form which is to be duplicated by the mimeograph process.
In planning the layout of the various items appearing on the form, it is LEAST important for you to know the
    A. amount of information which the form is to contain
    B. purpose for which the form will be used
    C. size of the form
    D. number of copies of the form which are required

20.____

21. The supervisor is responsible for the accuracy of the work performed by her subordinates.
Of the following procedures which she might adopt to insure the accurate copying of long reports from rough draft originals, the MOST effective one is to
    A. examine the rough draft for errors in grammar, punctuation, and spelling before assigning it to a typist to copy
    B. glance through each typed report before it leaves her bureau to detect any obvious errors made by the typist
    C. have another employee read the rough draft original to the typist who typed the report, and have the typist make whatever corrections are necessary
    D. rotate assignments involving the typing of long reports equally among all the typists in the unit

21.____

22. The total number of errors made during the month, or other period studied, indicates, in a general way, whether the work has been performed with reasonable accuracy. However, this is not in itself a true measure, but must be considered in relation to the total volume of work produced.
On the basis of this statement, the accuracy of work performed is MOST truly measured by the
    A. total number of errors made during a specified period
    B. comparison of the number of errors made and the quantity of work produced during a specified period
    C. average amount of work produced by the unit during each month or other designated period of time
    D. none of the above answers

22.____

23. In the course of your duties, you receive a letter which, you believe, should be called to the attention of your supervisor.
Of the following, the BEST reason for attaching previous correspondence to this letter before giving it to your supervisor is that
    A. there is less danger, if such a procedure is followed, of misplacing important letters
    B. this letter can probably be better understood in the light of previous correspondence

23.____

C. your supervisor is probably in a better position to understand the letter than you
D. this letter will have to be filed eventually so there is no additional work involved

24. Suppose that you are requested to transmit to the stenographers in your bureau an order curtailing certain privileges that they have been enjoying. You anticipate that your staff may resent curtailment of such privileges.
Of the following, the BEST action for you to take is to
A. impress upon your staff that an order is an order and must be obeyed
B. attempt to explain to your staff the probable reasons for curtailing their privileges
C. excuse the curtailment of privileges by saying that the welfare of the staff was evidently not considered
D. warn your staff that violation of an order may be considered sufficient cause for immediate dismissal

24._____

25. Suppose that a stenographer recently appointed to your bureau submits a memorandum suggesting a change in office procedure that has been tried before and has been found unsuccessful.
Of the following, the BEST action for you to take is to
A. send the stenographer a note acknowledging receipt of the suggestion, but do not attempt to carry out the suggestion
B. point out that suggestions should come from her supervisor, who has a better knowledge of the problems of the office
C. try out the suggested change a second time, lest the stenographer lose interest in her work
D. call the stenographer in, explain that the change if not practicable, and compliment her for her interest and alertness

25._____

26. Suppose that you are assistant to one of the important administrators in your department. You receive a note from the head of department asking your supervisor to assist with a pressing problem that has arisen by making an immediate recommendation. Your supervisor is out of town on official business for a few days and cannot be reached. The head of department, evidently, is not aware of his absence.
Of the following, the BEST action for you to take is to
A. send the note back to the head of department without comment so as not to incriminate your supervisor
B. forward the note to one of the administrators in another division of the department
C. wait until your supervisor returns and bring the note to his attention immediately
D. get in touch with the head of department immediately and inform him that your supervisor is out of town

26._____

27. One of your duties may be to estimate the budget of your unit for the next fiscal year. Suppose that you expect no important changes in the work of your unit during the next year.

27._____

Of the following, the MOST appropriate basis for estimating next year's budget is the
- A. average budget of your unit for the last five years
- B. budget of your unit for the current year plus fifty percent to allow for possible expansion
- C. average current budget of units in your department
- D. budget of your unit for the current fiscal year

28. As a supervisor, you should realize that the work of a stenographer ordinarily requires a higher level of intelligence than the work of a typist CHIEFLY because
    - A. the salary range of stenographers is, in most government and business offices, lower than the salary range of typists
    - B. greater accuracy and skill is ordinarily required of a typist
    - C. the stenographer must understand what is being dictated to enable her to write it out in shorthand
    - D. typists are required to do more technical and specialized work

28.____

29. Suppose that you are acting as assistant to an important administrator in your department.
    Of the following, the BEST reason for keeping a separate "pending" file of letters to which answers are expected very soon is that
    - A. important correspondence should be placed in a separate, readily accessible file
    - B. a periodic check of the "pending" file will indicate the possible need for follow-up letters
    - C. correspondence is never final, so provision should be made for keeping files open
    - D. there is seldom sufficient room in the permanent files to permit filing all letters

29.____

30. For a busy executive in a government department, the services of an assistant are valuable and almost indispensable.
    Of the following, the CHIEF value of an assistant PROBABLY lies in her
    - A. ability to assume responsibility for making major decisions
    - B. familiarity with the general purpose and functions of civil service
    - C. special education
    - D. familiarity with the work and detail involved in the duties of the executive whom she assists

30.____

31. The supervisor should set a good example.
    Of the following, the CHIEF implication of the above statement is that the supervisor should
    - A. behave as he expects his workers to behave
    - B. know as much about the worker as his workers do
    - C. keep his workers informed of what he is doing
    - D. keep ahead of his workers

31.____

32. Of the following, the LEAST desirable procedure for the competent supervisor to follow is to
    A. organize his work before taking responsibility for helping others with theirs
    B. avoid schedules and routines when he is busy
    C. be flexible in planning and carrying out his responsibilities
    D. secure the support of his staff in organizing the total job of the unit

33. Evaluation helps the worker by increasing his security.
    Of the following, the BEST justification for this statement is that
    A. security and growth depend upon knowledge by the worker of the agency's evaluation
    B. knowledge of his evaluation by agency and supervisor will stimulate the worker to better performance
    C. evaluation enables the supervisor and worker to determine the reasons for the worker's strengths and weaknesses
    D. the supervisor and worker together can usually recognize and deal with any worker's insecurity

34. Systematizing for efficiency means MOST NEARLY
    A. performing an assignment despite all interruptions
    B. leaving difficult assignments until the next day
    C. having a definite time schedule for certain daily duties
    D. trying to do as little work as possible

35. The CHIEF reason for an employee training program is to
    A. increase the efficiency of the employee's work
    B. train the employee for promotion examinations
    C. to meet and talk with each new employee
    D. to give the supervisor an opportunity to reprimand the employee for his lack of knowledge

36. A supervisor may encourage his subordinates to make suggestions by
    A. keeping a record of the number of suggestions an employee makes
    B. providing a suggestion box
    C. outlining a list of possible suggestions
    D. giving credit to a subordinate whose suggestion has been accepted and used

37. The statement that accuracy is of greater importation than speed means MOST NEARLY that
    A. slower work increases employment
    B. fast workers may be inferior workers
    C. there are many varieties of work to do in an office
    D. the slow worker is the most efficient person

9 (#2)

38. To print tabular material is always much more expensive than to print straight text.
It follows MOST NEARLY that
   A. the more columns and subdivisions there are in a table, the more expensive is the printing
   B. the omission of the number and title from a table reduces printing costs
   C. it is always desirable to only print straight text
   D. do not print tabular material as it is too expensive

38.____

39. If you were required to give service ratings to employees under your supervision, you should consider as MOST important, during the current period, the
   A. personal characteristics and salary and grade of an employee
   B. length of service and the volume of work performed
   C. previous service rating given him
   D. personal characteristics and the quality of work of an employee

39.____

40. If a representative committee of employees in a large department is to meet with an administrative officer for the purpose of improving staff relations and of handling grievances, it is BEST that these meetings be held
   A. at regular intervals
   B. whenever requested b an aggrieved employee
   C. whenever the need arises
   D. at the discretion of the administrative officer

40.____

41. In order to be best able to teach a newly appointed employee who must learn to do a type of work which is unfamiliar to him, his supervisor should realize that during this first stage in the learning process the subordinate is GENERALLY characterized by
   A. acute consciousness of self
   B. acute consciousness of subject matter, with little interest in persons or personalities
   C. inertness or passive acceptance of assigned role
   D. understanding of problems without understanding of the means of solving them

41.____

42. The MOST accurate of the following principles of education and learning for a supervisor to keep in mind when planning a training program for the assistant supervisors under her supervision is that
   A. assistant supervisors, like all other individuals, vary in the rate at which they learn new material and in the degree to which they can retain what they do learn
   B. experienced assistant supervisors who have the same basic college education and agency experience will be able to learn new material at approximately the same rate of speed
   C. the speed with which assistant supervisors can learn new material after the age of forty is half as rapid as at ages twenty to thirty
   D. with regard to any specific task, it is easier and takes less time to break an experienced assistant supervisor of old, unsatisfactory work habits than it is to teach him new, acceptable ones

42.____

43. A supervisor has been transferred from supervision of one group of units to another group of units in the same center. She spends the first three weeks in her new assignment in getting acquainted with her new subordinates, their caseload problems and their work. In this process, she notices that some of the cash records and forms which are submitted to her by two of the assistant supervisors are carelessly or improperly prepared.
   The BEST of the following actions for the supervisor to take in this situation is to
   A. carefully check the work submitted by these assistant supervisors during an additional three weeks before taking any more positive action
   B. confer with these offending workers and show each one where her work needs improvement and how to go about achieving it
   C. institute an in-service training program specifically designed to solve such a problem and instruct the entire subordinate staff in proper work methods
   D. make a note of these errors for documentary use in preparing the annual service rating reports and advise the workers involved to prepare their work more carefully

43._____

44. A supervisor, who was promoted to this position a year ago, has supervised a certain assistant supervisor for this one year. The work of the assistant supervisor has been very poor because he has done a minimum of work, refused to take sufficient responsibility, been difficult to handle, and required very close supervision. Apparently due to the increasing insistence by his supervisor that he improve the caliber of his work, the assistant supervisor tenders his resignation, stating that the demands of the job are too much for him. The opinion of the previous supervisor, who had supervised this assistant supervisor for two years, agrees substantially with that of the new supervisor. Under such circumstances, the BEST of the following actions the supervisor can take, in general, is to
   A. recommend that the resignation be accepted and that he be rehired should he later apply when he feels able to do the job
   B. recommend that the resignation be accepted and that he not be rehired should he later so apply
   C. refuse to accept the resignation but try to persuade the assistant supervisor to accept psychiatric help
   D. refuse to accept the resignation, promising the assistant supervisor that he will be less closely supervised in the future since he is now so experienced

44._____

45. Rumors have arisen to the effect that one of the staff investigators under your supervision has been attending classes at a local university during afternoon hours when he is supposed to be making field visits.
   The BEST of the following ways for you to approach this problem is to
   A. disregard the rumors since, like most rumors, they probably have no actual foundation in fact
   B. have a discreet investigation made in order to determine the actual facts prior to taking any other action

45._____

C. inform the investigator that you know what he has been doing and that such behavior is overt dereliction of duty and is punishable by dismissal
D. review the investigator's work record, spot check his cases, and take no further action unless the quality of his work is below average for the unit

46. A supervisor must consider many factors in evaluating a worker whom he has supervised for a considerable time.
In evaluating the capacity of such a worker to use independent judgment, the one of the following to which the supervisor should generally give MOST consideration is the worker's
    A. capacity to establish good relationships with people (clients, colleagues)
    B. educational background
    C. emotional stability
    D. the quality and judgment shown by the worker in previous work situations known to the supervisor

46.____

47. A supervisor is conducting a special meeting with the assistant supervisors under her supervision to read and discuss some major complex changes in the rules and procedures. She notices that one of the assistant supervisors who is normally attentive at meetings seems to be paying no attention to what is being said. The supervisor stops reading the rules and asks the assistant supervisor a couple of questions about the changed procedure, to which she gets satisfactory answers.
The BEST action of the following for the supervisor to take at the meeting is to
    A. advise the assistant supervisor gently but firmly that these changes are complex and that her undivided attention is required in order to fully comprehend them
    B. avoid further embarrassment to the assistant supervisor by asking the group as a whole to pay more attention to what is being read
    C. discontinue the questioning and resume reading the procedure
    D. politely request the assistant supervisor to stop giving those present the impression that she is uninterested in what goes on about her

47.____

48. A supervisor becomes aware that one of her very competent experienced workers never takes notes during an interview with a client except to note an occasional name, address, or date. When asked about this practice by the supervisor, the worker states that she has a good memory for important details and has always been able to satisfactorily record an interview after the client has left.
It would generally be BEST for the supervisor to handle this situation by
    A. discussing with her that more extensive note-taking may sometimes be desirable with a client who believes note-taking to be evidence that his problem will receive serious consideration
    B. agreeing with this practice since note-taking interferes with the establishment of a proper worker-client relationship
    C. explaining that, since interviewing is an art form rather than an exact science, a good worker must devise her own personal rules for interviewing and not be bound by general principles

48.____

D. warning the worker that memory is too uncertain a thing to be relied upon and, therefore, notes should be taken during an interview of all matters

49. When an experienced subordinate who has the authority and information necessary to make a decision on a certain difficult matter brings the matter to his supervisor without having made the decision, it would generally be BEST for the supervisor to
    A. agree to make the decision for the subordinate after the subordinate has explained why he finds it difficult to make the decision and after he has made a recommendation
    B. make the decision for the subordinate, explaining to him the reasons for arriving at the decision
    C. refuse to make the decision, but discuss the various alternatives with the subordinate in order to clarify the issues involved
    D. refuse to make the decision, explaining to the subordinate that he is deemed to be fully qualified and competent to make the decision

50. The one of the following instances when it is MOST important for an upper level supervisor to follow the chain of command is when he is
    A. communicating decisions
    B. communicating information
    C. receiving suggestions
    D. seeking information

KEY (CORRECT ANSWERS)

1. C	11. D	21. C	31. A	41. A
2. D	12. B	22. B	32. B	42. A
3. D	13. B	23. B	33. C	43. B
4. A	14. C	24. B	34. C	44. B
5. D	15. D	25. D	35. A	45. B
6. A	16. B	26. D	36. D	46. D
7. D	17. C	27. D	37. B	47. C
8. C	18. D	28. C	38. A	48. A
9. D	19. B	29. B	39. D	49. C
10. B	20. D	30. D	40. A	50. A

TEST 3

DIRECTIONS: Each question or incomplete statement is followed by several suggested answers or completions. Select the one that BEST answers the question or completes the statement. *PRINT THE LETTER OF THE CORRECT ANSWER IN THE SPACE AT THE RIGHT.*

1. Experts in the field of personnel relations feel that it is generally bad practice for subordinate employees to become aware of pending or contemplated changes in policy or organizational set-up via the "grapevine" CHIEFLY because
   A. evidence that one or more responsible officials have proved untrustworthy will undermine confidence in the agency
   B. the information disseminated by this method is seldom entirely accurate and generally spreads needless unrest among the subordinate staff
   C. the subordinate staff may conclude that the administration feels the staff cannot be trusted with the true information
   D. the subordinate staff may conclude that the administration lacks the courage to make an unpopular announcement through officials channels

1.____

2. In order to maintain a proper relationship with a worker who is assigned to staff rather than line functions, a line supervisor should
   A. accept all recommendations of the staff worker
   B. include the staff worker in the conferences called by the supervisor for his subordinates
   C. keep the staff worker informed of developments in the area of his staff assignment
   D. require that the staff worker's recommendations be communicated to the supervisor through the supervisor's own superior

2.____

3. Of the following, the GREATEST disadvantage of placing a worker in a staff position under the direct supervision of the supervisor whom he advises is the possibility that the
   A. staff worker will tend to be insubordinate because of a feeling of superiority over the supervisor
   B. staff worker will tend to give advice of the type which the supervisor wants to hear or finds acceptable
   C. supervisor will tend to be mistrustful of the advice of a worker of subordinate rank
   D. supervisor will tend to derive little benefit from the advice because to supervise properly he should know at least as much as his subordinate

3.____

4. One factor which might be given consideration in deciding upon the optimum span of control of a supervisor over his immediate subordinates is the position of the supervisor in the hierarchy of the organization. It is generally considered proper that the number of subordinates immediately supervised by a higher, upper echelon, supervisor
   A. is unrelated to and tends to form no pattern with the number supervised by lower level supervisors
   B. should be about the same as the number supervised by a lower level supervisor

4.____

C. should be larger than the number supervised by a lower level supervisor
D. should be smaller than the number supervised by a lower level supervisor

5. An important administrative problem is how precisely to define the limits on authority that is delegated to subordinate supervisors.
Such definition of limits of authority should be
   A. as precise as possible and practicable in all areas
   B. as precise as possible and practicable in areas of function, but should allow considerable flexibility in the area of personnel management
   C. as precise as possible and practicable in the area of personnel management, but should allow considerable flexibility in the areas of function
   D. in general terms so as to allow considerable flexibility both in the areas of function and in the areas of personnel management

6. The LEAST important of the following reasons why a particular activity should be assigned to a unit which performs activities dissimilar to it is that
   A. close coordination is needed between the particular activity and other activities performed by the unit
   B. it will enhance the reputation and prestige of the unit supervisor
   C. the unit makes frequent use of the results of this particular activity
   D. the unit supervisor has a sound knowledge and understanding of the particular activity

7. A supervisor is put in charge of a special unit. She is exceptionally well-qualified for this assignment by her training and experience. One of her very close personal friends has been working for some time as a field investigator in this unit. Both the supervisor and investigator are certain that the rest of the investigators in the unit, many of whom have been in the bureau for a long time, know of this close relationship.
Under these circumstances, the MOST advisable action for the supervisor to take is to
   A. ask that either she be allowed to return to her old assignment, or, if that cannot be arranged, that her friend be transferred to another unit in the center
   B. avoid any overt sign of favoritism by acting impartially and with greater reserve when dealing with this investigator than the rest of the staff
   C. discontinue any socializing with this investigator either inside or outside the office so as to eliminate any gossip or dissatisfaction
   D. talk the situation over with the other investigators and arrive at a mutually acceptable plan of proper office decorum

8. The one of the following causes of clerical error which is usually considered to be LEAST attributable to faulty supervision or inefficient management is
   A. inability to carry out instructions
   B. too much work to do
   C. an inappropriate record-keeping system
   D. continual interruptions

9. Assume that you are the supervisor of a clerical unit in a government agency. One of your subordinates violates a rule of the agency, a violation which requires that the employee be suspended from his work for one day. The violated rule is one that you have found to be unduly strict and you have recommended to the management of the agency that the rule be changed or abolished. The management has been considering your recommendation but has not yet reached a decision on the matter.
In these circumstances, you should
   A. not initiate disciplinary action, but, instead explain to the employee that the rule may be changed shortly
   B. delay disciplinary action on the violation until the management has reached a decision on changing the rule
   C. modify the disciplinary action by reprimanding the employee and informing him that further action may be taken when the management has reached a decision on changing the rule
   D. initiate the prescribed disciplinary action without commenting on the strictness of the rule or on your recommendation

10. Assume that a supervisor praises his subordinates for satisfactory aspects of their work only when he is about to criticize them for unsatisfactory aspects of their work.
Such a practice is undesirable PRIMARILY because
   A. his subordinates may expect to be praised for their work even if it is unsatisfactory
   B. praising his subordinates for some aspects of their work while criticizing other aspects will weaken the effects of the criticisms
   C. his subordinates would be more receptive to criticism if it were followed by praise
   D. his subordinates may come to disregard praise and wait for criticism to be given

11. The one of the following which would be the BEST reason for an agency to eliminate a procedure for obtaining and recording certain information is that
   A. it is no longer legally required to obtain the information
   B. there is an advantage in obtaining the information
   C. the information could be compiled on the basis of other information available
   D. the information obtained is sometimes incorrect

12. In determining the type and number of records to be kept in an agency, it is important to recognize that records are of value PRIMARILY as
   A. raw material to be used in statistical analysis
   B. sources of information about the agency's activities
   C. by-products of the activities carried on by the agency
   D. data for evaluating the effectiveness of the agency

Questions 13-17.

DIRECTIONS: Each of Questions 13 through 17 consists of a statement which contains one word that is incorrectly used because it is not in keeping with the meaning that the statement is evidently intended to convey. For each of these questions, you are to select the incorrectly used word and substitute for it one of the words lettered A, B, C, or D, which helps BEST to convey the meaning of the statement.

13. There has developed in recent years an increasing awareness of the need to measure the quality of management in all enterprises and to seek the principles that can serve as a basis for this improvement.
    A. growth   B. raise   C. efficiency   D. define

14. It is hardly an exaggeration to deny that the permanence, productivity, and humanity of any industrial system depend upon its ability to utilize the positive and constructive impulses of all who work and upon its ability to arouse and continue interest in the necessary activities.
    A. develop   B. efficiency   C. state   D. inspiration

15. The selection of managers on the basis of technical knowledge alone seems to recognize that the essential characteristic of management is getting things done through others, thereby demanding skills that are essential in coordinating the activities of subordinates.
    A. training   B. fails
    C. organization   D. improving

16. Only when it is deliberate and when it is clearly understood what impressions the ease of communication will probably create in the minds of employees and subordinate management, should top management refrain from commenting on a subject that is of general concern.
    A. obvious   B. benefit   C. doubt   D. absence

17. Scientific planning of work requires careful analysis of facts and a precise plan of action for the whims and fancies of executives that often provide only a vague indication of work to be done.
    A. substitutes   B. development
    C. preliminary   D. comprehensive

18. Assume that you are a supervisor. One of the workers under your supervision is careless about the routine aspects of his work.
    Of the following, the action MOST likely to develop in this worker a better attitude toward job routines is to demonstrate that
    A. it is just as easy to do his job the right way
    B. organization of his job will leave more time for field work
    C. the routine part of the job is essential to performing a good piece of work
    D. job routines are a responsibility of the worker

19. A supervisor can MOST effectively secure necessary improvement in a worker's office work by
    A. encouraging the worker to keep abreast of his work
    B. relating the routine part of his job to the total job to be done
    C. helping the worker to establish a good system for covering his office work and holding him to it
    D. informing the worker that he will be required to organize his work more efficiently

20. A supervisor should offer criticism in such a manner that the criticisms is helpful and not overwhelming.
    Of the following, the LEAST valid inference that can be drawn on the basis of the above statement is that a supervisor should
    A. demonstrate that the criticism is partial and not total
    B. give criticism in such a way that it does not undermine the worker's self-confidence
    C. keep his relationships with the worker objective
    D. keep criticism directed towards general work performance

21. The one of the following areas in which a worker may LEAST reasonably expect direct assistance from the supervisor is in
    A. building up rapport with all clients
    B. gaining insight into the unmet needs of clients
    C. developing an understanding of community resources
    D. interpreting agency policies and procedures

22. You are informed that a worker under your supervision has submitted a letter complaining of unfair service rating.
    Of the following, the MOST valid assumption for you to make concerning this worker is that he should be
    A. more adequately supervised in the future
    B. called in for a supervisory conference
    C. given a transfer to some other unit where he may be more happy
    D. given no more consideration than any other inefficient worker

23. Assume that you are a supervisor. You find that a somewhat bewildered worker, newly appointed to the department, hesitates to ask questions for fear of showing his ignorance and jeopardizing his position.
    Of the following, the BEST procedure for you to follow is to
    A. try to discover the reason for his evident fear of authority
    B. tell him that when he is in doubt about a procedure or a policy he should consult his fellow workers
    C. develop with the worker a plan for more frequent supervisory conferences
    D. explain why each staff member is eager to give him available information that will help him do a good job

24. Of the following, the MOST effective method of helping a newly-appointed employee adjust to his new job is to
    A. assure him that with experience his uncertain attitudes will be replaced by a professional approach
    B. help him, by accepting him as he is, to have confidence in his ability to handle the job
    C. help him to be on guard against the development of punitive attitudes
    D. help him to recognize the mutability of the agency's policies and procedures

25. Suppose that, as a supervisor, you have scheduled an individual conference with an experienced employee under your supervision.
    Of the following, the BEST plan of action for this conference is to
    A. discuss the work that the employee is most interested in
    B. plan with the employee to cover any problems that are difficult for him
    C. advise the employee that the conference is his to do with as he sees fit
    D. spot check the employee's work in advance and select those areas for discussion in which the employee has done poor work

26. Of the following, the CHIEF function of a supervisor should be to
    A. assist in the planning of new policies and the evaluation of existing ones
    B. promote congenial relationships among members of the staff
    C. achieve optimum functioning of each unit and each worker
    D. promote the smooth functioning of job routines

27. The competent supervisor must realize the importance of planning.
    Of the following, the aspect of planning which is LEAST appropriately considered a responsibility of the supervisor is
    A. long-range planning for the proper functioning of his unit
    B. planning to take care of peak and slack periods
    C. planning to cover agency policies in group conferences
    D. long-range planning to develop community resources

28. The one of the following objectives which should be of LEAST concern to the supervisor in the performance of his duties is to
    A. help the worker to make friends with all of his fellow employees
    B. be impartial and fair to all members of the staff
    C. stimulate the worker's growth on the job
    D. meet the needs of the individual employee

29. The one of the following which is LEAST properly considered a direct responsibility of the supervisor is
    A. liaison between the staff and the administrator
    B. interpreting administrative orders and procedures to the employees
    C. training new employees
    D. maintaining staff morale at a high level

30. In order to teach the employee to develop an objective approach, the BEST action for the supervisor to take is to help the worker to
    A. develop a sincere interest in his job
    B. understand the varied responsibilities that are an integral part of his job
    C. differentiate clearly between himself as a friend and as an employee
    D. find satisfaction in his work

31. If the employee shows excessive submission which indicates a need for dependence on the supervisor in handling an assignment, it would be MOST advisable for the supervisor to
    A. indicate firmly that the employee-supervisor relationship does not call for submission
    B. define areas of responsibility of employee and supervisor
    C. recognize the employee's need and of supervisor
    D. recognize the employee's need to be sustained and supported and help him by making decisions for him

32. Assume that, as a supervisor, you are conducting a group conference.
    Of the following, the BEST procedure for you to follow in order to stimulate group discussion is to
    A. permit the active participation of all members
    B. direct the discussion to an acceptable conclusion
    C. resolve conflicts of opinion among members of the group
    D. present a question for discussion on which the group members have some knowledge or experience

33. Suppose that, as a new supervisor, you wish to inform the staff under your supervision of your methods of operation.
    Of the following, the BEST procedure for you to follow is to
    A. advise the staff that they will learn gradually from experience
    B. inform each employee in an individual conference
    C. call a group conference for this purpose
    D. distribute a written memorandum among all members of the staff

34. The MOST constructive and effective method of correcting an employee who has made a mistake is, in general, to
    A. explain that his evaluation is related to his errors
    B. point out immediately where he erred and tell him how it should have been done
    C. show him how to readjust his methods so as to avoid similar errors in the future
    D. try to discover by an indirect method why the error was made

35. The MOST effective method for the supervisor to follow in order to obtain the cooperation of an employee under his supervision is, wherever possible, to
    A. maintain a careful record of performance in order to keep the employee on his toes
    B. give the employee recognition in order to promote greater effort and give him more satisfaction in his work

C. try to gain the employee's cooperation for the good of the service
D. advise the employee that his advancement on the job depends on his cooperation

36. Of the following, the MOST appropriate initial course for an employee to take when he is unable to clarify a policy with his supervisor is to
    A. bring up the problem at the next group conference
    B. discuss the policy immediately with his fellow employees
    C. accept the supervisor's interpretation as final
    D. determine what responsibility he has for putting the policy into effect

37. Good administration allows for different treatment of different workers.
    Of the following, the CHIEF implication of this statement is that
    A. it would be unfair for the supervisor not to treat all staff members alike
    B. fear of favoritism tends to undermine staff morale
    C. best results are obtained by individualization within the limits of fair treatment
    D. difficult problems call for a different kind of approach

38. The MOST effective and appropriate method of building efficiency and morale in a group of employees is, in general,
    A. by stressing the economic motive
    B. through use of the authority inherent in the position
    C. by a friendly approach to all
    D. by a discipline that is fair but strict

39. Of the following, the LEAST valid basis for the assignment of work to an employee is the
    A. kind of service to be rendered
    B. experience and training of the employee
    C. health and capacity of the employee
    D. racial composition of the community where the office is located

40. The CHIEF justification for staff education, consisting of in-service training, lies in its contribution to
    A. improvement in the quality of work performed
    B. recruitment of a better type of employee
    C. employee morale, accruing from a feeling of growth on the job
    D. the satisfaction that the employee gets on his job

41. Suppose that you are a supervisor. An employee no longer with your department requests you, as his former supervisor, to write a letter recommending him for a position with a private organization.
    Of the following the BEST procedure for you to follow is to include in the letter only information that
    A. will help the applicant get the job
    B. is clear, factual, and substantiated
    C. is known to you personally
    D. can readily be corroborated by personal interview

9 (#3)

42. Of the following, the MOST important item on which to base the efficiency evaluation of an employee under your supervision is
    A. the nature of the relationship that he has built up with his fellow employees
    B. how he gets along with his supervisors
    C. his personal habits and skills
    D. the effectiveness of his control over his work

32.____

43. According to generally accepted personnel practice, the MOST effective method of building morale in a new employee is to
    A. exercise caution in praising the employee, lest he become overconfident
    B. give sincere and frank recommendation whenever possible in order to stimulate interest and effort
    C. praise the employee highly even for mediocre performance so that he will be stimulated to do better
    D. warn the employee frequently that he cannot hope to succeed unless he puts forth his best efforts

43.____

44. Errors made by newly-appointed employees often follow a predictable pattern. The one of the following errors likely to have LEAST serious consequences is the tendency of a new employee to
    A. discuss problems that are outside his province with the client
    B. persuade the client to accept the worker's solution of a problem
    C. be two strict in carrying out departmental policy and procedure
    D. depend upon the use of authority due to his inexperience and lack of skill in working with people

44.____

45. The MOST effective way for a supervisor to break down a worker's defensive stand against supervisory guidance is to
    A. come to an understanding with him on the mutual responsibilities involved in the job of the employee and that of the supervisor
    B. tell him he must feel free to express his opinions and to discuss basic problems
    C. show him how to develop toward greater objectivity, sensitivity, and understanding
    D. advise him that it is necessary to carry out agency policy and procedures in order to do a good job

45.____

46. Of the following, the LEAST essential function of the supervisor who is conducting a group conference should be to
    A. keep attention focused on the purpose of the conference
    B. encourage discussion of controversial points
    C. make certain that all possible viewpoints are discussed
    D. be thoroughly prepared in advance

46.____

47. When conducting a group conference, the supervisor should be LEAST concerned with
    A. providing an opportunity for the free interchange of ideas
    B. imparting knowledge and understanding of the work

47.____

C. leading the discussion toward a planned goal
D. pointing out where individual workers have erred in work practice

48. If the participants in a group conference are unable to agree on the proper application of a concept to the work of a department, the MOST suitable temporary procedure for the supervisor to follow is to
    A. suggest that each member think the subject through before the next meeting
    B. tell the group to examine their differences for possible conflicts with present policies
    C. suggest that practices can be changed because of new conditions
    D. state the acceptable practice in the agency and whether deviations from such practice can be permitted

48._____

49. If an employee is to participate constructively in any group discussion, it is MOST important that he have
    A. advance notice of the agenda for the meeting
    B. long experience in the department
    C. knowledge and experience in the particular work
    D. the ability to assume a leadership role

49._____

50. Of the following, the MOST important principle for the supervisor to follow when conducting a group discussion is that he should
    A. move the discussion toward acceptance by the group of a particular point of view
    B. express his ideas clearly and succinctly
    C. lead the group to accept the authority inherent in his position
    D. contribute to the discussion from his knowledge and experience

50._____

KEY (CORRECT ANSWERS)

1. B	11. C	21. A	31. B	41. B
2. C	12. B	22. B	32. D	42. D
3. B	13. B	23. C	33. C	43. B
4. D	14. C	24. B	34. C	44. C
5. A	15. B	25. B	35. B	45. A
6. B	16. D	26. C	36. D	46. B
7. A	17. A	27. D	37. C	47. D
8. A	18. D	28. A	38. D	48. D
9. D	19. B	29. A	39. D	49. A
10. D	20. D	30. C	40. A	50. D

PHILOSOPHY, PRINCIPLES, PRACTICES, AND TECHNICS OF SUPERVISION, ADMINISTRATION, MANAGEMENT, AND ORGANIZATION

TABLE OF CONTENTS

	Page
MEANING OF SUPERVISION	1
THE OLD AND THE NEW SUPERVISION	1
THE EIGHT (8) BASIC PRINCIPLES OF THE NEW SUPERVISION	1
I. Principle of Responsibility	1
II. Principle of Authority	2
III. Principle of Self-Growth	2
IV. Principle of Individual Worth	2
V. Principle of Creative Leadership	2
VI. Principle of Success and Failure	2
VII. Principle of Science	3
VIII. Principle of Cooperation	3
WHAT IS ADMINISTRATION?	3
I. Practices Commonly Classed as "Supervisory"	3
II. Practices Commonly Classed as "Administrative"	3
III. Practices Commonly Classed as Both "Supervisory" and "Administrative"	4
RESPONSIBILITIES OF THE SUPERVISOR	4
COMPETENCIES OF THE SUPERVISOR	4
THE PROFESSIONAL SUPERVISOR-EMPLOYEE RELATIONSHIP	4
MINI-TEXT IN SUPERVISION, ADMINISTRATION, MANAGEMENT, AND ORGANIZATION	5
I. Brief Highlights	5
A. Levels of Management	6
B. What the Supervisor Must Learn	6
C. A Definition of Supervision	6
D. Elements of the Team Concept	6
E. Principles of Organization	6
F. The Four Important Parts of Every Job	7
G. Principles of Delegation	7
H. Principles of Effective Communications	7
I. Principles of Work Improvement	7
J. Areas of Job Improvement	7
K. Seven Key Points in Making Improvements	8

	L.	Corrective Techniques for Job Improvement	8
	M.	A Planning Checklist	8
	N.	Five Characteristics of Good Directions	9
	O.	Types of Directions	9
	P.	Controls	9
	Q.	Orienting the New Employee	9
	R.	Checklist for Orienting New Employees	9
	S.	Principles of Learning	10
	T.	Causes of Poor Performance	10
	U.	Four Major Steps in On-the-Job Instructions	10
	V.	Employees Want Five Things	10
	W.	Some Don'ts in Regard to Praise	11
	X.	How to Gain Your Workers' Confidence	11
	Y.	Sources of Employee Problems	11
	Z.	The Supervisor's Key to Discipline	11
	AA.	Five Important Processes of Management	12
	BB.	When the Supervisor Fails to Plan	12
	CC.	Fourteen General Principles of Management	12
	DD.	Change	12
II.	Brief Topical Summaries		13
	A.	Who/What is the Supervisor?	13
	B.	The Sociology of Work	13
	C.	Principles and Practices of Supervision	14
	D.	Dynamic Leadership	14
	E.	Processes for Solving Problems	15
	F.	Training for Results	15
	G.	Health, Safety, and Accident Prevention	16
	H.	Equal Employment Opportunity	16
	I.	Improving Communications	16
	J.	Self-Development	17
	K.	Teaching and Training	17
		1. The Teaching Process	17
		a. Preparation	17
		b. Presentation	18
		c. Summary	18
		d. Application	18
		e. Evaluation	18
		2. Teaching Methods	18
		a. Lecture	18
		b. Discussion	18
		c. Demonstration	19
		d. Performance	19
		e. Which Method to Use	19

PHILOSOPHY, PRINCIPLES, PRACTICES, AND TECHNICS
OF
SUPERVISION, ADMINISTRATION, MANAGEMENT, AND ORGANIZATION

MEANING OF SUPERVISION

The extension of the democratic philosophy has been accompanied by an extension in the scope of supervision. Modern leaders and supervisors no longer think of supervision in the narrow sense of being confined chiefly to visiting employees, supplying materials, or rating the staff. They regard supervision as being intimately related to all the concerned agencies of society, they speak of the supervisor's function in terms of "growth," rather than the "improvement" of employees.

This modern concept of supervision may be defined as follows: Supervision is leadership and the development of leadership within groups which are cooperatively engaged in inspection, research, training, guidance, and evaluation.

THE OLD AND THE NEW SUPERVISION

TRADITIONAL
1. Inspection
2. Focused on the employee
3. Visitation
4. Random and haphazard
5. Imposed and authoritarian
6. One person usually

MODERN
1. Study and analysis
2. Focused on aims, materials, methods, supervisors, employees, environment
3. Demonstrations, intervisitation, workshops, directed reading, bulletins, etc.
4. Definitely organized and planned (scientific)
5. Cooperative and democratic
6. Many persons involved (creative)

THE EIGHT (8) BASIC PRINCIPLES OF THE NEW SUPERVISION

I. Principle of Responsibility
Authority to act and responsibility for acting must be joined.
A. If you give responsibility, give authority.
B. Define employee duties clearly.
C. Protect employees from criticism by others.
D. Recognize the rights as well as obligations of employees.
E. Achieve the aims of a democratic society insofar as it is possible within the area of your work.
F. Establish a situation favorable to training and learning.
G. Accept ultimate responsibility for everything done in your section, unit, office, division, department.
H. Good administration and good supervision are inseparable.

II. Principle of Authority
The success of the supervisor is measured by the extent to which the power of authority is not used.
   A. Exercise simplicity and informality in supervision
   B. Use the simplest machinery of supervision
   C. If it is good for the organization as a whole, it is probably justified.
   D. Seldom be arbitrary or authoritative.
   E. Do not base your work on the power of position or of personality.
   F. Permit and encourage the free expression of opinions.

III. Principle of Self-Growth
The success of the supervisor is measured by the extent to which, and the speed with which, he is no longer needed.
   A. Base criticism on principles, not on specifics.
   B. Point out higher activities to employees.
   C. Train for self-thinking by employees to meet new situations.
   D. Stimulate initiative, self-reliance, and individual responsibility
   E. Concentrate on stimulating the growth of employees rather than on removing defects.

IV. Principle of Individual Worth
Respect for the individual is a paramount consideration in supervision.
   A. Be human and sympathetic in dealing with employees.
   B. Don't nag about things to be done.
   C. Recognize the individual differences among employees and seek opportunities to permit best expression of each personality.

V. Principle of Creative Leadership
The best supervision is that which is not apparent to the employee.
   A. Stimulate, don't drive employees to creative action.
   B. Emphasize doing good things.
   C. Encourage employees to do what they do best.
   D. Do not be too greatly concerned with details of subject or method.
   E. Do not be concerned exclusively with immediate problems and activities.
   F. Reveal higher activities and make them both desired and maximally possible.
   G. Determine procedures in the light of each situation but see that these are derived from a sound basic philosophy.
   H. Aid, inspire, and lead so as to liberate the creative spirit latent in all good employees.

VI. Principle of Success and Failure
There are no unsuccessful employees, only unsuccessful supervisors who have failed to give proper leadership.
   A. Adapt suggestions to the capacities, attitudes, and prejudices of employees.
   B. Be gradual, be progressive, be persistent.
   C. Help the employee find the general principle; have the employee apply his own problem to the general principle.
   D. Give adequate appreciation for good work and honest effort.
   E. Anticipate employee difficulties and help to prevent them.
   F. Encourage employees to do the desirable things they will do anyway.
   G. Judge your supervision by the results it secures.

VII. Principle of Science
Successful supervision is scientific, objective, and experimental. It is based on facts, not on prejudices.
   A. Be cumulative in results.
   B. Never divorce your suggestions from the goals of training.
   C. Don't be impatient of results.
   D. Keep all matters on a professional, not a personal, level.
   E. Do not be concerned exclusively with immediate problems and activities.
   F. Use objective means of determining achievement and rating where possible.

VIII. Principle of Cooperation
Supervision is a cooperative enterprise between supervisor and employee.
   A. Begin with conditions as they are.
   B. Ask opinions of all involved when formulating policies.
   C. Organization is as good as its weakest link.
   D. Let employees help to determine policies and department programs.
   E. Be approachable and accessible—physically and mentally.
   F. Develop pleasant social relationships.

WHAT IS ADMINISTRATION

Administration is concerned with providing the environment, the material facilities, and the operational procedures that will promote the maximum growth and development of supervisors and employees. (Organization is an aspect and a concomitant of administration.)

There is no sharp line of demarcation between supervision and administration; these functions are intimately interrelated and, often, overlapping. They are complementary activities.

I. Practices Commonly Classed as "Supervisory"
   A. Conducting employees' conferences
   B. Visiting sections, units, offices, divisions, departments
   C. Arranging for demonstrations
   D. Examining plans
   E. Suggesting professional reading
   F. Interpreting bulletins
   G. Recommending in-service training courses
   H. Encouraging experimentation
   I. Appraising employee morale
   J. Providing for intervisitation

II. Practices Commonly Classified as "Administrative"
   A. Management of the office
   B. Arrangement of schedules for extra duties
   C. Assignment of rooms or areas
   D. Distribution of supplies
   E. Keeping records and reports
   F. Care of audio-visual materials
   G. Keeping inventory records
   H. Checking record cards and books

    I. Programming special activities
    J. Checking on the attendance and punctuality of employees

III. Practices Commonly Classified as Both "Supervisory" and "Administrative"
    A. Program construction
    B. Testing or evaluating outcomes
    C. Personnel accounting
    D. Ordering instructional materials

RESPONSIBILITIES OF THE SUPERVISOR

A person employed in a supervisory capacity must constantly be able to improve his own efficiency and ability. He represent the employer to the employees and only continuous self-examination can make him a capable supervisor.

Leadership and training are the supervisor's responsibility. An efficient working unit is one in which the employees work with the supervisor. It is his job to bring out the best in his employees. He must always be relaxed, courteous, and calm in his association with his employees. Their feelings are important, and a harsh attitude does not develop the most efficient employees.

COMPETENCES OF THE SUPERVISOR

   I. Complete knowledge of the duties and responsibilities of his position.
  II. To be able to organize a job, plan ahead, and carry through.
 III. To have self-confidence and initiative.
  IV. To be able to handle the unexpected situation and make quick decisions.
   V. To be able to properly train subordinates in the positions they are best suited for.
  VI. To be able to keep good human relations among his subordinates.
 VII. To be able to keep good human relations between his subordinates and himself and to earn their respect and trust.

THE PROFESSIONAL SUPERVISOR-EMPLOYEE RELATIONSHIP

There are two kinds of efficiency: one kind is only apparent and is produced in organizations through the exercise of mere discipline; this is but a simulation of the second, or true, efficiency which springs from spontaneous cooperation. If you are a manager, no matter how great or small your responsibility, it is your job, in the final analysis, to create and develop this involuntary cooperation among the people whom you supervise. For, no matter how powerful a combination of money, machines, and materials a company may have, this is a dead and sterile thing without a team of willing, thinking, and articulate people to guide it.

The following 21 points are presented as indicative of the exemplary basic relationship that should exist between supervisor and employee:

1. Each person wants to be liked and respected by his fellow employee and wants to be treated with consideration and respect by his superior.
2. The most competent employee will make an error. However, in a unit where good relations exist between the supervisor and his employees, tenseness and fear do not exist. Thus, errors are not hidden or covered up, and the efficiency of a unit is not impaired.

3. Subordinates resent rules, regulations, or orders that are unreasonable or unexplained.
4. Subordinates are quick to resent unfairness, harshness, injustices, and favoritism.
5. An employee will accept responsibility if he knows that he will be complimented for a job well done, and not too harshly chastised for failure; that his supervisor will check the cause of the failure, and, if it was the supervisor's fault, he will assume the blame therefore. If it was the employee's fault, his supervisor will explain the correct method or means of handling the responsibility.
6. An employee wants to receive credit for a suggestion he has made, that is used. If a suggestion cannot be used, the employee is entitled to an explanation. The supervisor should not say "no" and close the subject.
7. Fear and worry slow up a worker's ability. Poor working environment can impair his physical and mental health. A good supervisor avoids forceful methods, threats, and arguments to get a job done.
8. A forceful supervisor is able to train his employees individually and as a team, and is able to motivate them in the proper channels.
9. A mature supervisor is able to properly evaluate his subordinates and to keep them happy and satisfied.
10. A sensitive supervisor will never patronize his subordinates.
11. A worthy supervisor will respect his employees' confidences.
12. Definite and clear-cut responsibilities should be assigned to each executive.
13. Responsibility should always be coupled with corresponding authority.
14. No change should be made in the scope or responsibilities of a position without a definite understanding to that effect on the part of all persons concerned.
15. No executive or employee, occupying a single position in the organization, should be subject to definite orders from more than one source.
16. Orders should never be given to subordinates over the head of a responsible executive. Rather than do this, the officer in question should be supplanted.
17. Criticisms of subordinates should, whoever possible, be made privately, and in no case should a subordinate be criticized in the presence of executives or employees of equal or lower rank.
18. No dispute or difference between executives or employees as to authority or responsibilities should be considered too trivial for prompt and careful adjudication.
19. Promotions, wage changes, and disciplinary action should always be approved by the executive immediately superior to the one directly responsible.
20. No executive or employee should ever be required, or expected, to be at the same time an assistant to, and critic of, another.
21. Any executive whose work is subject to regular inspection should, wherever practicable, be given the assistance and facilities necessary to enable him to maintain an independent check of the quality of his work.

MINI-TEXT IN SUPERVISION, ADMINISTRATION, MANAGEMENT, AND ORGANIZATION

I. Brief Highlights

Listed concisely and sequentially are major headings and important data in the field for quick recall and review.

A. Levels of Management
Any organization of some size has several levels of management. In terms of a ladder, the levels are:

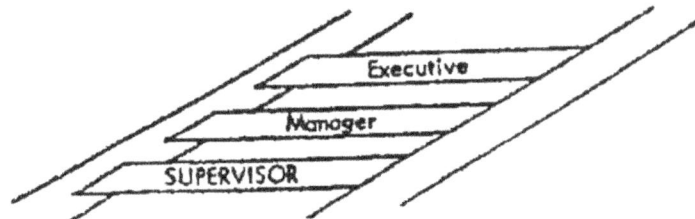

The first level is very important because it is the beginning point of management leadership.

B. What the Supervisor Must Learn
A supervisor must learn to:
1. Deal with people and their differences
2. Get the job done through people
3. Recognize the problems when they exist
4. Overcome obstacles to good performance
5. Evaluate the performance of people
6. Check his own performance in terms of accomplishment

C. A Definition of Supervisor
The term supervisor means any individual having authority, in the interests of the employer, to hire, transfer, suspend, lay-off, recall, promote, discharge, assign, reward, or discipline other employees or responsibility to direct them, or to adjust their grievances, or effectively to recommend such action, if, in connection with the foregoing, exercise of such authority is not of a merely routine or clerical nature but requires the use of independent judgment.

D. Elements of the Team Concept
What is involved in teamwork? The component parts are:
1. Members
2. A leader
3. Goals
4. Plans
5. Cooperation
6. Spirit

E. Principles of Organization
1. A team member must know what his job is.
2. Be sure that the nature and scope of a job are understood.
3. Authority and responsibility should be carefully spelled out.
4. A supervisor should be permitted to make the maximum number of decisions affecting his employees.
5. Employees should report to only one supervisor.
6. A supervisor should direct only as many employees as he can handle effectively.
7. An organization plan should be flexible.

8. Inspection and performance of work should be separate.
9. Organizational problems should receive immediate attention.
10. Assign work in line with ability and experience.

F. The Four Important Parts of Every Job
1. Inherent in every job is the *accountability* for results.
2. A second set of factors in every job is *responsibilities*.
3. Along with duties and responsibilities one must have the *authority* to act within certain limits without obtaining permission to proceed.
4. No job exists in a vacuum. The supervisor is surrounded by key *relationships*.

G. Principles of Delegation
Where work is delegated for the first time, the supervisor should think in terms of these questions:
1. Who is best qualified to do this?
2. Can an employee improve his abilities by doing this?
3. How long should an employee spend on this?
4. Are there any special problems for which he will need guidance?
5. How broad a delegation can I make?

H. Principles of Effective Communications
1. Determine the media.
2. To whom directed?
3. Identification and source authority.
4. Is communication understood?

I. Principles of Work Improvement
1. Most people usually do only the work which is assigned to them.
2. Workers are likely to fit assigned work into the time available to perform it.
3. A good workload usually stimulates output.
4. People usually do their best work when they know that results will be reviewed or inspected.
5. Employees usually feel that someone else is responsible for conditions of work, workplace layout, job methods, type of tools/equipment, and other such factors.
6. Employees are usually defensive about their job security.
7. Employees have natural resistance to change.
8. Employees can support or destroy a supervisor.
9. A supervisor usually earns the respect of his people through his personal example of diligence and efficiency.

J. Areas of Job Improvement
The areas of job improvement are quite numerous, but the most common ones which a supervisor can identify and utilize are:
1. Departmental layout
2. Flow of work
3. Workplace layout
4. Utilization of manpower
5. Work methods
6. Materials handling

7. Utilization
8. Motion economy

K. Seven Key Points in Making Improvements
1. Select the job to be improved
2. Study how it is being done now
3. Question the present method
4. Determine actions to be taken
5. Chart proposed method
6. Get approval and apply
7. Solicit worker participation

l. Corrective Techniques of Job Improvement
Specific Problems
1. Size of workload
2. Inability to meet schedules
3. Strain and fatigue
4. Improper use of men and skills
5. Waste, poor quality, unsafe conditions
6. Bottleneck conditions that hinder output
7. Poor utilization of equipment and machine
8. Efficiency and productivity of labor

General Improvement
1. Departmental layout
2. Flow of work
3. Work plan layout
4. Utilization of manpower
5. Work methods
6. Materials handling
7. Utilization of equipment
8. Motion economy

Corrective Techniques
1. Study with scale model
2. Flow chart study
3. Motion analysis
4. Comparison of units produced to standard allowance
5. Methods analysis
6. Flow chart and equipment study
7. Down time vs. running time
8. Motion analysis

M. A Planning Checklist
1. Objectives
2. Controls
3. Delegations
4. Communications
5. Resources
6. Manpower

7. Equipment
8. Supplies and materials
9. Utilization of time
10. Safety
11. Money
12. Work
13. Timing of improvements

N. Five Characteristics of Good Directions
In order to get results, directions must be:
1. Possible of accomplishment
2. Agreeable with worker interests
3. Related to mission
4. Planned and complete
5. Unmistakably clear

O. Types of Directions
1. Demands or direct orders
2. Requests
3. Suggestion or implication
4. volunteering

P. Controls
A typical listing of the overall areas in which the supervisor should establish controls might be:
1. Manpower
2. Materials
3. Quality of work
4. Quantity of work
5. Time
6. Space
7. Money
8. Methods

Q. Orienting the New Employee
1. Prepare for him
2. Welcome the new employee
3. Orientation for the job
4. Follow-up

R. Checklist for Orienting New Employees   Yes   No
1. Do you appreciate the feelings of new employees
   when they first report for work?   ___   ___
2. Are you aware of the fact that the new employee must
   make a big adjustment to his job?   ___   ___
3. Have you given him good reasons for liking the job and
   the organization?   ___   ___
4. Have you prepared for his first day on the job?   ___   ___
5. Did you welcome him cordially and make him feel needed?   ___   ___

		Yes	No
6.	Did you establish rapport with him so that he feels free to talk and discuss matters with you?	___	___
7.	Did you explain his job to him and his relationship to you?	___	___
8.	Does he know that his work will be evaluated periodically on a basis that is fair and objective?	___	___
9.	Did you introduce him to his fellow workers in such a way that they are likely to accept him?	___	___
10.	Does he know what employee benefits he will receive?	___	___
11.	Does he understand the importance of being on the job and what to do if he must leave his duty station?	___	___
12.	Has he been impressed with the importance of accident prevention and safe practice?	___	___
13.	Does he generally know his way around the department?	___	___
14.	Is he under the guidance of a sponsor who will teach the right way of doing things?	___	___
15.	Do you plan to follow-up so that he will continue to adjust successfully to his job?	___	___

S. Principles of Learning
1. Motivation
2. Demonstration or explanation
3. Practice

T. Causes of Poor Performance
1. Improper training for job
2. Wrong tools
3. Inadequate directions
4. Lack of supervisory follow-up
5. Poor communications
6. Lack of standards of performance
7. Wrong work habits
8. Low morale
9. Other

U. Four Major Steps in On-The-Job Instruction
1. Prepare the worker
2. Present the operation
3. Tryout performance
4. Follow-up

V. Employees Want Five Things
1. Security
2. Opportunity
3. Recognition
4. Inclusion
5. Expression

W. Some Don'ts in Regard to Praise
1. Don't praise a person for something he hasn't done.
2. Don't praise a person unless you can be sincere.
3. Don't be sparing in praise just because your superior withholds it from you.
4. Don't let too much time elapse between good performance and recognition of it

X. How to Gain Your Workers' Confidence
Methods of developing confidence include such things as:
1. Knowing the interests, habits, hobbies of employees
2. Admitting your own inadequacies
3. Sharing and telling of confidence in others
4. Supporting people when they are in trouble
5. Delegating matters that can be well handled
6. Being frank and straightforward about problems and working conditions
7. Encouraging others to bring their problems to you
8. Taking action on problems which impede worker progress

Y. Sources of Employee Problems
On-the-job causes might be such things as:
1. A feeling that favoritism is exercised in assignments
2. Assignment of overtime
3. An undue amount of supervision
4. Changing methods or systems
5. Stealing of ideas or trade secrets
6. Lack of interest in job
7. Threat of reduction in force
8. Ignorance or lack of communications
9. Poor equipment
10. Lack of knowing how supervisor feels toward employee
11. Shift assignments

Off-the-job problems might have to do with:
1. Health
2. Finances
3. Housing
4. Family

Z. The Supervisor's Key to Discipline
There are several key points about discipline which the supervisor should keep in mind:
1. Job discipline is one of the disciplines of life and is directed by the supervisor.
2. It is more important to correct an employee fault than to fix blame for it.
3. Employee performance is affected by problems both on the job and off.
4. Sudden or abrupt changes in behavior can be indications of important employee problems.
5. Problems should be dealt with as soon as possible after they are identified.
6. The attitude of the supervisor may have more to do with solving problems than the techniques of problem solving.
7. Correction of employee behavior should be resorted to only after the supervisor is sure that training or counseling will not be helpful.

8. Be sure to document your disciplinary actions.
9. Make sure that you are disciplining on the basis of facts rather than personal feelings.
10. Take each disciplinary step in order, being careful not to make snap judgments, or decisions based on impatience.

AA. Five Important Processes of Management
1. Planning
2. Organizing
3. Scheduling
4. Controlling
5. Motivating

BB. When the Supervisor Fails to Plan
1. Supervisor creates impression of not knowing his job
2. May lead to excessive overtime
3. Job runs itself—supervisor lacks control
4. Deadlines and appointments missed
5. Parts of the work go undone
6. Work interrupted by emergencies
7. Sets a bad example
8. Uneven workload creates peaks and valleys
9. Too much time on minor details at expense of more important tasks

CC. Fourteen General Principles of Management
1. Division of work
2. Authority and responsibility
3. Discipline
4. Unity of command
5. Unity of direction
6. Subordination of individual interest to general interest
7. Remuneration of personnel
8. Centralization
9. Scalar chain
10. Order
11. Equity
12. Stability of tenure of personnel
13. Initiative
14. Esprit de corps

DD. Change

Bringing about change is perhaps attempted more often, and yet less well understood, than anything else the supervisor does. How do people generally react to change? (People tend to resist change that is imposed upon them by other individuals or circumstances.

Change is characteristic of every situation. It is a part of every real endeavor where the efforts of people are concerned.

1. Why do people resist change?
   People may resist change because of:
   a. Fear of the unknown
   b. Implied criticism
   c. Unpleasant experiences in the past
   d. Fear of loss of status
   e. Threat to the ego
   f. Fear of loss of economic stability

2. How can we best overcome the resistance to change?
   In initiating change, take these steps:
   a. Get ready to sell
   b. Identify sources of help
   c. Anticipate objections
   d. Sell benefits
   e. Listen in depth
   f. Follow up

II. Brief Topical Summaries

   A. Who/What is the Supervisor?
      1. The supervisor is often called the "highest level employee and the lowest level manager."
      2. A supervisor is a member of both management and the work group. He acts as a bridge between the two.
      3. Most problems in supervision are in the area of human relations, or people problems.
      4. Employees expect: Respect, opportunity to learn and to advance, and a sense of belonging, and so forth.
      5. Supervisors are responsible for directing people and organizing work. Planning is of paramount importance.
      6. A position description is a set of duties and responsibilities inherent to a given position.
      7. It is important to keep the position description up-to-date and to provide each employee with his own copy.

   B. The Sociology of Work
      1. People are alike in many ways; however, each individual is unique.
      2. The supervisor is challenged in getting to know employee differences. Acquiring skills in evaluating individuals is an asset.
      3. Maintaining meaningful working relationships in the organization is of great importance.
      4. The supervisor has an obligation to help individuals to develop to their fullest potential.
      5. Job rotation on a planned basis helps to build versatility and to maintain interest and enthusiasm in work groups.
      6. Cross training (job rotation) provides backup skills.

7. The supervisor can help reduce tension by maintaining a sense of humor, providing guidance to employees, and by making reasonable and timely decisions. Employees respond favorably to working under reasonably predictable circumstances.
8. Change is characteristic of all managerial behavior. The supervisor must adjust to changes in procedures, new methods, technological changes, and to a number of new and sometimes challenging situations.
9. To overcome the natural tendency for people to resist change, the supervisor should become more skillful in initiating change.

C. Principles and Practices of Supervision
1. Employees should be required to answer to only one superior.
2. A supervisor can effectively direct only a limited number of employees, depending upon the complexity, variety, and proximity of the jobs involved.
3. The organizational chart presents the organization in graphic form. It reflects lines of authority and responsibility as well as interrelationships of units within the organization.
4. Distribution of work can be improved through an analysis using the "Work Distribution Chart."
5. The "Work Distribution Chart" reflects the division of work within a unit in understandable form.
6. When related tasks are given to an employee, he has a better chance of increasing his skills through training.
7. The individual who is given the responsibility for tasks must also be given the appropriate authority to insure adequate results.
8. The supervisor should delegate repetitive, routine work. Preparation of recurring reports, maintaining leave and attendance records are some examples.
9. Good discipline is essential to good task performance. Discipline is reflected in the actions of employees on the job in the absence of supervision.
10. Disciplinary action may have to be taken when the positive aspects of discipline have failed. Reprimand, warning, and suspension are examples of disciplinary action.
11. If a situation calls for a reprimand, be sure it is deserved and remember it is to be done in private.

D. Dynamic Leadership
1. A style is a personal method or manner of exerting influence.
2. Authoritarian leaders often see themselves as the source of power and authority.
3. The democratic leader often perceives the group as the source of authority and power.
4. Supervisors tend to do better when using the pattern of leadership that is most natural for them.
5. Social scientists suggest that the effective supervisor use the leadership style that best fits the problem or circumstances involved.
6. All four styles—telling, selling, consulting, joining—have their place. Using one does not preclude using the other at another time.

7. The theory X point of view assumes that the average person dislikes work, will avoid it whenever possible, and must be coerced to achieve organizational objectives.
8. The theory Y point of view assumes that the average person considers work to be a natural as play, and, when the individual is committed, he requires little supervision or direction to accomplish desired objectives.
9. The leader's basic assumptions concerning human behavior and human nature affect his actions, decisions, and other managerial practices.
10. Dissatisfaction among employees is often present, but difficult to isolate. The supervisor should seek to weaken dissatisfaction by keeping promises, being sincere and considerate, keeping employees informed, and so forth.
11. Constructive suggestions should be encouraged during the natural progress of the work.

E. Processes for Solving Problems
1. People find their daily tasks more meaningful and satisfying when they can improve them.
2. The causes of problems, or the key factors, are often hidden in the background. Ability to solve problems often involves the ability to isolate them from their backgrounds. There is some substance to the cliché that some persons "can't see the forest for the trees."
3. New procedures are often developed from old ones. Problems should be broken down into manageable parts. New ideas can be adapted from old one.
4. People think differently in problem-solving situations. Using a logical, patterned approach is often useful. One approach found to be useful includes these steps:
   a. Define the problem
   b. Establish objectives
   c. Get the facts
   d. Weigh and decide
   e. Take action
   f. Evaluate action

F. Training for Results
1. Participants respond best when they feel training is important to them.
2. The supervisor has responsibility for the training and development of those who report to him.
3. When training is delegated to others, great care must be exercised to insure the trainer has knowledge, aptitude, and interest for his work as a trainer.
4. Training (learning) of some type goes on continually. The most successful supervisor makes certain the learning contributes in a productive manner to operational goals.
5. New employees are particularly susceptible to training. Older employees facing new job situations require specific training, as well as having need for development and growth opportunities.
6. Training needs require continuous monitoring.
7. The training officer of an agency is a professional with a responsibility to assist supervisors in solving training problems.

8. Many of the self-development steps important to the supervisor's own growth are equally important to the development of peers and subordinates. Knowledge of these is important when the supervisor consults with others on development and growth opportunities.

G. Health, Safety, and Accident Prevention
1. Management-minded supervisors take appropriate measures to assist employees in maintaining health and in assuring safe practices in the work environment.
2. Effective safety training and practices help to avoid injury and accidents.
3. Safety should be a management goal. All infractions of safety which are observed should be corrected without exception.
4. Employees' safety attitude, training and instruction, provision of safe tools and equipment, supervision, and leadership are considered highly important factors which contribute to safety and which can be influenced directly by supervisors.
5. When accidents do occur, they should be investigated promptly for very important reasons, including the fact that information which is gained can be used to prevent accidents in the future.

H. Equal Employment Opportunity
1. The supervisor should endeavor to treat all employees fairly, without regard to religion, race, sex, or national origin.
2. Groups tend to reflect the attitude of the leader. Prejudice can be detected even in very subtle form. Supervisors must strive to create a feeling of mutual respect and confidence in every employee.
3. Complete utilization of all human resources is a national goal. Equitable consideration should be accorded women in the work force, minority-group members, the physically and mentally handicapped, and the older employee. The important question is: "Who can do the job?"
4. Training opportunities, recognition for performance, overtime assignments, promotional opportunities, and all other personnel actions are to be handled on an equitable basis.

I. Improving Communications
1. Communications is achieving understanding between the sender and the receiver of a message. It also means sharing information—the creation of understanding.
2. Communication is basic to all human activity. Words are means of conveying meanings; however, real meanings are in people.
3. There are very practical differences in the effectiveness of one-way, impersonal, and two-way communications. Words spoken face-to-face are better understood. Telephone conversations are effective, but lack the rapport of person-to-person exchanges. The whole person communicates.
4. Cooperation and communication in an organization go hand in hand. When there is a mutual respect between people, spelling out rules and procedures for communicating is unnecessary.
5. There are several barriers to effective communications. These include failure to listen with respect and understanding, lack of skill in feedback, and misinterpreting the meanings of words used by the speaker. It is also common

practice to listen to what we want to hear, and tune out things we do not want to hear.
6. Communication is management's chief problem. The supervisor should accept the challenge to communicate more effectively and to improve interagency and intra-agency communications.
7. The supervisor may often plan for and conduct meetings. The planning phase is critical and may determine the success or the failure of a meeting.
8. Speaking before groups usually requires extra effort. Stage fright may never disappear completely, but it can be controlled.

J. Self-Development
1. Every employee is responsible for his own self-development.
2. Toastmaster and toastmistress clubs offer opportunities to improve skills in oral communications.
3. Planning for one's own self-development is of vital importance. Supervisors know their own strengths and limitations better than anyone else.
4. Many opportunities are open to aid the supervisor in his developmental efforts, including job assignments; training opportunities, both governmental and non-governmental—to include universities and professional conferences and seminars.
5. Programmed instruction offers a means of studying at one's own rate.
6. Where difficulties may arise from a supervisor's being away from his work for training, he may participate in televised home study or correspondence courses to meet his self-development needs.

K. Teaching and Training
1. The Teaching Process
Teaching is encouraging and guiding the learning activities of students toward established goals. In most cases this process consists of five steps: preparation, presentation, summarization, evaluation, and application.

   a. Preparation
   Preparation is two-fold in nature; that of the supervisor and the employee. Preparation by the supervisor is absolutely essential to success. He must know what, when, where, how, and whom he will teach. Some of the factors that should be considered are:
   1) The objectives
   2) The materials needed
   3) The methods to be used
   4) Employee participation
   5) Employee interest
   6) Training aids
   7) Evaluation
   8) Summarization

   Employee preparation consists in preparing the employee to receive the material. Probably the most important single factor in the preparation of the employee is arousing and maintaining his interest. He must know the objectives of the training, why he is there, how the material can be used, and its importance to him.

b. Presentation
In presentation, have a carefully designed plan and follow it. The plan should be accurate and complete, yet flexible enough to meet situations as they arise. The method of presentation will be determined by the particular situation and objectives.

c. Summary
A summary should be made at the end of every training unit and program. In addition, there may be internal summaries depending on the nature of the material being taught. The important thing is that the trainee must always be able to understand how each part of the new material relates to the whole.

d. Application
The supervisor must arrange work so the employee will be given a chance to apply new knowledge or skills while the material is still clear in his mind and interest is high. The trainee does not really know whether he has learned the material until he has been given a chance to apply it. If the material is not applied, it loses most of its value.

e. Evaluation
The purpose of all training is to promote learning. To determine whether the training has been a success or failure, the supervisor must evaluate this learning.
In the broadest sense, evaluation includes all the devices, methods, skills, and techniques used by the supervisor to keep himself and the employees informed as to their progress toward the objectives they are pursuing. The extent to which the employee has mastered the knowledge, skills, and abilities, or changed his attitudes, as determined by the program objectives, is the extent to which instruction has succeeded or failed.
Evaluation should not be confined to the end of the lesson, day, or program but should be used continuously. We shall note later the way this relates to the rest of the teaching process.

2. Teaching Methods
A teaching method is a pattern of identifiable student and instructor activity used in presenting training material.
All supervisors are faced with the problem of deciding which method should be used at a given time.

a. Lecture
The lecture is direct oral presentation of material by the supervisor. The present trend is to place less emphasis on the trainer's activity and more on that of the trainee.

b. Discussion
Teaching by discussion or conference involves using questions and other techniques to arouse interest and focus attention upon certain areas, and by doing so creating a learning situation. This can be one of the most

valuable methods because it gives the employees an opportunity to express their ideas and pool their knowledge.

c. Demonstration
The demonstration is used to teach how something works or how to do something. It can be used to show a principle or what the results of a series of actions will be. A well-staged demonstration is particularly effective because it shows proper methods of performance in a realistic manner.

d. Performance
Performance is one of the most fundamental of all learning techniques or teaching methods. The trainee may be able to tell how a specific operation should be performed but he cannot be sure he knows how to perform the operation until he has done so.
As with all methods, there are certain advantages and disadvantages to each method.

e. Which Method to Use
Moreover, there are other methods and techniques of teaching. It is difficult to use any method without other methods entering into it. In any learning situation, a combination of methods is usually more effective than any one method alone.

Finally, evaluation must be integrated into the other aspects of the teaching-learning process.

It must be used in the motivation of the trainees; it must be used to assist in developing understanding during the training; and it must be related to employee application of the results of training.

This is distinctly the role of the supervisor.

GLOSSARY OF LEGAL TERMS

TABLE OF CONTENTS

	Page
Action ... Affiant	1
Affidavit ... At Bar	2
At Issue ... Burden of Proof	3
Business ... Commute	4
Complainant ... Conviction	5
Cooperative ... Demur (v.)	6
Demurrage ... Endorsement	7
Enjoin ... Facsimile	8
Factor ... Guilty	9
Habeas Corpus ... Incumbrance	10
Indemnify ... Laches	11
Landlord and Tenant ... Malice	12
Mandamus ... Obiter Dictum	13
Object (v.) ... Perjury	14
Perpetuity ... Proclamation	15
Proffered Evidence ... Referee	16
Referendum ... Stare Decisis	17
State ... Term	18
Testamentary ... Warrant (Warranty) (v.)	19
Warrant (n.) ... Zoning	20

GLOSSARY OF LEGAL TERMS

A

ACTION - "Action" includes a civil action and a criminal action.

A FORTIORI - A term meaning you can reason one thing from the existence of certain facts.

A POSTERIORI - From what goes after; from effect to cause.

A PRIORI - From what goes before; from cause to effect.

AB INITIO - From the beginning.

ABATE - To diminish or put an end to.

ABET - To encourage the commission of a crime.

ABEYANCE - Suspension, temporary suppression.

ABIDE - To accept the consequences of.

ABJURE - To renounce; give up.

ABRIDGE - To reduce; contract; diminish.

ABROGATE - To annul, repeal, or destroy.

ABSCOND - To hide or absent oneself to avoid legal action.

ABSTRACT - A summary.

ABUT - To border on, to touch.

ACCESS - Approach; in real property law it means the right of the owner of property to the use of the highway or road next to his land, without obstruction by intervening property owners.

ACCESSORY - In criminal law, it means the person who contributes or aids in the commission of a crime.

ACCOMMODATED PARTY - One to whom credit is extended on the strength of another person signing a commercial paper.

ACCOMMODATION PAPER - A commercial paper to which the accommodating party has put his name.

ACCOMPLICE - In criminal law, it means a person who together with the principal offender commits a crime.

ACCORD - An agreement to accept something different or less than that to which one is entitled, which extinguishes the entire obligation.

ACCOUNT - A statement of mutual demands in the nature of debt and credit between parties.

ACCRETION - The act of adding to a thing; in real property law, it means gradual accumulation of land by natural causes.

ACCRUE - To grow to; to be added to.

ACKNOWLEDGMENT - The act of going before an official authorized to take acknowledgments, and acknowledging an act as one's own.

ACQUIESCENCE - A silent appearance of consent.

ACQUIT - To legally determine the innocence of one charged with a crime.

AD INFINITUM - Indefinitely.

AD LITEM - For the suit.

AD VALOREM - According to value.

ADJECTIVE LAW - Rules of procedure.

ADJUDICATION - The judgment given in a case.

ADMIRALTY - Court having jurisdiction over maritime cases.

ADULT - Sixteen years old or over (in criminal law).

ADVANCE - In commercial law, it means to pay money or render other value before it is due.

ADVERSE - Opposed; contrary.

ADVOCATE - (v.) To speak in favor of;
(n.) One who assists, defends, or pleads for another.

AFFIANT - A person who makes and signs an affidavit.

AFFIDAVIT - A written and sworn to declaration of facts, voluntarily made.
AFFINITY - The relationship between persons through marriage with the kindred of each other; distinguished from consanguinity, which is the relationship by blood.
AFFIRM - To ratify; also when an appellate court affirms a judgment, decree, or order, it means that it is valid and right and must stand as rendered in the lower court.
AFOREMENTIONED; AFORESAID - Before or already said.
AGENT - One who represents and acts for another.
AID AND COMFORT - To help; encourage.
ALIAS - A name not one's true name.
ALIBI - A claim of not being present at a certain place at a certain time.
ALLEGE - To assert.
ALLOTMENT - A share or portion.
AMBIGUITY - Uncertainty; capable of being understood in more than one way.
AMENDMENT - Any language made or proposed as a change in some principal writing.
AMICUS CURIAE - A friend of the court; one who has an interest in a case, although not a party in the case, who volunteers advice upon matters of law to the judge. For example, a brief amicus curiae.
AMORTIZATION - To provide for a gradual extinction of (a future obligation) in advance of maturity, especially, by periodical contributions to a sinking fund which will be adequate to discharge a debt or make a replacement when it becomes necessary.
ANCILLARY - Aiding, auxiliary.
ANNOTATION - A note added by way of comment or explanation.
ANSWER - A written statement made by a defendant setting forth the grounds of his defense.
ANTE - Before.
ANTE MORTEM - Before death.
APPEAL - The removal of a case from a lower court to one of superior jurisdiction for the purpose of obtaining a review.
APPEARANCE - Coming into court as a party to a suit.
APPELLANT - The party who takes an appeal from one court or jurisdiction to another (appellate) court for review.
APPELLEE - The party against whom an appeal is taken.
APPROPRIATE - To make a thing one's own.
APPROPRIATION - Prescribing the destination of a thing; the act of the legislature designating a particular fund, to be applied to some object of government expenditure.
APPURTENANT - Belonging to; accessory or incident to.
ARBITER - One who decides a dispute; a referee.
ARBITRARY - Unreasoned; not governed by any fixed rules or standard.
ARGUENDO - By way of argument.
ARRAIGN - To call the prisoner before the court to answer to a charge.
ASSENT - A declaration of willingness to do something in compliance with a request.
ASSERT - Declare.
ASSESS - To fix the rate or amount.
ASSIGN - To transfer; to appoint; to select for a particular purpose.
ASSIGNEE - One who receives an assignment.
ASSIGNOR - One who makes an assignment.
AT BAR - Before the court.

AT ISSUE - When parties in an action come to a point where one asserts something and the other denies it.
ATTACH - Seize property by court order and sometimes arrest a person.
ATTEST - To witness a will, etc.; act of attestation.
AVERMENT - A positive statement of facts.

B

BAIL - To obtain the release of a person from legal custody by giving security and promising that he shall appear in court; to deliver (goods, etc.) in trust to a person for a special purpose.
BAILEE - One to whom personal property is delivered under a contract of bailment.
BAILMENT - Delivery of personal property to another to be held for a certain purpose and to be returned when the purpose is accomplished.
BAILOR - The party who delivers goods to another, under a contract of bailment.
BANC (OR BANK) - Bench; the place where a court sits permanently or regularly; also the assembly of all the judges of a court.
BANKRUPT - An insolvent person, technically, one declared to be bankrupt after a bankruptcy proceeding.
BAR - The legal profession.
BARRATRY - Exciting groundless judicial proceedings.
BARTER - A contract by which parties exchange goods for other goods.
BATTERY - Illegal interfering with another's person.
BEARER - In commercial law, it means the person in possession of a commercial paper which is payable to the bearer.
BENCH - The court itself or the judge.
BENEFICIARY - A person benefiting under a will, trust, or agreement.
BEST EVIDENCE RULE, THE - Except as otherwise provided by statute, no evidence other than the writing itself is admissible to prove the content of a writing. This section shall be known and may be cited as the best evidence rule.
BEQUEST - A gift of personal property under a will.
BILL - A formal written statement of complaint to a court of justice; also, a draft of an act of the legislature before it becomes a law; also, accounts for goods sold, services rendered, or work done.
BONA FIDE - In or with good faith; honestly.
BOND - An instrument by which the maker promises to pay a sum of money to another, usually providing that upon performances of a certain condition the obligation shall be void.
BOYCOTT - A plan to prevent the carrying on of a business by wrongful means.
BREACH - The breaking or violating of a law, or the failure to carry out a duty.
BRIEF - A written document, prepared by a lawyer to serve as the basis of an argument upon a case in court, usually an appellate court.
BURDEN OF PRODUCING EVIDENCE - The obligation of a party to introduce evidence sufficient to avoid a ruling against him on the issue.
BURDEN OF PROOF - The obligation of a party to establish by evidence a requisite degree of belief concerning a fact in the mind of the trier of fact or the court. The burden of proof may require a party to raise a reasonable doubt concerning the existence of nonexistence of a fact or that he establish the existence or nonexistence of a fact by a preponderance of the evidence, by clear and convincing proof, or by proof beyond a reasonable doubt.

Except as otherwise provided by law, the burden of proof requires proof by a preponderance of the evidence.

BUSINESS, A - Shall include every kind of business, profession, occupation, calling or operation of institutions, whether carried on for profit or not.

BY-LAWS - Regulations, ordinances, or rules enacted by a corporation, association, etc., for its own government.

C

CANON - A doctrine; also, a law or rule, of a church or association in particular.

CAPIAS - An order to arrest.

CAPTION - In a pleading, deposition or other paper connected with a case in court, it is the heading or introductory clause which shows the names of the parties, name of the court, number of the case on the docket or calendar, etc.

CARRIER - A person or corporation undertaking to transport persons or property.

CASE - A general term for an action, cause, suit, or controversy before a judicial body.

CAUSE - A suit, litigation or action before a court.

CAVEAT EMPTOR - Let the buyer beware. This term expresses the rule that the purchaser of an article must examine, judge, and test it for himself, being bound to discover any obvious defects or imperfections.

CERTIFICATE - A written representation that some legal formality has been complied with.

CERTIORARI - To be informed of; the name of a writ issued by a superior court directing the lower court to send up to the former the record and proceedings of a case.

CHANGE OF VENUE - To remove place of trial from one place to another.

CHARGE - An obligation or duty; a formal complaint; an instruction of the court to the jury upon a case.

CHARTER - (n.) The authority by virtue of which an organized body acts;
(v.) in mercantile law, it means to hire or lease a vehicle or vessel for transportation.

CHATTEL - An article of personal property.

CHATTEL MORTGAGE - A mortgage on personal property.

CIRCUIT - A division of the country, for the administration of justice; a geographical area served by a court.

CITATION - The act of the court by which a person is summoned or cited; also, a reference to legal authority.

CIVIL (ACTIONS)- It indicates the private rights and remedies of individuals in contrast to the word "criminal" (actions) which relates to prosecution for violation of laws.

CLAIM (n.) - Any demand held or asserted as of right.

CODICIL - An addition to a will.

CODIFY - To arrange the laws of a country into a code.

COGNIZANCE - Notice or knowledge.

COLLATERAL - By the side; accompanying; an article or thing given to secure performance of a promise.

COMITY - Courtesy; the practice by which one court follows the decision of another court on the same question.

COMMIT - To perform, as an act; to perpetrate, as a crime; to send a person to prison.

COMMON LAW - As distinguished from law created by the enactment of the legislature (called statutory law), it relates to those principles and rules of action which derive their authority solely from usages and customs of immemorial antiquity, particularly with reference to the ancient unwritten law of England. The written pronouncements of the common law are found in court decisions.

COMMUTE - Change punishment to one less severe.

COMPLAINANT - One who applies to the court for legal redress.
COMPLAINT - The pleading of a plaintiff in a civil action; or a charge that a person has committed a specified offense.
COMPROMISE - An arrangement for settling a dispute by agreement.
CONCUR - To agree, consent.
CONCURRENT - Running together, at the same time.
CONDEMNATION - Taking private property for public use on payment therefor.
CONDITION - Mode or state of being; a qualification or restriction.
CONDUCT - Active and passive behavior; both verbal and nonverbal.
CONFESSION - Voluntary statement of guilt of crime.
CONFIDENTIAL COMMUNICATION BETWEEN CLIENT AND LAWYER - Information transmitted between a client and his lawyer in the course of that relationship and in confidence by a means which, so far as the client is aware, discloses the information to no third persons other than those who are present to further the interest of the client in the consultation or those to whom disclosure is reasonably necessary for the transmission of the information or the accomplishment of the purpose for which the lawyer is consulted, and includes a legal opinion formed and the advice given by the lawyer in the course of that relationship.
CONFRONTATION - Witness testifying in presence of defendant.
CONSANGUINITY - Blood relationship.
CONSIGN - To give in charge; commit; entrust; to send or transmit goods to a merchant, factor, or agent for sale.
CONSIGNEE - One to whom a consignment is made.
CONSIGNOR - One who sends or makes a consignment.
CONSPIRACY - In criminal law, it means an agreement between two or more persons to commit an unlawful act.
CONSPIRATORS - Persons involved in a conspiracy.
CONSTITUTION - The fundamental law of a nation or state.
CONSTRUCTION OF GENDERS - The masculine gender includes the feminine and neuter.
CONSTRUCTION OF SINGULAR AND PLURAL - The singular number includes the plural; and the plural, the singular.
CONSTRUCTION OF TENSES - The present tense includes the past and future tenses; and the future, the present.
CONSTRUCTIVE - An act or condition assumed from other parts or conditions.
CONSTRUE - To ascertain the meaning of language.
CONSUMMATE - To complete.
CONTIGUOUS - Adjoining; touching; bounded by.
CONTINGENT - Possible, but not assured; dependent upon some condition.
CONTINUANCE - The adjournment or postponement of an action pending in a court.
CONTRA - Against, opposed to; contrary.
CONTRACT - An agreement between two or more persons to do or not to do a particular thing.
CONTROVERT - To dispute, deny.
CONVERSION - Dealing with the personal property of another as if it were one's own, without right.
CONVEYANCE - An instrument transferring title to land.
CONVICTION - Generally, the result of a criminal trial which ends in a judgment or sentence that the defendant is guilty as charged.

COOPERATIVE - A cooperative is a voluntary organization of persons with a common interest, formed and operated along democratic lines for the purpose of supplying services at cost to its members and other patrons, who contribute both capital and business.
CORPUS DELICTI - The body of a crime; the crime itself.
CORROBORATE - To strengthen; to add weight by additional evidence.
COUNTERCLAIM - A claim presented by a defendant in opposition to or deduction from the claim of the plaintiff.
COUNTY - Political subdivision of a state.
COVENANT - Agreement.
CREDIBLE - Worthy of belief.
CREDITOR - A person to whom a debt is owing by another person, called the "debtor."
CRIMINAL ACTION - Includes criminal proceedings.
CRIMINAL INFORMATION - Same as complaint.
CRITERION (sing.)
CRITERIA (plural) - A means or tests for judging; a standard or standards.
CROSS-EXAMINATION - Examination of a witness by a party other than the direct examiner upon a matter that is within the scope of the direct examination of the witness.
CULPABLE - Blamable.
CY-PRES - As near as (possible). The rule of *cy-pres* is a rule for the construction of instruments in equity by which the intention of the party is carried out *as near as may be*, when it would be impossible or illegal to give it literal effect.

D

DAMAGES - A monetary compensation, which may be recovered in the courts by any person who has suffered loss, or injury, whether to his person, property or rights through the unlawful act or omission or negligence of another.
DECLARANT - A person who makes a statement.
DE FACTO - In fact; actually but without legal authority.
DE JURE - Of right; legitimate; lawful.
DE MINIMIS - Very small or trifling.
DE NOVO - Anew; afresh; a second time.
DEBT - A specified sum of money owing to one person from another, including not only the obligation of the debtor to pay, but the right of the creditor to receive and enforce payment.
DECEDENT - A dead person.
DECISION - A judgment or decree pronounced by a court in determination of a case.
DECREE - An order of the court, determining the rights of all parties to a suit.
DEED - A writing containing a contract sealed and delivered; particularly to convey real property.
DEFALCATION - Misappropriation of funds.
DEFAMATION - Injuring one's reputation by false statements.
DEFAULT - The failure to fulfill a duty, observe a promise, discharge an obligation, or perform an agreement.
DEFENDANT - The person defending or denying; the party against whom relief or recovery is sought in an action or suit.
DEFRAUD - To practice fraud; to cheat or trick.
DELEGATE (v.)- To entrust to the care or management of another.
DELICTUS - A crime.
DEMUR (v.) - To dispute the sufficiency in law of the pleading of the other side.

DEMURRAGE - In maritime law, it means, the sum fixed or allowed as remuneration to the owners of a ship for the detention of their vessel beyond the number of days allowed for loading and unloading or for sailing; also used in railroad terminology.

DENIAL - A form of pleading; refusing to admit the truth of a statement, charge, etc.

DEPONENT - One who gives testimony under oath reduced to writing.

DEPOSITION - Testimony given under oath outside of court for use in court or for the purpose of obtaining information in preparation for trial of a case.

DETERIORATION - A degeneration such as from decay, corrosion or disintegration.

DETRIMENT - Any loss or harm to person or property.

DEVIATION - A turning aside.

DEVISE - A gift of real property by the last will and testament of the donor.

DICTUM (sing.)
DICTA (plural) - Any statements made by the court in an opinion concerning some rule of law not necessarily involved nor essential to the determination of the case.

DIRECT EVIDENCE - Evidence that directly proves a fact, without an inference or presumption, and which in itself if true, conclusively establishes that fact.

DIRECT EXAMINATION - The first examination of a witness upon a matter that is not within the scope of a previous examination of the witness.

DISAFFIRM - To repudiate.

DISMISS - In an action or suit, it means to dispose of the case without any further consideration or hearing.

DISSENT - To denote disagreement of one or more judges of a court with the decision passed by the majority upon a case before them.

DOCKET (n.) - A formal record, entered in brief, of the proceedings in a court.

DOCTRINE - A rule, principle, theory of law.

DOMICILE - That place where a man has his true, fixed and permanent home to which whenever he is absent he has the intention of returning.

DRAFT (n.) - A commercial paper ordering payment of money drawn by one person on another.

DRAWEE - The person who is requested to pay the money.

DRAWER - The person who draws the commercial paper and addresses it to the drawee.

DUPLICATE - A counterpart produced by the same impression as the original enlargements and miniatures, or by mechanical or electronic re-recording, or by chemical reproduction, or by other equivalent technique which accurately reproduces the original.

DURESS - Use of force to compel performance or non-performance of an act.

E

EASEMENT - A liberty, privilege, or advantage without profit, in the lands of another.

EGRESS - Act or right of going out or leaving; emergence.

EIUSDEM GENERIS - Of the same kind, class or nature. A rule used in the construction of language in a legal document.

EMBEZZLEMENT - To steal; to appropriate fraudulently to one's own use property entrusted to one's care.

EMBRACERY - Unlawful attempt to influence jurors, etc., but not by offering value.

EMINENT DOMAIN - The right of a state to take private property for public use.

ENACT - To make into a law.

ENDORSEMENT - Act of writing one's name on the back of a note, bill or similar written instrument.

ENJOIN - To require a person, by writ of injunction from a court of equity, to perform or to abstain or desist from some act.
ENTIRETY - The whole; that which the law considers as one whole, and not capable of being divided into parts.
ENTRAPMENT - Inducing one to commit a crime so as to arrest him.
ENUMERATED - Mentioned specifically; designated.
ENURE - To operate or take effect.
EQUITY - In its broadest sense, this term denotes the spirit and the habit of fairness, justness, and right dealing which regulate the conduct of men.
ERROR - A mistake of law, or the false or irregular application of law as will nullify the judicial proceedings.
ESCROW - A deed, bond or other written engagement, delivered to a third person, to be delivered by him only upon the performance or fulfillment of some condition.
ESTATE - The interest which any one has in lands, or in any other subject of property.
ESTOP - To stop, bar, or impede.
ESTOPPEL - A rule of law which prevents a man from alleging or denying a fact, because of his own previous act.
ET AL. (alii) - And others.
ET SEQ. (sequential) - And the following.
ET UX. (uxor) - And wife.
EVIDENCE - Testimony, writings, material objects, or other things presented to the senses that are offered to prove the existence or non-existence of a fact.
    Means from which inferences may be drawn as a basis of proof in duly constituted judicial or fact finding tribunals, and includes testimony in the form of opinion and hearsay.
EX CONTRACTU
EX DELICTO - In law, rights and causes of action are divided into two classes, those arising *ex contractu* (from a contract) and those arising *ex delicto* (from a delict or tort).
EX OFFICIO - From office; by virtue of the office.
EX PARTE - On one side only; by or for one.
EX POST FACTO - After the fact.
EX POST FACTO LAW - A law passed after an act was done which retroactively makes such act a crime.
EX REL. (relations) - Upon relation or information.
EXCEPTION - An objection upon a matter of law to a decision made, either before or after judgment by a court.
EXECUTOR (male)
EXECUTRIX (female) - A person who has been appointed by will to execute the will.
EXECUTORY - That which is yet to be executed or performed.
EXEMPT - To release from some liability to which others are subject.
EXONERATION - The removal of a burden, charge or duty.
EXTRADITION - Surrender of a fugitive from one nation to another.

F

F.A.S.- "Free alongside ship"; delivery at dock for ship named.
F.O.B.- "Free on board"; seller will deliver to car, truck, vessel, or other conveyance by which goods are to be transported, without expense or risk of loss to the buyer or consignee.
FABRICATE - To construct; to invent a false story.
FACSIMILE - An exact or accurate copy of an original instrument.

FACTOR - A commercial agent.
FEASANCE - The doing of an act.
FELONIOUS - Criminal, malicious.
FELONY - Generally, a criminal offense that may be punished by death or imprisonment for more than one year as differentiated from a misdemeanor.
FEME SOLE - A single woman.
FIDUCIARY - A person who is invested with rights and powers to be exercised for the benefit of another person.
FIERI FACIAS - A writ of execution commanding the sheriff to levy and collect the amount of a judgment from the goods and chattels of the judgment debtor.
FINDING OF FACT - Determination from proof or judicial notice of the existence of a fact. A ruling implies a supporting finding of fact; no separate or formal finding is required unless required by a statute of this state.
FISCAL - Relating to accounts or the management of revenue.
FORECLOSURE (sale) - A sale of mortgaged property to obtain satisfaction of the mortgage out of the sale proceeds.
FORFEITURE - A penalty, a fine.
FORGERY - Fabricating or producing falsely, counterfeited.
FORTUITOUS - Accidental.
FORUM - A court of justice; a place of jurisdiction.
FRAUD - Deception; trickery.
FREEHOLDER - One who owns real property.
FUNGIBLE - Of such kind or nature that one specimen or part may be used in the place of another.

G

GARNISHEE - Person garnished.
GARNISHMENT - A legal process to reach the money or effects of a defendant, in the possession or control of a third person.
GRAND JURY - Not less than 16, not more than 23 citizens of a county sworn to inquire into crimes committed or triable in the county.
GRANT - To agree to; convey, especially real property.
GRANTEE - The person to whom a grant is made.
GRANTOR - The person by whom a grant is made.
GRATUITOUS - Given without a return, compensation or consideration.
GRAVAMEN - The grievance complained of or the substantial cause of a criminal action.
GUARANTY (n.) - A promise to answer for the payment of some debt, or the performance of some duty, in case of the failure of another person, who, in the first instance, is liable for such payment or performance.
GUARDIAN - The person, committee, or other representative authorized by law to protect the person or estate or both of an incompetent (or of a *sui juris* person having a guardian) and to act for him in matters affecting his person or property or both. An incompetent is a person under disability imposed by law.
GUILTY - Establishment of the fact that one has committed a breach of conduct; especially, a violation of law.

H

HABEAS CORPUS - You have the body; the name given to a variety of writs, having for their object to bring a party before a court or judge for decision as to whether such person is being lawfully held prisoner.
HABENDUM - In conveyancing; it is the clause in a deed conveying land which defines the extent of ownership to be held by the grantee.
HEARING - A proceeding whereby the arguments of the interested parties are heared.
HEARSAY - A type of testimony given by a witness who relates, not what he knows personally, but what others have told hi, or what he has heard said by others.
HEARSAY RULE, THE - (a) "Hearsay evidence" is evidence of a statement that was made other than by a witness while testifying at the hearing and that is offered to prove the truth of the matter stated; (b) Except as provided by law, hearsay evidence is inadmissible; (c) This section shall be known and may be cited as the hearsay rule.
HEIR - Generally, one who inherits property, real or personal.
HOLDER OF THE PRIVILEGE - (a) The client when he has no guardian or conservator; (b) A guardian or conservator of the client when the client has a guardian or conservator; (c) The personal representative of the client if the client is dead; (d) A successor, assign, trustee in dissolution, or any similar representative of a firm, association, organization, partnership, business trust, corporation, or public entity that is no longer in existence.
HUNG JURY - One so divided that they can't agree on a verdict.
HUSBAND-WIFE PRIVILEGE - An accused in a criminal proceeding has a privilege to prevent his spouse from testifying against him.
HYPOTHECATE - To pledge a thing without delivering it to the pledgee.
HYPOTHESIS - A supposition, assumption, or toehry.

I

I.E. (id est) - That is.
IB., OR IBID.(ibidem) - In the same place; used to refer to a legal reference previously cited to avoid repeating the entire citation.
ILLICIT - Prohibited; unlawful.
ILLUSORY - Deceiving by false appearance.
IMMUNITY - Exemption.
IMPEACH - To accuse, to dispute.
IMPEDIMENTS - Disabilities, or hindrances.
IMPLEAD - To sue or prosecute by due course of law.
IMPUTED - Attributed or charged to.
IN LOCO PARENTIS - In place of parent, a guardian.
IN TOTO - In the whole; completely.
INCHOATE - Imperfect; unfinished.
INCOMMUNICADO - Denial of the right of a prisoner to communicate with friends or relatives.
INCOMPETENT - One who is incapable of caring for his own affairs because he is mentally deficient or undeveloped.
INCRIMINATION - A matter will incriminate a person if it constitutes, or forms an essential part of, or, taken in connection with other matters disclosed, is a basis for a reasonable inference of such a violation of the laws of this State as to subject him to liability to punishment therefor, unless he has become for any reason permanently immune from punishment for such violation.
INCUMBRANCE - Generally a claim, lien, charge or liability attached to and binding real property.

INDEMNIFY - To secure against loss or damage; also, to make reimbursement to one for a loss already incurred by him.
INDEMNITY - An agreement to reimburse another person in case of an anticipated loss falling upon him.
INDICIA - Signs; indications.
INDICTMENT - An accusation in writing found and presented by a grand jury charging that a person has committed a crime.
INDORSE - To write a name on the back of a legal paper or document, generally, a negotiable instrument
INDUCEMENT - Cause or reason why a thing is done or that which incites the person to do the act or commit a crime; the motive for the criminal act.
INFANT - In civil cases one under 21 years of age.
INFORMATION - A formal accusation of crime made by a prosecuting attorney.
INFRA - Below, under; this word occurring by itself in a publication refers the reader to a future part of the publication.
INGRESS - The act of going into.
INJUNCTION - A writ or order by the court requiring a person, generally, to do or to refrain from doing an act.
INSOLVENT - The condition of a person who is unable to pay his debts.
INSTRUCTION - A direction given by the judge to the jury concerning the law of the case.
INTERIM - In the meantime; time intervening.
INTERLOCUTORY - Temporary, not final; something intervening between the commencement and the end of a suit which decides some point or matter, but is not a final decision of the whole controversy.
INTERROGATORIES - A series of formal written questions used in the examination of a party or a witness usually prior to a trial.
INTESTATE - A person who dies without a will.
INURE - To result, to take effect.
IPSO FACTO - By the fact iself; by the mere fact.
ISSUE (n.) The disputed point or question in a case,

J

JEOPARDY - Danger, hazard, peril.
JOINDER - Joining; uniting with another person in some legal steps or proceeding.
JOINT - United; combined.
JUDGE - Member or members or representative or representatives of a court conducting a trial or hearing at which evidence is introduced.
JUDGMENT - The official decision of a court of justice.
JUDICIAL OR JUDICIARY - Relating to or connected with the administration of justice.
JURAT - The clause written at the foot of an affidavit, stating when, where and before whom such affidavit was sworn.
JURISDICTION - The authority to hear and determine controversies between parties.
JURISPRUDENCE - The philosophy of law.
JURY - A body of persons legally selected to inquire into any matter of fact, and to render their verdict according to the evidence.

L

LACHES - The failure to diligently assert a right, which results in a refusal to allow relief.

LANDLORD AND TENANT - A phrase used to denote the legal relation existing between the owner and occupant of real estate.
LARCENY - Stealing personal property belonging to another.
LATENT - Hidden; that which does not appear on the face of a thing.
LAW - Includes constitutional, statutory, and decisional law.
LAWYER-CLIENT PRIVILEGE - (1) A "client" is a person, public officer, or corporation, association, or other organization or entity, either public or private, who is rendered professional legal services by a lawyer, or who consults a lawyer with a view to obtaining professional legal services from him; (2) A "lawyer" is a person authorized, or reasonably believed by the client to be authorized, to practice law in any state or nation; (3) A "representative of the lawyer" is one employed to assist the lawyer in the rendition of professional legal services; (4) A communication is "confidential" if not intended to be disclosed to third persons other than those to whom disclosure is in furtherance of the rendition of professional legal services to the client or those reasonably necessary for the transmission of the communication.

General rule of privilege - A client has a privilege to refuse to disclose and to prevent any other person from disclosing confidential communications made for the purpose of facilitating the rendition of professional legal services to the client, (1) between himself or his representative and his lawyer or his lawyer's representative, or (2) between his lawyer and the lawyer's representative, or (3) by him or his lawyer to a lawyer representing another in a matter of common interest, or (4) between representatives of the client or between the client and a representative of the client, or (5) between lawyers representing the client.
LEADING QUESTION - Question that suggests to the witness the answer that the examining party desires.
LEASE - A contract by which one conveys real estate for a limited time usually for a specified rent; personal property also may be leased.
LEGISLATION - The act of enacting laws.
LEGITIMATE - Lawful.
LESSEE - One to whom a lease is given.
LESSOR - One who grants a lease
LEVY - A collecting or exacting by authority.
LIABLE - Responsible; bound or obligated in law or equity.
LIBEL (v.) - To defame or injure a person's reputation by a published writing.
(n.) - The initial pleading on the part of the plaintiff in an admiralty proceeding.
LIEN - A hold or claim which one person has upon the property of another as a security for some debt or charge.
LIQUIDATED - Fixed; settled.
LIS PENDENS - A pending civil or criminal action.
LITERAL - According to the language.
LITIGANT - A party to a lawsuit.
LITATION - A judicial controversy.
LOCUS - A place.
LOCUS DELICTI - Place of the crime.
LOCUS POENITENTIAE - The abandoning or giving up of one's intention to commit some crime before it is fully completed or abandoning a conspiracy before its purpose is accomplished.

M

MALFEASANCE - To do a wrongful act.
MALICE - The doing of a wrongful act Intentionally without just cause or excuse.

MANDAMUS - The name of a writ issued by a court to enforce the performance of some public duty.
MANDATORY (adj.) Containing a command.
MARITIME - Pertaining to the sea or to commerce thereon.
MARSHALING - Arranging or disposing of in order.
MAXIM - An established principle or proposition.
MINISTERIAL - That which involves obedience to instruction, but demands no special discretion, judgment or skill.
MISAPPROPRIATE - Dealing fraudulently with property entrusted to one.
MISDEMEANOR - A crime less than a felony and punishable by a fine or imprisonment for less than one year.
MISFEASANCE - Improper performance of a lawful act.
MISREPRESENTATION - An untrue representation of facts.
MITIGATE - To make or become less severe, harsh.
MITTIMUS - A warrant of commitment to prison.
MOOT (adj.) Unsettled, undecided, not necessary to be decided.
MORTGAGE - A conveyance of property upon condition, as security for the payment of a debt or the performance of a duty, and to become void upon payment or performance according to the stipulated terms.
MORTGAGEE - A person to whom property is mortgaged.
MORTGAGOR - One who gives a mortgage.
MOTION - In legal proceedings, a "motion" is an application, either written or oral, addressed to the court by a party to an action or a suit requesting the ruling of the court on a matter of law.
MUTUALITY - Reciprocation.

N

NEGLIGENCE - The failure to exercise that degree of care which an ordinarily prudent person would exercise under like circumstances.
NEGOTIABLE (instrument) - Any instrument obligating the payment of money which is transferable from one person to another by endorsement and delivery or by delivery only.
NEGOTIATE - To transact business; to transfer a negotiable instrument; to seek agreement for the amicable disposition of a controversy or case.
NOLLE PROSEQUI - A formal entry upon the record, by the plaintiff in a civil suit or the prosecuting officer in a criminal action, by which he declares that he "will no further prosecute" the case.
NOLO CONTENDERE - The name of a plea in a criminal action, having the same effect as a plea of guilty; but not constituting a direct admission of guilt.
NOMINAL - Not real or substantial.
NOMINAL DAMAGES - Award of a trifling sum where no substantial injury is proved to have been sustained.
NONFEASANCE - Neglect of duty.
NOVATION - The substitution of a new debt or obligation for an existing one.
NUNC PRO TUNC - A phrase applied to acts allowed to be done after the time when they should be done, with a retroactive effect.("Now for then.")

O

OATH - Oath includes affirmation or declaration under penalty of perjury.
OBITER DICTUM - Opinion expressed by a court on a matter not essentially involved in a case and hence not a decision; also called dicta, if plural.

OBJECT (v.) - To oppose as improper or illegal and referring the question of its propriety or legality to the court.
OBLIGATION - A legal duty, by which a person is bound to do or not to do a certain thing.
OBLIGEE - The person to whom an obligation is owed.
OBLIGOR - The person who is to perform the obligation.
OFFER (v.) - To present for acceptance or rejection.
    (n.) - A proposal to do a thing, usually a proposal to make a contract.
OFFICIAL INFORMATION - Information within the custody or control of a department or agency of the government the disclosure of which is shown to be contrary to the public interest.
OFFSET - A deduction.
ONUS PROBANDI - Burden of proof.
OPINION - The statement by a judge of the decision reached in a case, giving the law as applied to the case and giving reasons for the judgment; also a belief or view.
OPTION - The exercise of the power of choice; also a privilege existing in one person, for which he has paid money, which gives him the right to buy or sell real or personal property at a given price within a specified time.
ORDER - A rule or regulation; every direction of a court or judge made or entered in writing but not including a judgment.
ORDINANCE - Generally, a rule established by authority; also commonly used to designate the legislative acts of a municipal corporation.
ORIGINAL - Writing or recording itself or any counterpart intended to have the same effect by a person executing or issuing it. An "original" of a photograph includes the negative or any print therefrom. If data are stored in a computer or similar device, any printout or other output readable by sight, shown to reflect the data accurately, is an "original."
OVERT - Open, manifest.

P

PANEL - A group of jurors selected to serve during a term of the court.
PARENS PATRIAE - Sovereign power of a state to protect or be a guardian over children and incompetents.
PAROL - Oral or verbal.
PAROLE - To release one in prison before the expiration of his sentence, conditionally.
PARITY - Equality in purchasing power between the farmer and other segments of the economy.
PARTITION - A legal division of real or personal property between one or more owners.
PARTNERSHIP - An association of two or more persons to carry on as co-owners a business for profit.
PATENT (adj.) - Evident.
    (n.) - A grant of some privilege, property, or authority, made by the government or sovereign of a country to one or more individuals.
PECULATION - Stealing.
PECUNIARY - Monetary.
PENULTIMATE - Next to the last.
PER CURIAM - A phrase used in the report of a decision to distinguish an opinion of the whole court from an opinion written by any one judge.
PER SE - In itself; taken alone.
PERCEIVE - To acquire knowledge through one's senses.
PEREMPTORY - Imperative; absolute.
PERJURY - To lie or state falsely under oath.

PERPETUITY - Perpetual existence; also the quality or condition of an estate limited so that it will not take effect or vest within the period fixed by law.
PERSON - Includes a natural person, firm, association, organization, partnership, business trust, corporation, or public entity.
PERSONAL PROPERTY - Includes money, goods, chattels, things in action, and evidences of debt.
PERSONALTY - Short term for personal property.
PETITION - An application in writing for an order of the court, stating the circumstances upon which it is founded and requesting any order or other relief from a court.
PLAINTIFF - A person who brings a court action.
PLEA - A pleading in a suit or action.
PLEADINGS - Formal allegations made by the parties of their respective claims and defenses, for the judgment of the court.
PLEDGE - A deposit of personal property as a security for the performance of an act.
PLEDGEE - The party to whom goods are delivered in pledge.
PLEDGOR - The party delivering goods in pledge.
PLENARY - Full; complete.
POLICE POWER - Inherent power of the state or its political subdivisions to enact laws within constitutional limits to promote the general welfare of society or the community.
POLLING THE JURY - Call the names of persons on a jury and requiring each juror to declare what his verdict is before it is legally recorded.
POST MORTEM - After death.
POWER OF ATTORNEY - A writing authorizing one to act for another.
PRECEPT - An order, warrant, or writ issued to an officer or body of officers, commanding him or them to do some act within the scope of his or their powers.
PRELIMINARY FACT - Fact upon the existence or nonexistence of which depends the admissibility or inadmissibility of evidence. The phrase "the admissibility or inadmissibility of evidence" includes the qualification or disqualification of a person to be a witness and the existence or nonexistence of a privilege.
PREPONDERANCE - Outweighing.
PRESENTMENT - A report by a grand jury on something they have investigated on their own knowledge.
PRESUMPTION - An assumption of fact resulting from a rule of law which requires such fact to be assumed from another fact or group of facts found or otherwise established in the action.
PRIMA FACUE - At first sight.
PRIMA FACIE CASE - A case where the evidence is very patent against the defendant.
PRINCIPAL - The source of authority or rights; a person primarily liable as differentiated from "principle" as a primary or basic doctrine.
PRO AND CON - For and against.
PRO RATA - Proportionally.
PROBATE - Relating to proof, especially to the proof of wills.
PROBATIVE - Tending to prove.
PROCEDURE - In law, this term generally denotes rules which are established by the Federal, State, or local Governments regarding the types of pleading and courtroom practice which must be followed by the parties involved in a criminal or civil case.
PROCLAMATION - A public notice by an official of some order, intended action, or state of facts.

PROFFERED EVIDENCE - The admissibility or inadmissibility of which is dependent upon the existence or nonexistence of a preliminary fact.
PROMISSORY (NOTE) - A promise in writing to pay a specified sum at an expressed time, or on demand, or at sight, to a named person, or to his order, or bearer.
PROOF - The establishment by evidence of a requisite degree of belief concerning a fact in the mind of the trier of fact or the court.
PROPERTY - Includes both real and personal property.
PROPRIETARY (adj.) - Relating or pertaining to ownership; usually a single owner.
PROSECUTE - To carry on an action or other judicial proceeding; to proceed against a person criminally.
PROVISO - A limitation or condition in a legal instrument.
PROXIMATE - Immediate; nearest
PUBLIC EMPLOYEE - An officer, agent, or employee of a public entity.
PUBLIC ENTITY - Includes a national, state, county, city and county, city, district, public authority, public agency, or any other political subdivision or public corporation, whether foreign or domestic.
PUBLIC OFFICIAL - Includes an official of a political dubdivision of such state or territory and of a municipality.
PUNITIVE - Relating to punishment.

Q

QUASH - To make void.
QUASI - As if; as it were.
QUID PRO QUO - Something for something; the giving of one valuable thing for another.
QUITCLAIM (v.) - To release or relinquish claim or title to, especially in deeds to realty.
QUO WARRANTO - A legal procedure to test an official's right to a public office or the right to hold a franchise, or to hold an office in a domestic corporation.

R

RATIFY - To approve and sanction.
REAL PROPERTY - Includes lands, tenements, and hereditaments.
REALTY - A brief term for real property.
REBUT - To contradict; to refute, especially by evidence and arguments.
RECEIVER - A person who is appointed by the court to receive, and hold in trust property in litigation.
RECIDIVIST - Habitual criminal.
RECIPROCAL - Mutual.
RECOUPMENT - To keep back or get something which is due; also, it is the right of a defendant to have a deduction from the amount of the plaintiff's damages because the plaintiff has not fulfilled his part of the same contract.
RECROSS EXAMINATION - Examination of a witness by a cross-examiner subsequent to a redirect examination of the witness.
REDEEM - To release an estate or article from mortgage or pledge by paying the debt for which it stood as security.
REDIRECT EXAMINATION - Examination of a witness by the direct examiner subsequent to the cross-examination of the witness.
REFEREE - A person to whom a cause pending in a court is referred by the court, to take testimony, hear the parties, and report thereon to the court.

REFERENDUM - A method of submitting an important legislative or administrative matter to a direct vote of the people.
RELEVANT EVIDENCE - Evidence including evidence relevant to the credulity of a witness or hearsay declarant, having any tendency in reason to prove or disprove any disputed fact that is of consequence to the determination of the action.
REMAND - To send a case back to the lower court from which it came, for further proceedings.
REPLEVIN - An action to recover goods or chattels wrongfully taken or detained.
REPLY (REPLICATION) - Generally, a reply is what the plaintiff or other person who has instituted proceedings says in answer to the defendant's case.
RE JUDICATA - A thing judicially acted upon or decided.
RES ADJUDICATA - Doctrine that an issue or dispute litigated and determined in a case between the opposing parties is deemed permanently decided between these parties.
RESCIND (RECISSION) - To avoid or cancel a contract.
RESPONDENT - A defendant in a proceeding in chancery or admiralty; also, the person who contends against the appeal in a case.
RESTITUTION - In equity, it is the restoration of both parties to their original condition (when practicable), upon the rescission of a contract for fraud or similar cause.
RETROACTIVE (RETROSPECTIVE) - Looking back; effective as of a prior time.
REVERSED - A term used by appellate courts to indicate that the decision of the lower court in the case before it has been set aside.
REVOKE - To recall or cancel.
RIPARIAN (RIGHTS) - The rights of a person owning land containing or bordering on a water course or other body of water, such as lakes and rivers.

S

SALE - A contract whereby the ownership of property is transferred from one person to another for a sum of money or for any consideration.
SANCTION - A penalty or punishment provided as a means of enforcing obedience to a law; also, an authorization.
SATISFACTION - The discharge of an obligation by paying a party what is due to him; or what is awarded to him by the judgment of a court or otherwise.
SCIENTER - Knowingly; also, it is used in pleading to denote the defendant's guilty knowledge.
SCINTILLA - A spark; also the least particle.
SECRET OF STATE - Governmental secret relating to the national defense or the international relations of the United States.
SECURITY - Indemnification; the term is applied to an obligation, such as a mortgage or deed of trust, given by a debtor to insure the payment or performance of his debt, by furnishing the creditor with a resource to be used in case of the debtor's failure to fulfill the principal obligation.
SENTENCE - The judgment formally pronounced by the court or judge upon the defendant after his conviction in a criminal prosecution.
SET-OFF - A claim or demand which one party in an action credits against the claim of the opposing party.
SHALL and MAY - "Shall" is mandatory and "may" is permissive.
SITUS - Location.
SOVEREIGN - A person, body or state in which independent and supreme authority is vested.
STARE DECISIS - To follow decided cases.

STATE - "State" means this State, unless applied to the different parts of the United States. In the latter case, it includes any state, district, commonwealth, territory or insular possession of the United States, including the District of Columbia.
STATEMENT - (a) Oral or written verbal expression or (b) nonverbal conduct of a person intended by him as a substitute for oral or written verbal expression.
STATUTE - An act of the legislature. Includes a treaty.
STATUTE OF LIMITATION - A statute limiting the time to bring an action after the right of action has arisen.
STAY - To hold in abeyance an order of a court.
STIPULATION - Any agreement made by opposing attorneys regulating any matter incidental to the proceedings or trial.
SUBORDINATION (AGREEMENT) - An agreement making one's rights inferior to or of a lower rank than another's.
SUBORNATION - The crime of procuring a person to lie or to make false statements to a court.
SUBPOENA - A writ or order directed to a person, and requiring his attendance at a particular time and place to testify as a witness.
SUBPOENA DUCES TECUM - A subpoena used, not only for the purpose of compelling witnesses to attend in court, but also requiring them to bring with them books or documents which may be in their possession, and which may tend to elucidate the subject matter of the trial.
SUBROGATION - The substituting of one for another as a creditor, the new creditor succeeding to the former's rights.
SUBSIDY - A government grant to assist a private enterprise deemed advantageous to the public.
SUI GENERIS - Of the same kind.
SUIT - Any civil proceeding by a person or persons against another or others in a court of justice by which the plaintiff pursues the remedies afforded him by law.
SUMMONS - A notice to a defendant that an action against him has been commenced and requiring him to appear in court and answer the complaint.
SUPRA - Above; this word occurring by itself in a book refers the reader to a previous part of the book.
SURETY - A person who binds himself for the payment of a sum of money, or for the performance of something else, for another.
SURPLUSAGE - Extraneous or unnecessary matter.
SURVIVORSHIP - A term used when a person becomes entitled to property by reason of his having survived another person who had an interest in the property.
SUSPEND SENTENCE - Hold back a sentence pending good behavior of prisoner.
SYLLABUS - A note prefixed to a report, especially a case, giving a brief statement of the court's ruling on different issues of the case.

T

TALESMAN - Person summoned to fill a panel of jurors.
TENANT - One who holds or possesses lands by any kind of right or title; also, one who has the temporary use and occupation of real property owned by another person (landlord), the duration and terms of his tenancy being usually fixed by an instrument called "a lease."
TENDER - An offer of money; an expression of willingness to perform a contract according to its terms.
TERM - When used with reference to a court, it signifies the period of time during which the court holds a session, usually of several weeks or months duration.

TESTAMENTARY - Pertaining to a will or the administration of a will.
TESTATOR (male)
TESTATRIX (female) - One who makes or has made a testament or will.
TESTIFY (TESTIMONY) - To give evidence under oath as a witness.
TO WIT - That is to say; namely.
TORT - Wrong; injury to the person.
TRANSITORY - Passing from place to place.
TRESPASS - Entry into another's ground, illegally.
TRIAL - The examination of a cause, civil or criminal, before a judge who has jurisdiction over it, according to the laws of the land.
TRIER OF FACT - Includes (a) the jury and (b) the court when the court is trying an issue of fact other than one relating to the admissibility of evidence.
TRUST - A right of property, real or personal, held by one party for the benefit of another.
TRUSTEE - One who lawfully holds property in custody for the benefit of another.

U

UNAVAILABLE AS A WITNESS - The declarant is (1) Exempted or precluded on the ground of privilege from testifying concerning the matter to which his statement is relevant; (2) Disqualified from testifying to the matter; (3) Dead or unable to attend or to testify at the hearing because of then existing physical or mental illness or infirmity; (4) Absent from the hearing and the court is unable to compel his attendance by its process; or (5) Absent from the hearing and the proponent of his statement has exercised reasonable diligence but has been unable to procure his attendance by the court's process.
ULTRA VIRES - Acts beyond the scope and power of a corporation, association, etc.
UNILATERAL - One-sided; obligation upon, or act of one party.
USURY - Unlawful interest on a loan.

V

VACATE - To set aside; to move out.
VARIANCE - A discrepancy or disagreement between two instruments or two aspects of the same case, which by law should be consistent.
VENDEE - A purchaser or buyer.
VENDOR - The person who transfers property by sale, particularly real estate; the term "seller" is used more commonly for one who sells personal property.
VENIREMEN - Persons ordered to appear to serve on a jury or composing a panel of jurors.
VENUE - The place at which an action is tried, generally based on locality or judicial district in which an injury occurred or a material fact happened.
VERDICT - The formal decision or finding of a jury.
VERIFY - To confirm or substantiate by oath.
VEST - To accrue to.
VOID - Having no legal force or binding effect.
VOIR DIRE - Preliminary examination of a witness or a juror to test competence, interest, prejudice, etc.

W

WAIVE - To give up a right.
WAIVER - The intentional or voluntary relinquishment of a known right.
WARRANT (WARRANTY) (v.) - To promise that a certain fact or state of facts, in relation to the subject matter, is, or shall be, as it is represented to be.

WARRANT (n.) - A writ issued by a judge, or other competent authority, addressed to a sheriff, or other officer, requiring him to arrest the person therein named, and bring him before the judge or court to answer or be examined regarding the offense with which he is charged.

WRIT - An order or process issued in the name of the sovereign or in the name of a court or judicial officer, commanding the performance or nonperformance of some act.

WRITING - Handwriting, typewriting, printing, photostating, photographing and every other means of recording upon any tangible thing any form of communication or representation, including letters, words, pictures, sounds, or symbols, or combinations thereof.

WRITINGS AND RECORDINGS - Consists of letters, words, or numbers, or their equivalent, set down by handwriting, typewriting, printing, photostating, photographing, magnetic impulse, mechanical or electronic recording, or other form of data compilation.

Y

YEA AND NAY - Yes and no.

YELLOW DOG CONTRACT - A contract by which employer requires employee to sign an instrument promising as condition that he will not join a union during its continuance, and will be discharged if he does join.

Z

ZONING - The division of a city by legislative regulation into districts and the prescription and application in each district of regulations having to do with structural and architectural designs of buildings and of regulations prescribing use to which buildings within designated districts may be put.

COURTROOM TERMS

A/K/A: Acronym that stands for "also known as" and introduces any alternative or assumed names or aliases of an individual. A term to indicate another name by which a person is known.

Arraignment: The bringing of a defendant before the court to answer the matters charged against him in an indictment or information. The defendant is read the charges and must respond with his plea.

Arrest: Deprivation of one's liberty by legal authority.

Bail: An amount of money set by the court to procure the release of a person from legal custody; this money is to be forfeited if the defendant fails to appear for trial.

Beyond a Reasonable Doubt: The standard of proof required for a finding of guilty in a criminal matter. Satisfied to a moral certainty. This is a higher standard of proof than that required in a civil matter (preponderance of the evidence).

Co-Defendant: Any additional defendant or respondent in the same case.

Confession: A voluntary statement made by a person charged with a crime wherein said person acknowledges his/her guilt of the offense charged and discloses participation in the act.

Controlled Dangerous Substance: That group of legally designated drugs, which, by statute, it is illegal to possess or distribute.

Criminal complaint: The initial written notice to a defendant that he/she is being charged with a public offense.

Due Process of Law: The exercise of the powers of the government with the safeguards for the protection of individual rights as set forth in the constitution, statutes, and common case law.

Felony: A crime of a more serious nature than a misdemeanor, the exact nature of which is defined by state statute and which is punishable by a term of imprisonment exceeding one year or by death.

Grand Jury: A jury of inquiry whose duty is to receive complaints and accusations in criminal cases, hear the evidence presented on the part of the state, and determine whether to indict (see "indictment" below).

Impeach: As used in the Law of Evidence, to call into question the truthfulness of a witness, by means of introducing evidence to discredit him or her.

Indictment: A written accusation presented by a grand jury after having been presented with evidence, charging that a person named therein has done some act, or has been guilty of some omission that by law is a public offense.

Miranda Warnings: The compulsory advisement of a person's rights prior to any custodial interrogation; these include: a) the right to remain silent; b) that any statement made may be used against him/her; c) the right to an attorney; d) the appointment of counsel if the accused cannot afford his or her own attorney. Unless these rights are given, any evidence obtained in an interrogation cannot be used in the individual's trial against him/her.

Misdemeanor: Offense lower than felony and generally punishable by a fine or imprisonment other than in a penitentiary.

Motion to Quash: Application to the court to set aside the complaint, indictment or subpoena due to a lack of probable cause to arrest the defendant, or in matters heard by a grand jury, due to evidence not properly presented to the grand jury.

Motion to Sever: Application to the court made when there are two defendants charged with the same crimes or who acted jointly in the commission of a crime, when their attorneys feel it would be in their best interest if they had separate trials.

Motion to Suppress Evidence: Application to the court to prevent evidence from being presented at trial when said evidence has been obtained by illegal means. It applies to physical evidence, statements made by defendant when not advised by counsel or through wiretapping, prior convictions, etc..

Parole: A conditional release from custody at the discretion of the paroling authority prior to his or her completing the prison sentence imposed. During said release the offender is required to observe conditions of this status under the supervision of a parole agency.

Plea: A defendant's formal answer in court to the charges contained in a charging document.

Guilty: A plea by the defendant in which he acknowledges guilt either of the offense charged or of a less serious offense pursuant to an agreement with the prosecuting attorney. It should be understood, however, that the court may not be obliged to recognize this.

Nolo Contendere: A plea that is admissible in some jurisdictions, in which the defendant states that he does not contest the charges against him. Also called "no contest", this plea has the same effect as a guilty plea, except that it cannot be used against the defendant in civil actions arising out of the same incident which gave rise to the criminal charges.

Not Guilty: A plea of innocence by the defendant.

Not Guilty by Reason of Insanity: A plea that is sometimes entered in conjunction with the "not guilty" plea.

Double Jeopardy: A plea entered by a defendant who has been tried for an offense wherein he asserts that he cannot be tried a second time for said offense, unless he successfully secured a new trial after an appeal, or after a motion for a new trial was granted by the trial court.

Police Report: The official report made by any police officer involved with the incident or appearing after the incident, setting forth the officer's observations and statements of parties and witnesses. It can be used as evidence in a trial.

Pre-Trial Intervention: Utilized in some states when a defendant is accused of a first offense, to divert the defendant from the criminal justice system.

Probation: To allow a person convicted of a minor offense to go at large, under a suspension of sentence, during good behavior, and generally under the supervision of a probation officer.

Prosecutor: The attorney who prosecutes defendants for crimes, in the name of the government.

Search Warrant: A written order, issued by the court, directing the police to search a specified location for particular personal property (stolen or illegally possessed).

Speedy Trial: Mandate by the government that all criminal trials must take place within a specified time after arrest.

Writ of Habeas Corpus: A mandate issued from a court requiring that an individual be brought before the court.